Violín

Afrodescendant religious music in the Caribbean and Latin America typically foregrounds drumming and centuries-old songs of praise to spirit deities. In recent years, a new form of worship has gained popularity in Cuba known as a *violín* or *toque de violín*, which features the violin alongside the guitar, electronic piano, and/or other instruments commonly associated with popular music. *Violines* can be understood as loosely defined spaces for performance that developed in a context of cultural oppression and dominance. They can be viewed as a concession to Eurocentric and secular tastes, or as a blackening/creolizing of those same practices, or both. They express religious faith in pluralistic ways, incorporating repertoire from various Black religions alongside influences from folk Catholicism, and classical, commercial, and folkloric music. Drawing from an encyclopedic knowledge of Cuban music, ethnographic work, and interviews, Robin D. Moore's groundbreaking book is the first to explore the compelling *violín* ceremony in detail.

Robin D. Moore is Professor of Ethnomusicology at the University of Texas at Austin. He is the editor and co-author of *Music and Revolution: Cultural Change in Socialist Cuba*, *Musics of Latin America*, *College Music Curricula for a New Century*, and *Fernando Ortiz on Music*.

Afro-Latin America

Series Editors

George Reid Andrews, *University of Pittsburgh*
Alejandro de la Fuente, *Harvard University*

This series reflects the coming of age of the new, multidisciplinary field of Afro-Latin American Studies which centers on the histories, cultures, and experiences of people of African descent in Latin America. The series aims to showcase scholarship produced by different disciplines, including history, political science, sociology, ethnomusicology, anthropology, religious studies, art, law, and cultural studies. It covers the full temporal span of the African Diaspora in Latin America, from the early colonial period to the present and includes continental Latin America, the Caribbean, and other key areas in the region where Africans and their descendants have made a significant impact.

A full list of titles published in the series can be found at:
www.cambridge.org/afro-latin-america

Violín

Mediating Musical Style and Devotional Practice in Twenty-First-Century Cuba

ROBIN D. MOORE
University of Texas at Austin

Shaftesbury Road, Cambridge CB2 8EA, United Kingdom

One Liberty Plaza, 20th Floor, New York, NY 10006, USA

477 Williamstown Road, Port Melbourne, VIC 3207, Australia

314–321, 3rd Floor, Plot 3, Splendor Forum, Jasola District Centre,
New Delhi – 110025, India

103 Penang Road, #05–06/07, Visioncrest Commercial, Singapore 238467

Cambridge University Press is part of Cambridge University Press & Assessment,
a department of the University of Cambridge.

We share the University's mission to contribute to society through the pursuit of
education, learning and research at the highest international levels of excellence.

www.cambridge.org
Information on this title: www.cambridge.org/9781009584036

DOI: 10.1017/9781009584029

© Robin D. Moore 2026

This publication is in copyright. Subject to statutory exception and to the provisions
of relevant collective licensing agreements, no reproduction of any part may take
place without the written permission of Cambridge University Press & Assessment.

When citing this work, please include a reference to the DOI: 10.1017/9781009584029

First published 2026

A catalogue record for this publication is available from the British Library

A Cataloging-in-Publication data record for this book is available from the Library of Congress

ISBN 978-1-009-58403-6 Hardback
ISBN 978-1-009-58401-2 Paperback

Cambridge University Press & Assessment has no responsibility for the persistence
or accuracy of URLs for external or third-party internet websites referred to in this
publication and does not guarantee that any content on such websites is, or will remain,
accurate or appropriate.

For EU product safety concerns, contact us at Calle José Abascal, 56, 1°, 28003
Madrid, Spain or email eugpsr@cambridge.org

Cover credit: Yunior Terry performing in New York City in a *violín* organized by
Octavio "El Papa" Soto Tongo, 2014. Photo by Juan Cabellero.

To Lorraine and Eva, with love. And in memory of Tomás Fernández Robaina, a passionate scholar, advocate for the Afro-Cuban community, mentor, and friend.

Contents

List of Figures	*page* viii
Acknowledgments	xi
Glossary	xv
1 Introduction	1
2 Situating *Violines*	21
3 Spiritism and *Violines Espirituales*	52
4 *Violines a Ochún* and *Orisha* Praise	98
5 Performance Dynamics in *Toques de Violín*	133
6 *Violines* Abroad	165
Conclusion	195
References	210
Index	222

Figures

2.1 A *brindis* or toast in honor of the *orisha* Ochún.   page 23
2.2 A *violín* in the Cabildo de Santa Teresa, Matanzas.   26
2.3 The *violín* ensemble Los Águilas.   28
2.4 Percussionist Rafael Espinosa Casanova (left) performing in a *violín* ensemble.   31
2.5 Roy Vázquez and María Teresa Gómez Noguera performing in East Havana.   35
2.6 The *cajón* ensemble San Cristóbal de Regla directed by Andres Jacinto Balaez-Chinicle.   45
3.1 A Spiritist altar featuring water glasses, fresh flowers, perfume, carefully dressed dolls representing spirit guides, and a lit candle.   56
3.2 "Sea el Santísimo."   63
3.3 "La luz redentora."   65
3.4 "O venid protectores."   66
3.5 "O María" (or "Ave María").   70
3.6 "San Miguel bendito."   71
3.7 "Canción a San Lázaro."   74
3.8 Transcription of "Marinero, marinero."   75
3.9 "Corre el agua."   76
3.10 "La gitana."   77
3.11 "Canto al indio."   78
3.12 "Mamá Francisca," initial melody.   81
3.13 "Congo de Guinea soy," initial melody and *montuno*.   82
3.14 "Lumbe lumbe."   84
3.15 A musical rendition of the Spiritist Padrenuestro by Ramón Negrón Flores.   87

3.16	Excerpt of vocal and flute countermelody of "O María" (or "Ave María") as performed in a *violín espiritual*.	90
3.17	Violin double stops behind "Canción a San Lázaro."	91
3.18	"Ole con ole, gitana" with chordal accompaniment.	93
3.19	"Gitana de mis amores, bendíceme."	94
3.20	"Francisca" with chordal accompaniment.	95
4.1	Yenny's altar, prepared for her *violín* dedicated to Ochún.	108
4.2	"Ochiminí," a traditional praise song to Elegguá as interpreted by the Orquesta Estrellas Cubanas.	112
4.3	"Porque soy tan chiquitico," melody and antiphonal refrain.	113
4.4	Chorus to Margarita Lecuona's "Babalú."	116
4.5	"Plegaria a Obatalá."	118
4.6	"Obatalá kunawa" as sung traditionally.	119
4.7	"Obatalá kunawa" sung in duple meter and with its melody altered so that it conforms to a i-iv-V-i minor harmonic vamp.	119
4.8	"Oyansa ma terema," played in duple meter, transitioning briefly to 6/8 time.	121
4.9	"El hombre de la guayabera" chorus.	122
4.10	"Onileo" vamp, alternating between a lead singer and chorus.	123
4.11	"Plegaria a Yemayá."	124
4.12	The traditional Lucumí chant to Yemayá "Awoyó aé" accompanied by rumba clave on bell, guitar chords, and a percussion solo on the bongo.	126
4.13	"Beroní abebe Ochún" as sung traditionally in triple meter.	127
4.14	"Beroní abebe Ochún" as performed by a typical *violín* ensemble with string *guajeos* and in duple meter.	128
5.1	Danai Pérez Domínguez relaxing with invited guests following her *violín* and *brindis*.	136
5.2	Repertoire in Danai's *violín*.	137
5.3	Musicians performing in Yenny's *violín*.	139
5.4	Performers in Eduar's *violín*.	140
5.5	A duple-meter rhythm accompanying *orisha* songs in Eduar's *violín*.	141
5.6	Eduar's *violín* repertoire.	142
5.7	A triple-meter rhythm accompanying *orisha* songs in Eduar's *violín*, apparently representing an adaptation of the batá's *ñongo* pattern.	144
5.8	Sketch of a simple bongo drum break used to call in the chorus of a new praise song for Elegguá, "Sosa sokere."	147

5.9	Straight quarter-notes on the bongo, used instead of a standard *martillo* pattern to generate musical interest during call–response singing.	147
5.10	"Voy a hacer un violín."	150
5.11	Nadia's *violín*.	151
5.12	"A remar," one of many *plegarias* devoted to Yemayá, usually performed in alternation between a chorus and lead singer.	152
5.13	A segment of music accompanying the "Todo lo malo" antiphonal segment in 6/8 following the *oru* to Yemayá.	155
5.14	Sample chorus and lead line of "Vuela la paloma."	158
5.15	"Estaba la langosta" chorus as performed in Ileana's *violín*, in full and shorter versions.	159
6.1	Yunior Terry (left), performing in 2014 in an event organized by Octavio "El Papa" Sotolongo (top right) and his cousin (lower right).	168
6.2	Tania and Abraham Rivero.	172
6.3	A vocal and harmonic transcription of Tania and Abraham's video "Oshun yeyé moro."	175
6.4	The "Ko ko ko iroko omo iyesá" melody, as arranged by Tania and Abraham in their "Oshun iyesá" video.	177
6.5	The praise rhythm to Osain known as Borotitilawa, used as percussive accompaniment to the traditional "Ko ko ko iroko omo iyesá" chant arranged by Tania and Abraham.	177
6.6	Yilian Orama, photographed during a *violín* in Miami.	179
6.7	"Elegguá, Elegguá asokere kere-kere meyé" chant to Elegguá, performed instrumentally on violin and djembe.	183
6.8	Instrumental "Cheke cheke" chant to Ochún on violin and djembe in 6/8 time.	183
6.9	Lisbet Soto, performing for *santero* Robert Sánchez on his birthday *en santo* in the Venezuelan littoral near the town of Todasana.	185
6.10	"Fantasía Yoruba" featuring Luis Peña, percussion, and Miguel Amín, violin.	190
6.11	Luis Peña's modified Borotitilawa/Obanla rhythm performed solo on all three *batá* drums.	193

Acknowledgments

The drafting of this book has been a complex and humbling process, and has underscored how much I have yet to learn about many aspects of Cuban culture and religion. What seemed to me at first a topic engaging heavily with popular music and somewhat tangential to traditional Afrodiasporic worship soon came to intersect with profound religious beliefs as well as broader philosophies, practices, and musical spheres. In this sense, the project took me into unfamiliar territory and involved ever more frequent consultation with religious practitioners and specialists. I found many of my initial assumptions inaccurate. During my first years investigating the topic, I was frequently forced to reframe my understandings, develop new lines of questioning, and reflect further on the relationship between *violín* worship and other forms of devotion.

Research began in 2018 during a month spent in Cuba, primarily in Havana. At that time I worked through personal contacts, and the help of friends and colleagues at the Casa de las Américas (especially musicologist Layda Ferrando), to conduct interviews on *violines* and to attend performances. Initially I was unsure how much information I would find, and thought that perhaps I would only write an article or two on the topic. After returning home, I continued to read available literature on Spiritism and related practices, slowly learning more and hoping to return the following year. But with heavy commitments at the University of Texas and, later, the onset of the Covid-19 pandemic, travel to Cuba for follow-up work proved difficult. Eventually, I contracted the help of others on the island to film *violines* and to conduct interviews for me. The initial researcher I worked with was Ms. Rosy Bayona Mojena, an employee at the Centro Cultural Juan Marinello, an important locus of interdisciplinary scholarship (https://icic.cult.cu/). Rosy and I worked together for about six months, but she later relocated to Pinar del Río in order to help care for members of her family. Shortly thereafter I began collaborating with Ms. Melena Francis Valdés, a partnership that has been fundamental to this project. It eventually became clear that the topic of *violines* merited a book-length publication.

Melena (https://melena.com/home) is many things: a Cuban-American, a professional percussionist specializing in Afro-Latin instruments who has performed with many renowned artists, a member of the Ocha religious community, a music educator, and a researcher in her own right who has undertaken studies of Abakuá communities. Melena's knowledge of respect for local practitioners and many personal contacts made her a key collaborator. She recorded and transcribed most of the interviews supporting this study, as well as taking photos, filming, and recording many performances. She followed up with interviewees to ask additional questions of them when necessary. She often provided her own pithy insights into the dynamics surrounding religious events, and she offered clarifications about ritual language and countless other topics by querying her spiritual elders and friends. Her frequent presence in Cuba (she divides her time between Havana and Los Angeles) was central to the realization of this research. I simply could not have written the book without you, Melena. Thank you!

The distanced nature of my data-gathering and my lack of direct interaction with many interviewees created problems that, in retrospect, I should have worked harder to avoid. I did not show interviewees copies of draft text for their commentary early on, for instance. Some interviewees did not know I planned to publish an academic book until it was almost finished, and I should have made sure they were aware of this. As the manuscript was nearing completion, it occurred to me that it would be helpful to create a website with footage of *violines* and interviews on the topic so that interested readers could access more of the material I had used in creating the manuscript. Melena began to help me toward that end by contacting performers and interviewees to ask permission in advance of uploading their materials. Many were surprised to hear about the book publication, wanted to see how their interviews had been used, and many expressed concern with how I had quoted or represented them in the text. In some cases this was because I misinterpreted their statements, attributing meanings to them that I perceived but that they didn't intend. In others, interviewees did not agree with the broader arguments I was making and didn't want their statements used to support them. In still other cases, they indicated that my statements about religious practice were imprecise or inaccurate and needed additional elaboration. Thus, the final months prior to publication have involved numerous – and, at times, tense – interactions with interviewees, and I have removed or edited many statements. During that process, some interviewees asked that their names be removed from the text and/or expressed a desire to be made anonymous. A few had made statements that could be considered problematic or biased by others, so Melena and I pre-emptively anonymized them for their protection. Though it has been a difficult process, I know the manuscript is stronger for the changes made through these interactions. I thank everyone willing to provide suggested edits or comments for their input.

Regarding the website: a few key individuals who were filmed did not want their performances or images shared; for that reason I am not able to make public all of the audio and video footage that I once hoped to and have therefore paused the initiative. Several of the performers discussed in the following chapters have authorized the dissemination of their *violines*, however; if you have an interest in particular events or musical sequences that are discussed, feel free to contact me directly and, if I am permitted to share them, I will happily make them available.

Countless other friends and colleagues helped with aspects of this project and deserve mention. My wife, Lorraine Leu, exposed me to Fred Moten's writings on fugitivity and helped me develop my theoretical framing as well as fashion the book's title. Johnny Frías facilitated contact with *violín* performers in the Miami area, spoke with them for me, and provided film clips of music making he had seen. Johnny, Melena, Richard Huntley, Michael Spiro, Nolan Warden, and David Font-Navarrete all shared invaluable insights into performance from their perspective as *batá* drummers (most *omo Añá*) and percussionists. Nadia Milad Issa filmed her own *violín* in Havana and provided access to the footage.

Many friends and colleagues helped me track down people and/or resources related to the project or provided insights into the analysis of *violines* and Cuban cultural history. They include David Brown, Jorge Duany, Radamés and Isabel Giró, Liliana González Moreno, Niurca Márquez, Nicolás Martínez Palacios, Ramón "Mongui" Torres Zayas, and Nolan Warden. Marc Gidal provided access to his work on Spiritist music in Brazil for purposes of comparison. Ivor Miller offered field notes, interviews, photos, and videos of *violines* he attended in the 1990s. José "Pepe" Reyes Jr. provided insights into his performances with the

Orquesta Estrellas Cubanas. Many others helped me with the interpretation of song texts and determining the origin of particular song choruses incorporated into *violines*. They include Nelson Aboy Domingo, Mercedes Almirall, Alira Ashvo-Muñoz, Abilio Betancourt Bejerano, Rodolfo de la Fuente, Alexis Esquivel, Reynaldo Fernández Pavón, David Font-Navarrete, Melena Francis Valdés, Agustín González, Verónica González, Rafael Lam, Ben Lapidus, Rolando Pérez, Ramón Torres Zayas, and Amanda Villepasteur. Scholars of religion provided crucial advice as well, including Aisha Beliso-de Jesús, Brent Crosson, the late Ana Stela Cunha, Diana Espírito Santo, Arisbel López Atraca, Solimar Otero, and Stefan Palmié.

Volunteer undergraduate researcher Audrey Huber helped me conduct web searches and find video posts of *violines* on YouTube, Instagram, and other platforms. Many colleagues and graduate students helped with the transcription of musical examples, including Eli Castillo Mena, Richard Huntley, Sarah Lahasky, Kevin Parme, J. A. Strub, and Fernando Véliz Corado (the latter a University of Texas Humanities Institute research assistant). Several colleagues provided invaluable help by reading and commenting on draft chapters, including David Font-Navarrete, Melena Francis Valdés and Solimar Otero (both of whom read the entire manuscript), Johnny Frías, Daniel Party, and Sonia Seeman.

Thanks are due to my letter writers: Aisha Beliso-de Jesús, Alejandro de la Fuente, and Timothy Rommen. With their help, I received summer research support in 2019 from the Center for Mexican American Studies and later a semester's teaching leave in Fall 2023 provided by the Lozano Long Institute of Latin American Studies at the University of Texas. Both grants provided the chance to read more widely on Cuban religion and to draft book chapters. Thanks to my anonymous external reviewers who provided helpful feedback, and to Cecelia Cancellaro, Victoria Phillips, Helen B. Cooper, and the staff at Cambridge University Press for their efforts to see the book to publication.

Glossary

Abakuá A member of a male secret society in Cuba derived from traditions on the border between present-day Nigeria and Cameroon
Abasí Supreme god of the Abakuá
Abebé A ritual fan held by Ochún, one of her sacred objects
Aberikula Unconsecrated. A term usually associated with *batá* drums that have not been ritually prepared for use in sacred ceremonies
Aché A term for spiritual force or power
Akpwon A lead singer in ritual contexts
Aleyo The term for a religious practitioner in Regla de Ocha/Santería, but someone who has not yet been initiated
Altares de cruz celebrations A form of folk Catholicism associated with patron saint festivals in Cuba, especially prior to 1959. It involves the creation of altars and the singing of devotional music over a period of nine evenings. Some of these songs have influenced the music of *misas espirituales*
Arará A Cuban term describing people and religious traditions derived from present-day Dahomey in West Africa
Babalawo A spiritual advisor able to predict the future and offer advice by means of a Yoruba-derived divination system known as Ifá
Batá **drums** A set of three hourglass-shaped drums associated with Santería ceremony
Bataleros Batá drummers. *See also omo Añá; tambolero*
Bembé A form of music making and dance associated with less formal Santería worship and performed on unconsecrated drums

Bomba section   In contemporary Cuban dance music, a bomba section refers to a moment when melodic and harmonic instruments stop playing, leaving only percussion and voices

Botánica   A store devoted to providing materials needed for spiritual activities, including Santería and *espiritismo cruzado*

Bóveda **Also** *bóveda espiritual*   Literally, vault or crypt; this term is used to reference the altar or table where ritual objects are placed that serve as a focus of activities in *misas espirituales*. The contents of the *bóveda* include candles, water glasses, a crucifix, cigars, figurines, or dolls representing an individual's guiding spirits

Bozal   A form of pidgin Spanish mixed with elements of Kikongo or other African languages, imitating the speech of African slaves in colonial Cuba. It is incorporated frequently into Palo worship and some Ocha worship, and it is spoken by some spirits who appear in Spiritist rites

Buen ser **(pl.** *buenos seres***)**   A good or enlightened spirit being that guides and advises those in the physical world in the context of a *misa espiritual*

Cabeza   Literally, "head." The leader of a *misa espiritual*

Cabildo   A Black mutual aid society organized along ethnic lines. Most closely associated with the colonial era, free and enslaved Blacks organized *cabildos* in order to perpetuate traditional languages, religious expression, and music

Cajón **(pl.** *cajones***)**   A resonant wooden box used as a musical instrument. Also used as an abbreviated term for *cajón de muerto*

Cajón de muerto (*also cajón pa'l muerto* **or** *cajón al muerto*)   A musical performance on *cajón* instruments, as well as possibly others (claves, conga drums, *catá*), as a form of devotion or offering to the spirit world

Cajón para santo   A form of religious and musical devotion for the *orishas*, but performed on *cajones* as opposed to drums

Camino   Roughly, incarnation. Deities in Santería appear in many guises at different times in the many stories told about them. Each distinct manifestation is known as a *camino* or *patakí*

Campo material   The material world or material plane

Cascarilla   A preparation made of ground eggshells, known for its ability to break up negative spiritual energy. Sometimes it is scattered around the *bóveda* as well as rubbed onto the bodies of participants

Catá   A round and resonant piece of wood struck with sticks, used as a woodblock

Chachalokafun Also Ichachalekefun.   A rapid rhythm played on the *batá* drums in duple meter that often ends ritual song and dance sequences

Charanga   A Cuban dance band format featuring violins and flute

Chekeré   *See also* güiro. A dried gourd with a net of beads or seeds attached to the outside. The instrument is shaken and struck to produce sounds

Cinquillo   Literally, little group of five. A common, syncopated rhythmic figure in Afro-Cuban and Afro-Latin American music consisting of five notes. It is often written as: quarter-note, eighth-note, quarter-note, eighth-note, quarter-note

Claves   A pair of wooden sticks used as a musical instrument in Cuba. They are struck against each other to create various rhythmic patterns

Comisión   A grouping or collection of aligned spiritual forces recognized by Cuban Spiritists. Examples include the *comisión María* or the *comisión india*

Corriente   Spiritual flow, current, or tendency. Associated with *misas espirituales*, *corrientes* are spiritual currents that tie together similar forms of spiritual energy, such as Babalú Ayé and other spirit entities that perform acts of physical and spiritual healing

Cuadro espiritual   Spiritual cadre. A group of spirits who share certain affinities with a living person in terms of personality and who advise and guide them

Danzón   An instrumental dance music genre that developed in the late nineteenth century. It is characterized by rondo form and contrasting sections, as well as by a specific rhythm known as *danzón* clave

Despojo   An act of ritual purification

Diana   An improvised vocal segment using vocables, similar to scatting. Singers of rumba use the *diana* early in their performances to establish a tonal center before cueing in the chorus

Don de gracia   An offering of grace or gratitude, typically in the form of music. Also a subcategory of *violín*, usually involving events with less overtly religious content

Ebioso   The Arará term for Changó, African god of thunder, lightning, and warfare

Ebó   In Santería, an offering or sacrifice typically made to the *orishas*

Egun   A Lukumí term that refers to spirits of the dead, specifically one's direct ancestors and one's religious family (i.e. the lineage of one's *padrinos/madrinas* [spiritual godparents]). *See also muerto.* While the terms *egun* and *muerto* are sometimes used interchangeably, *egun* is linked to *orisha* worship and *muerto* or *guía* to Spiritism

Elekes Also collares   Ritual necklaces in the colors of particular *orishas* worn by *santeros*

Espiritismo   Spiritism

Espiritismo cruzado   Spiritism blended with other Afrodiasporic religious systems such as Santería, Palo, or Vodoun

Espiritismo de cordón   Literally, chain or cord Spiritism. A variant practiced widely in eastern Cuba, *espiritismo de cordón* is similar in some respects to the ring shout associated with early Black churches in the United States. Participants commune with ancestor spirits and seek spiritual cleansing while standing in a circle with others and chanting short call–response songs of praise while rhythmically moving their bodies. Such devotion usually lasts many hours

Espiritista   A practitioner of Spiritism

Fluido   Spiritual force or energy needed to facilitate communication with spirit beings in *misas espirituales*

Guataca   An iron hoe blade, sometimes used as a percussion instrument

Guajeo   A rhythmic, repeated melodic figure played by violinists in *charanga* dance bands during the final *montuno* segment. Often, *guajeos* incorporate double stops

Guía   Spirit guide. See also *muerto*

Güiro   See also *chekeré*. A musical instrument fashioned out of a dried and hollowed-out gourd. The sort used in dance music has grooves carved into one side of a gourd that are scraped with a wooden dowel to produce sound. *Güiro* instruments can also be made by fashioning a net of beads on the outside of a gourd and shaking it; this instrument is referred to both as a *güiro* and as a *chekeré* and is traditionally used in devotional contexts associated with Santería

Hembra   Literally, female. A term used to refer to the larger bongo drumhead

Ibeyí   The twin *orishas*, children of Changó and under his protection. All twins are viewed as spiritually charged in Lucumí religion

Ifá   A Yoruba-derived system of divining the future by means of interpreting ancient proverbs

Íreme   A masked Abakuá dancer representing an ancestor spirit

Iroko   The *orisha* associated with sacred ceiba trees and believed to dwell inside them

Iruke   A ritual whip or whisk associated with the *orisha* Oyá (as well as with the *orishas* Obatalá and Ochún Ololodí) that she holds in her hand as she dances

Itá   A spiritual reading or consultation conducted by a Lucumí high priest (Obá Oriate) by means of cowrie shells

Iyawó   A recent initiate into Santería

Iyere   Ritual praise songs to the *orishas*

Iyesá music   A form of drumming associated with Santería. It was initially associated with the devotion of a distinct ethnic group in Nigeria, but in Cuba has been incorporated into *bata* and other repetoires

Lucumí.   An adjective referencing Yoruba-influenced religious practices in Cuba. By extension, it also refers to the African-derived languages used in many prayers and songs

Lalubanché   Also alumbanche or olubanshe. The name of a *bata* rhythm often played in conjunction with *rezos* (nonmetrical praise songs) to Elegguá

Macho   Literally, male. A term used to describe the smaller bongo drumhead

Madama   The term for a "mammy" spirit that often appears as part of *misas espirituales*

Makut drums   Two- or three-drum ensembles associated with Kongo societies, especially in colonial-era Cuba. The unique rhythms associated with them are associated primarily with secular entertainment but can also accompany lighter moments of Kongo religious events. Makuta drums are said to be one of the antecedents to the modern conga drum

Mambises (singular *mambí*)   Insurgent fighters in Cuba's Wars of Independence

Manillas   Bracelets

Manto   A ritual cloth in the color of a particular *orisha* that *santeros* drape on their ceremonial altars (*tronos*)

Martillo   Literally, hammer. A term used to describe the basic rhythmic pattern played on the bongo drum in Cuban *son* and other dance music

Masacote   A term used to reference the interplay of various rhythms in modern Cuban dance music. See also *bomba*

Media unidad   Literally, half unit or half being, the term for a medium (an individual able to channel spirits)

Merengue   A style of dance music originating in the Dominican Republic. It is characterized by a brisk duple-meter tempo and characteristic rhythmic patterns on a metal scraper and the *tambora* drum

Misa espiritual   A creole form of séance and the most common form of religious devotion associated with *espiritismo cruzado*. It combines influences from multiple religious systems

Misa de coronación   The final ritual event that takes place prior to an individual's initiation into the Lucumí religion. It involves a spiritual coronation with flowers

Misa de desarrollo   A Spiritist séance intended to develop strong ties between an individual and the beings associated with their spiritual cadre

Misa de investigación   A ritual intended to determine the nature of one's unique cadre of spirit guides. The *muertos* or spirits contacted can confirm whether they agree the individual should become an initiate in Ocha or Palo, or whether to proceed with other ceremonies, such as receiving Olokun

Misas de recogimiento   Spiritist séances designed to collect and dispel negative influences or energies

Montuno   The fast, climactic, call–response section of Cuban folkloric music or dance music. *Montunos* usually feature prominent vocal and/or instrumental improvisation

Muerto   *See also guía*. A spirit guide, often associated with one's *cordón espiritual* or spiritual cadre. These forces typically accompany and watch over an individual; they may consist of Catholic saints or the spirits of Africans, Gypsies, Indians, and others

Música jíbara   Puerto Rican country music, played primarily on string instruments such as the *cuatro*

Nganga   Also known as *prenda*, *nganga* refers to a ritual iron pot used in Kongo-derived religions, filled with various ritual objects. It is used to control the spirits of the dead

Ngangulero   A Palo priest who controls the forces of a *prenda*

Ñáñigo   A pejorative term used in colonial times to refer to *íremes*, masked dancers who represent ancestor spirits associated with Abakuá secret societies

Ñongo   A relatively fast-paced rhythmic pattern in triple meter associated with the *batá* drums

Nsambi Mpungo   The supreme deity in Kongo-derived Palo religions

Ocha   *Also* Regla de Ocha, the "rule of the *orisha*." An alternate term for Santería

Odun   A ritual proverb used to interpret the future as part of the Ifá divination system

Ogó   A crooked staff typically held by the *orisha* Elegguá

Olokun   *Orisha* of the deep ocean, a realm also associated with the dead

Omo Añá   Literally, child of Añá. The name given to ritually consecrated *batá* players who are permitted to participate in formal ceremonies. Añá references the name of the *orisha* who resides in consecrated *batá* drums

Orishas   Spirit deities derived from Yoruba religions. They are tied to historical African figures and simultaneously understood to embody fundamental aspects of human life such as motherhood, masculinity, wisdom, sensuality, etcetera

Orquesta típica   A Cuban dance band of the nineteenth century featuring trombone, cornet, ophicleide, clarinet, violin, and *güiro*, among other instruments

Oru   A ritual sequence of devotional music or music and dance. *See also tratado*

Oru del Eyá Aránla   Literally "praise sequence on the patio." *Orisha* worship performance in a public space that involves drumming, song, and dance

Oru del Igbodú   Also known as *oru seco*. A private ceremony involving only drumming in a private room, usually in front of an altar. It involves a complex series of rhythms performed in honor of the *orishas*, in distinct order

Palero   A practitioner of Palo

Palo   A generic term for Kongo-influenced religions in Cuba. Also (when written in lower case) a style of folkloric drumming from the Dominican Republic

Plaza   The area in front of an altar or *trono* where gifts to the *orishas* are placed

Plegaria. Also transmisión.   The term for traditional praise hymns used in Spiritist traditions and more recently incorporated into *violines*. Many are believed to have come from eastern Cuba

Prenda   In Kongo-influenced religions, the name for sacred objects controlling spirit entities summoned and controlled by ritual specialists

Regla de Ocha *See also* **Santería.**   Literally, rule of the *orishas*, a term for Yoruba-influenced religious practices in Cuba

Religiosidad popular   Popular religiosity. A term referencing countless manifestations of largely Afrodescendant-influenced religious traditions in Cuba

Rezo   A nonmetrical sung prayer used in Santería worship

Rueda de casino   Literally, casino circle. The term for a style of salsa choreography involving couples arranged in a circle who perform simultaneous moves and pass partners around to others in the group

Rumbita de santo   A final, catchy song ending a musical praise sequence to an *orisha* in Santería

Rumba   A form of secular music and dance in Cuba, most often involving couples

Rumba guaguancó   A specific subgenre of rumba, the most common style

Rumba yambú   An older subgenre of rumba involving slower rhythms, less improvisation on the drums, and mimetic choreography

Salamalecum   A Cuban adaptation of the Arabic phrase "peace be with you." The greeting is often heard in Palo ceremonies or *cajón* performance and is associated with Kongo/African spirits

Santería   *See also* Ocha or Regla de Ocha. Religion of the saints. A common term for *orisha* worship

Santero/a   A practitioner of Santería

Santiguo   The act of blessing an individual in a *misa espiritual* by means of oil or holy water

Soca   A term from Trinidad and Tobago originally meaning "soul calypso," it now references a style of modern dance music

Son   Cuban *son* is a form of Black dance music that developed in eastern Cuba around 1900 and now serves as the basis of most popular music making

Tambolero   A drummer, often implicitly one who performs for religious events

Toque de santo   A devotional act devoted to the *orishas* involving drumming, song, and dance

Transmisión   See Plegaria

Tratado   A series of short religious songs in call–response format dedicated to a particular *orisha* and associated with Santería ceremony

Tres   A folkloric guitar-like instrument of Cuba that has three courses of double strings and plays syncopated melodies that outline chords

Trono   Literally, throne. A ritual altar used in *violín* and other celebrations associated with Santería

Tumbadora   Conga drum

Tumba francesa   A drumming, song, and dance tradition derived from Haiti and perpetuated by Haitian immigrants in eastern Cuba. The performances represent a "blackening" of elite francophone traditions; participants dress in fancy, colonial-era costumes and execute choreographies derived from the minuet and contradance to the accompaniment of drums

Villancico   A song associated with the Christmas season

Violín (also toque de violín)   A light devotional event to the *orishas* and/or spirits that is performed by small ensembles of violins and other instruments such as the guitar, bongo, hand percussion, and vocalists

Violines fusionados   *Violín* events involving worship of both *orishas* and other spirit entities

Yalodde   Literally, regal queen or great lady. A term of homage usually referring to Ochún

I

Introduction

An elderly guitarist/singer and violinist sit on plastic chairs in the back yard of a home in East Havana that has been rented by Cuban family members visiting from Miami. The musicians sip canned soda (a luxury in contemporary Cuba) as a few guests sit expectantly nearby. Others prepare food, chase after young children, play cards, or jump in and out of a small swimming pool. Almost all attendees at this event are white Cubans. The musicians have been hired to make an informal musical offering to the spirit world, and the guitarist asks his hosts whether they have any pieces in mind that they'd like to hear. They say "no"; whatever the duo chooses to play is fine. Musicians Roy Vázquez and María Teresa Gómez Noguera begin with an instrumental version of a bolero by Ernesto Lecuona from the early twentieth century: "Siempre en mi corazón" (Always in My Heart). They continue with a few *plegarias* or traditional hymns in Spanish from the local Spiritist tradition – "La luz redentora" (The Redeeming Light), "Misericordia" (Mercy), etcetera – then segue to a series of Cuban, Mexican, and Puerto Rican boleros: "Quiéreme mucho" (Love Me Deeply), "El reloj" (The Clock), "Madrigal" – before switching to a famous chachachá, "El bodeguero" (The Shopkeeper). Following a break, they continue with a *plegaria* to the Virgin of Charity, Cuba's mixed-race patron saint, then a popular song by Miguel Matamoros ("Mi veneración") about visiting the Virgin of Charity's shrine in El Cobre valley. Toward the end of their performance, as rum and beer circulate freely, the musicians increase the tempo of their music and incorporate catchy choral refrains into their set that reference the *orishas*[1]

---

[1] *Orishas* are spirit deities derived from Yoruba religions. They are tied to historical African figures and simultaneously understood to embody fundamental aspects of human life such as motherhood, masculinity, wisdom, sensuality, etcetera.

Ochún and Yemayá with phrases such as "*Deja que Yalodde te toque, y deja que Yalodde te pase la mano*" (Let the regal queen [Ochún] touch you, let her pass her hand over you").[2] To conclude, they have the crowd clap along with a series of choruses taken from commercial music of the mid-twentieth century: the refrain of "Amalia Batista" from the *zarzuela* of the same name: "*Amalia Batista, Amalia mayombe, ¿qué tiene esa negra que amarra a los hombres?*" (Amalia Batista, Amalia *mayombe*, what is it about that dark woman that attracts men so?);[3] "*Tranquilidad, Juan Francisco, tranquilidad, tranquilidad, ese revólver que tú tienes no tira ná*" (Relax, Juan Francisco, relax, that revolver you have there won't shoot at all);[4] "*Monta mi caballo que está en la puerta que da al Camino Real*" (Get on my horse that's in the door leading to the Royal Highway);[5] and others.

In another *violín* event organized near Havana's Almendares Park near the river, the crowd was racially mixed but Black participants predominated, as is more commonly the case. Several in attendance described themselves as daughters of Yemayá and the ocean but also *hijas de las dos aguas*, spiritually tied to Ochún and fresh water as well. The organizer chose to situate the event near a river because it was centrally located, and because as a forested park it represented all elements of nature.[6] She had hired a musical group including a guitarist, violinist, a flute player, and two percussionist-singers who alternated playing bongo, *güiro*, and clave. And she prepared for the activity by creating multiple altars on the ground

---

[2] A note on orthography: my study references many terms associated with Afro-Cuban religions and *violines* that exist primarily in oral tradition; they can be written or (or even pronounced) many different ways. For example, the word "Yalodde" that ritually salutes Ochún can also be written as "Iyalodde" (which many believe the most accurate spelling) or "Yalorde"; the Lucumí or Yoruba-influenced term for spirits of one's ancestors may be written as *egun*, *Eggun*, *eggún*, etc. When in doubt about which spelling to employ, I have chosen those found in Lydia Cabrera's (1970) collection of Yoruba/Lucumí vocabulary.

[3] This *zarzuela* features an attractive mixed-race woman as a protagonist who can pass as white and pursues affairs with elite white Cuban men. The term "*mayombe*" references Kongo religions and suggests that at least some of her appeal to men results from magic.

[4] This chorus comes from a *charanga* dance tune ("Tranquilidad, Juan Francisco" popularized by the Orquesta Jorrín in the mid-twentieth century). Its lyrics make joking metaphorical reference to Juan Francisco's sexual limitations, and may also represent an implicit plea for calm and nonviolence. It appears to have first been recorded on the Areito LP LD-4012 from 1981, *Con Jorrín en el Capri*. Thanks to Verónica González at FIUs Green Library for the reference.

[5] The refrain comes from the Miguel Matamoros composition "El fiel enamorado" ("The Faithful Romantic") from the late 1920s. The song's lyrics speak to unrequited love and a desire to elope with a young woman by riding off with her on a horse.

[6] Canto Herrera interview, December 2023.

dedicated to the four cardinal points of the compass and to the primary elements. One was filled with lit candles to represent fire and adorned with crystals of various colors, fresh flowers, and jewelry. A second contained small glasses of water and seashells; another used stones and pieces of wood to reference the earth. A spiritual leader opened the service by asking all individuals affiliated with religions to contribute with invocations of their choosing, and later invited anyone interested in praying to other ancestral sources of energy to do so. Two *babalawos*[7] spoke, then an *iyawó* or recent initiate into Regla de Ocha,[8] then a woman initiated in Palo.[9] The organizer continued by reciting an extended prayer with words unknown to me (she later described it as a unique spiritual expression inspired by her culturally diverse spirit guides).[10] Following this introduction, the musicians began to play, continuing for about an hour and a half. Initial pieces included repertoire associated with the Catholic Church and a song in Spanish dedicated to Elegguá. Later pieces included songs to Catholic saints, to Yemayá and Babalú Ayé, and others dedicated to Kongo spirits, Gypsy and Indian spirits, and to Changó.

As may be evident from these descriptions, the term *violín* (or *toque de violín*) references a range of musical performances with ties to multiple forms of spiritual practice and to sacred and secular music making. As someone who has studied more traditional forms of African-influenced religious worship for decades, I initially found the "in-betweenness" represented by *toques de violín* unintelligible. Rather than hearing complex rhythmic patterns on *batá* drums or other percussion and chants primarily sung in African-derived languages, I encountered instead a bewildering amalgam of repertoire. Instrumental music abounds in *violines*, such as waltzes, boleros, pop hits, Tin Pan Alley songs ("Blue Moon" and "Over the Rainbow"), and light classical pieces by Cuban and European composers. Cuban popular music features prominently too, such as guitar-based *trova* and *sones* from the early twentieth century. Devotional songs dedicated to a variety of saints and other spirit entities constitute much of the repertoire too: songs to San Miguel (a powerful warrior), San Lázaro (a healer), and others. Chants to the *orishas* may be performed in relatively traditional form, as instrumental melodies, or harmonized and arranged as

---

[7] A *babalawo* is a priest devoted to consulting the wisdom of the *orishas* through divination.
[8] Also known as Santería, a religious system influenced by traditions derived from present-day Nigeria.
[9] A Kongo-derived religion based on channelling the forces and wisdom of spirits of the dead.
[10] Canto Herrera, WhatsApp communication, February 18, 2024.

dance music. The ensembles accompanying such groups can include anything from accordion or synthesizer piano to cowbell. Overall, the mood associated with *violines* tends to be lighter and more festive than in sacred drumming performances. Participants enter and leave freely, many sitting passively and filming particular segments on their cell phones as if they were at a public concert. Compared with other rituals, *violines* also tend to be short, concluding within a couple of hours.

Despite their popularity today, *violín* history is poorly documented. Ethnographer Fernando Ortiz never mentions them in his expansive work from the mid-twentieth century, for instance, nor do other prominent ethnographers of the period (Lydia Cabrera, Rómulo Lachatañeré, Argeliers León).[11] The same is true of most other publications on religion and music that have appeared more recently (e.g., Bolívar 1990; Castellanos and Castellanos 1992; Barreal Fernández et al. 1998; Barnet 2001; Fernández Olmos and Paravisini-Gebert 2011). This lack of attention to *toques de violín* derives from multiple factors, one of which is their close ties to Spiritism as well as Santería, the former another under-researched form of worship. Diana Espírito Santo (2015, 33) describes Spiritism as "Cuba's most prolific ritual practice today," yet notes that few studies of it have been undertaken, possibly because many scholars of Caribbean religion prefer to explore traditions more exclusively tied to the African diaspora. Spiritism, and especially *espiritismo cruzado* (crossed or integrated Spiritism, the most common form), fuse influences from orthodox and folk Catholicism, Spiritism as practiced in Europe, and multiple West African-derived religions (Leé Llosas 2005, 11). Indeed, *espiritismo cruzado* has strongly influenced the structure and organization of all *violines* and inspired an entire subgenre of performance: the *violín espiritual* (see Chapter 3). Researchers may have also overlooked *violines* because of a tendency to study Cuban religions and religious music according to discrete taxonomies: Yoruba-influenced beliefs, Kongo rites, Abakuá rites, Dahomeyan practices, and so on (e.g., León 1984).[12] *Toques de violín*, representing an especially complex amalgam of diverse practices, do not fit neatly into any such category.

---

[11] See, for instance, Lachatañeré 1992 (a collection of works written the 1930s and 1940s), Ortiz 1981 [1951], and Barreal Fernández 1966.

[12] The same divisions are evident in many later works, based on earlier paradigms (e.g., Guanche 1983, Matibag 1996, Barnet 2001). All recognize mixture and change in local religious systems, but don't sufficiently emphasize their fundamentally interpenetrated nature.

It appears that devotees of Santería and Spiritism initially incorporated the violin into devotion in the early twentieth century because they associated its sound with sweetness, sophistication, maternity, and the sound of flowing water (Balbuena Gutiérrez 2003, 112; Cortes 2016). Thus, *violines* are often organized to venerate water deities and female *orishas*, especially Ochún, known for her love of sweet and elegant things. In Cuba, many now also honor Yemayá, Obatalá, Elegguá, and other deities or spirits with the same music. Early performances included only solo violins, but, as of at least the 1970s, ensembles expanded to incorporate additional instruments. An even more rapid expansion of *violín* performance took place with the religious opening in Cuba made possible by the Fourth Communist Party Congress in 1991 and its tolerant stance toward all devotion (Moore 2006, 220ff.). *Violines* (and other forms of worship) are now performed openly across the island and in its diaspora – Miami, Mexico, Venezuela, Ecuador, Toronto – and economic need has led more instrumentalists than before (including many classically trained nonbelievers) to form *violín* ensembles as a means of generating extra income.

The structure of *violines* varies, but most often incorporates ritual song sequences (*orus*) of various sorts. Most begin with a short initial set of pieces derived from the Catholic Church, the concert stage, and/or the Spiritist tradition that musicians play in front of an altar dedicated to whichever entity is being honored. These slower pieces, sometimes performed before other guests arrive, are followed by longer and livelier sequences intended for everyone to enjoy. In the case of *violines espirituales*, many *orus* typically begin with *plegarias* devoted to Catholic saints. Later sequences pay homage to locally recognized *comisiones* (families of related spirit beings), especially Kongos. *Violines* devoted primarily to the *orishas* follow a similar structure: they combine traditional songs in Lucumí (a Yoruba-influenced ritual language) with Spanish-language *plegarias* and other songs that reference the *orishas* indirectly. The *zarzuela* aria "Damisela encantadora," for example, is often performed in honor of Ochún since she is understood to be an enchanting damsel. The waltz "Sobre las olas" (Over the Waves) may serve as an offering for Yemayá because she is an ocean goddess. Or a *son* like "El huerfanito" (The Little Orphan) may be played to pay homage to Obatalá because he is believed to be a caretaker of the vulnerable, such as orphans. Later segments of *violín* celebrations tend to foreground popular repertoire or open-ended vamps that foreground improvisation. Many songs, even those with overtly religious lyrics, are accompanied by chordal harmonies on the guitar or keyboard, percussive grooves, and violin *guajeos* (syncopated, repeating melodic riffs) derived from dance music ensembles. This eclectic approach to music making, the foregrounding of pop music elements, and the fact that direct dialogue with spirits or *orishas* through possession is not the goal of *violines* all contribute to an informal atmosphere distinct from other religious rites.

Another, even looser category of performance associated with *violín* ensembles are *dones de gracia* – literally, gifts of grace or offerings of gratitude. This modality is most often organized by individuals who have not "made their saint" or have no formal religious affiliation, and they are especially common on Mother's Day. *Dones de gracia* accentuate the "festive" character of *violines* further and have virtually no formal structure (García Lacerra 2015, 45). Musicians describe them as *descargas*: free jam sessions based around repertoire with only loose ties to spirits, saints, *orishas*, or religious themes.

INTERPRETING THE VIOLÍN

How are we to interpret the emergence of *toques de violín*? What resources does this reformulation of Black religion offer to Cubans in the twenty-first century, a period of pandemic disruption and renewed economic crisis? What does the popularity of *violines* suggest about recent trends in Black religious practice, aesthetically and conceptually? Many forms of devotion combine and absorb diverse influences, of course; Johnson and Palmié (2018, 450–1) characterize Afro-Latin American religions especially as involving layered affiliations, the cultivation of "parallelisms" and "'double participation' … within larger, heterogeneous religious ecologies." Yet *violines* accentuate these tendencies in new ways, and their adoption by practitioners of Regla de Ocha is especially striking. Why are they performed regularly in tandem with or as a substitution for more traditional forms of drumming, dance, and song? I argue that *violines* express religious faith in more pluralistic ways than in the past, reconciling longstanding Afrodiasporic practices with commercial repertoire that younger worshippers are comfortable with, and that they effectively amalgamate a host of distinct belief systems into a single event. They appeal to devotees in part because their approach to worship strikes many as modern and urbane, and because they seamlessly elide the realms of the sacred and the secular, the popular and the folkloric. Following Fred Moten (2018), *violín* performance can be viewed as fugitive, moving beyond externally imposed boundaries or categories and weaving together cultural objects or elements that formerly had little relation to one another.

It is worth emphasizing that while practitioners of Afro-Cuban religious music have perpetuated some songs and dances across many generations with little change, the same repertoire has a long history of being transformed radically in commercial music contexts. Beginning at least in the 1920s and 1930s with the rise of the *afrocubanismo* movement, religious themes, melodies, and terminology began to appear in the recordings of ensembles such as the Septeto Habanero and Septeto Nacional, the compositions of Margarita Lecuona and Gilberto Valdés, as well as in poetry, prose, visual art, and other media (Moore 1997). The trend accelerated into the mid-twentieth century with commercial releases by Celia Cruz, Merceditas Valdés, Chano Pozo, Gina Martín, and Celina González, and has been perpetuated more recently in the music of Irakere, Batacumbele, Mezcla, Síntesis, NG La Banda, collaborations between Wynton Marsalis and Pedrito Martínez, etcetera.[13] On concert stages and elsewhere, performers have long blurred the boundaries between the sacred and the secular. Even so, the embrace of pop music in devotional contexts represents something new.

Practitioners view *violines* as a distinct form of expression not to be confused with drumming-based worship (*tambores*) that has the explicit goal of calling down the *orishas*. For the most part, the religious community has embraced *violines*, yet their approach to worship represents enough of a break with established practice to generate many differences of opinion. Certainly the harmonizing of Afrodescendant devotional chants with Western chord sequences and the "dancifying" of praise songs represent significant stylistic changes – and, some might say, radical ones. Hearing sacred songs performed as fun-loving dance tunes fundamentally affects the "interpretive moves" (Feld 1984) by which audience members evaluate them. Such an approach encourages participants to respond to sung prayers as a form of popular culture, both conceptually and in terms of physical movement. Many adaptations of repertoire seem to consciously blur the boundaries of spirituality, using sound as a means of generating affect and pleasure while they tack between references to mundane and religious themes.

Violines complicate any fixed sense of genre because of their amalgamated nature, the varied musical forms they incorporate, and their lack of

---

[13] Regarding Marsalis and Martínez, see their amazing Carnegie Hall performance from 2014, available on YouTube: www.YouTube.com/watch?v=huGNcMoXCkY&t=3055s (accessed September 21, 2023).

consistent structure from one event to the next. They could be described as taking Danilo Orozco's (2001) notion of "inter-genre" – denoting a musical style that foregrounds intertextuality – to new extremes. They might also be characterized as a "performance complex" (Madrid and Moore 2013, 10–11) in that they create only a loosely defined space of affect whose specific manifestations are determined by the needs of the organizer. The *violín* construct weaves together entirely distinct repertoires and stylistic referents, all of which may be emphasized or deemphasized at any given moment.

Moten's notion of fugitivity helps frame *violín* performance as part of a broader array of Afrodiasporic expression in the Americas. The essence of Black performance for Moten involves an ongoing refusal to accept externally imposed boundaries, categories, standards, or orthodoxies, the weaving together of cultural objects or elements that formerly had little relation to one another (Wallace 2018), and, in many cases, an embrace of the vernacular and apolitical in addition to the spiritual. In *Stolen Life* (2018), Moten writes that, in jazz and other forms of African American music, fugitivity entails "a desire for and a spirit of escape and transgression of the proper and the proposed. It's a desire for the outside, for a playing or being outside, an outlaw edge proper to the now always already improper voice or instrument" (131). Moten frames Black fugitivity as emergent, improvised, "a poesis of explicitly 'informal' form-giving in performance and music" (Schulman 2021, 274) and in everyday social practices. He views vitality and freedom as inherent to such expression, imagined not as chaos or an absence of structure but as an act that makes sense of things, moving across boundaries, weaving together diverse cultural realities. Moten (2018, 287) perceives "a structural antagonism between institutionalized (white) forms and informal (black) sociality" within jazz that also helps explain the dynamics of *violín* performance and its complex amalgams. *Violines* from this perspective can be viewed as transcending reified categories, challenging existing orthodoxies, working to unify the sacred and the secular, and refashioning spirituality to conform to the fractured realities of life in postslave and postcolonial contexts. Following this framing, I view *violines* as an antigenre of sorts that defy easy classification (perhaps to an even greater extent than jazz, since their meanings extend far beyond the sonic) and that change form constantly as they draw on multiple elements of Afrodiasporic and Eurodescendant music and religiosity. *Violines* contribute to a space of "elastic spirituality" that accommodates, welcomes, and reconciles diverse elements of primarily subaltern Caribbean experience.

This study contributes to scholarship on Cuban and Caribbean religions and music extending beyond the confines of current literature in various ways. Existing publications on the music of Santería, for instance, focus primarily on topics such as percussion instruments and rhythms, song forms, texts, cosmology, and traditional ritual practices (e.g., Murphy 1994, Amira and Cornelius 1999), the biographies of particular performers (Vélez 2000, Vaughan and Aldama 2012), the codification of Black religious practices and ideologies toward particular political ends (Palmié 2002), or government attempts to regulate and folklorize religious performance (Hagedorn 2001). By contrast, my study examines new entanglements between the sacred and the secular and new appropriations of Eurodescendant cultural forms on the part of practitioners. It thus re-examines the notion of Black religious music making itself. It analyzes a poorly documented form of expression and its relation to the many sociopolitical changes the country has experienced in recent decades. I argue that *violines* represent a fascinating point of intersection between repertoires and beliefs, and that participants engage with them in many ways and to different ends. On some level, *violines* attest to multiple tendencies simultaneously: the continued mainstreaming of Afrodescendant religious traditions and their ongoing engagement with other, more commercial forms of music and culture; the ever-wider influence of Spiritism on multiple forms of devotion; and perhaps also the gradual loss of esoteric Lucumí religious knowledge among present-day practitioners of Regla de Ocha and their preference for Spanish-language texts. Some now find it easier to pay homage to Ochún or Yemayá without learning as many traditional songs and dances, for instance.[14] Yet *violines* also attest to the creation of new spaces of worship for the initiated and the uninitiated, and to the expansion of religious communities and their music making.

Miraima García Lacerra's BA thesis from 2015 represents the most substantive investigation on *violines* to date and provides useful background information, as does Ana Koprivica's masters thesis (2002) and an article derived from it (2010). Cuban musicologists (Casanova Oliva 1988; Balbuena 2003) have discussed *violines* briefly in works devoted to broader topics. Filmmaker Ernesto Sotto released a documentary in 2009, *El misterio de las aguas*, about devotion to the Caridad del Cobre (closely associated with the *orisha* Ochún) and includes footage of a *toque de violín*.

---

[14] See also Ochoa 2020 for a discussion of more traditional *orisha* worship involving drumming that similarly incorporates phrases in Spanish.

He later wrote about the experience of attending that same event (Sotto 2012), during which at least one participant was possessed by a spirit guide. Afro-Cuban author Inés María Martiatu published a fictive short story (2008) describing *violines* from the perspective of a Black female musician. Johnny Frías (2015) published an article on *violines* as performed in Miami. Most recently, Finnish musicologist Ville Livari wrote a dissertation on forms of violin improvisation within the ceremonies (2023). Aside from these efforts, and one commercial CD release (Oviedo and Pinelli 2011), the only material readily available for consultation about *toques de violín* is the (substantial) video footage of them uploaded to YouTube by practitioners themselves and the webpages created by some performers to advertise their services. Related publications on the music of Cuban Spiritism are also scanty, though Axel Hesse's publications (1971, 1975) provide a useful point of departure.

Umbanda and Quimbanda in southern Brazil, as studied by Marc Gidal (2016), suggest many parallels between creole Caribbean religions and other Afrodiasporic practices. Gidal analyzes boundaries and boundary-crossing between various forms of religion, especially Batuque (a more heavily African-inspired drumming and song practice similar to Candomblé), Umbanda, and Quimbanda (also involving drumming traditions but more heavily influenced by Spiritism). *Violín* practitioners demonstrate less interest in maintaining boundaries and incorporate less drumming than the groups discussed by Gidal, yet the broad contours of such practices in Brazil – with their foregrounding of lineages (*linhas*) of spirit guides defined by race/ethnicity (including *ciganos* or Roma/Gypsies, *pretos velhos* or the spirits of African slaves, and Amerindian spirits such as *caboclos* or the *linha guarani*), and a heavy emphasis on devotional songs known as *pontos cantados* – bear a striking resemblance to *espiritismo cruzado* as practiced in Cuba.[15] The use of the *rabeca*, a northeastern Brazilian folk violin, in commercial recordings of Afro-Indigenous Jurema devotional songs by Maciel Salu parallel the Cuban practices discussed in this book to an extent as well,[16] though they represent the product of a single artist rather than a widespread tendency.

Some devotional practices in southern Haiti, particularly those dedicated to *lwa blâ* or white/foreign spirit deities, involve playing minuets

---

[15] See also Matory (2005, 30) for further discussion of the diverse spirits worshipped in Brazilian *caboclos* including Tupi Indians, mixed-race cowboys, and Turks.

[16] Cory LaFevers (2019) has discussed this phenomenon in Salu's recent release *Libertade*, drawing on the work of Cavalcante Rosa (2009) and others.

and contradances on the violin, accompanied by frame and hand drums and figure dancing (Lowenthal 1978, 401–2; see also Averill and Yi 2003, 278–80; Yi 1995, 419–72). This style of worship, part of an event known as a *bâboch violô* or all-night violin party/dance, suggests certain parallels with the Cuban *toque de violín*, though the repertoire derives primarily from instrumental European dance tunes as performed in colonial times. Averill notes[17] that Haitian *bâboch violô* is rare in the present day and is confined to small regions of the country. Colombian *violín caucano* tradition represents another form of Black violin repertoire derived from the colonial era, yet it has no religious ties. Also known locally as *violín negro*, its performers use either a standard violin or a folkloric variant made of guadua wood, a subspecies of bamboo.[18]

Finally, the *hatajo* (or *atajo*) *de negritos* from the southern coast of Peru deserves mention as a Black violin tradition that loosely parallels Cuban *violines* because of its religious associations. The term *hatajo* derives from the verb *atajar*, used to describe the herding of cattle. Ensembles consist of dozens of dancers and musicians (the latter performing primarily on guitars, violins, and hand percussion such as strings of bells) who process through the streets at Christmastime, most notably in towns such as El Carmen or San Regis. Performances combine elements of African, Andean/Indigenous, and European heritage. *Hatajo* music is performed in a brisk duple or triple meter; it incorporates prominent drone pitches accompanying short, repetitive melodic phrases and is danced *zapateado*-style. UNESCO recognizes *hatajo* as a form of Intangible Cultural Heritage, linked both to colonial-era religious devotion such as the *villancico* and to local histories of slavery and discrimination.[19]

VIOLINES AS AFRODIASPORIC RELIGION

Questions of terminology quickly come to the fore when analyzing Cuban *violines*, including the issue of whether they should be considered part of

---

[17] Personal email, April 28. 2021.
[18] Thanks to Cindia Arango López for bringing this practice to my attention. For more information, see the following links: www.youtube.com/watch?v=OcRTPoeK_xU (accessed May 21, 2024); https://bit.ly/4hCUPBT; https://bit.ly/41fGghN (accessed May 3, 2023).
[19] Representative performances can be viewed online: www.youtube.com/watch?v=VGsVGvwVsIY, www.youtube.com/watch?v=ow_hC-obaJI, and www.youtube.com/watch?v=VQqAbVZhOPg (accessed October 24, 2024). My thanks to Pilar Cáceres Cartagena for bringing the practice to my attention. More information about the practice is available here: https://bit.ly/3ECqjcu.

Black religious systems at all. Certainly the public for *violines* transcends racial boundaries, and much of the musical repertoire performed by *violín* ensembles derives from sources other than African or Black communities. Additionally, as Arisbel López Andraca notes, Caribbean religion and music making are both spheres of activity that have contributed to the erasure of racial barriers and social segregation. For these reasons, some scholars, especially within Cuba, take issue with terms like "Black religion" and avoid them.[20] Instead, researchers Lázara Menéndez Vázquez (2005a) and Jorge Ramírez Calzadilla (1997) employ phrases such as "religions of African origin" when referring to Ocha, Palo, and Abakuá rites, and, at least as often, broader terms without any racial referents, such as *religiosidad popular* (see also Leé Llosas 2005, 14; Carranza Fuentes 2011, 157). This may derive from a broader tendency within Cuba to downplay race as a determinant of social experience, and out of recognition that the racialization of religion was first used as a means of denying the legitimacy of and criminalizing Black devotion, for instance in Fernando Ortiz's early works (1973 [1906]). By contrast, terms such as "Afro-Cuban religion," "Black diasporic religion," "Yoruba-inspired," "African-imagined," or "African-inspired" are common in the writings of scholars based abroad, primarily when discussing Regla de Ocha and Palo (e.g., Beliso-De Jesús 2015, 2; Matibag 1996, vi–vii; Murphy 1994, 4; Ochoa 2010, 8; Fernández Olmos and Paravisini-Gebert 2011, 33). These authors underscore the origins of such worship among the slave population, in maroon encampments, and in urban *cabildos* (Black mutual aid societies) as a form of cultural resistance.

Literature on Spiritism in Latin America written by local and foreign scholars tends to even more consistently foreground Afrodescendant influences, perhaps to distinguish such practices from their European counterparts. Gidal (2016, 6) notes that practitioners of Umbanda (similar to *espiritismo cruzado*) refer to their religion as "Afro-gaucho"[21] in order to recognize its embrace of both African and European elements. He states (2016, 23) that spirits of Black ancestry are prominent in the devotional pantheon and underscores the degree to which it has been influenced by the African diaspora. Brandon (1993, 3) views Cuban Spiritism and even Latin American Catholicism as strongly influenced by African religions and thus

---

[20] Thanks to López Andraca for corresponding with me about these issues in September and October of 2019, and for introducing me to the recent works of many Cubanist scholars of religion.

[21] The term "gaucho" emphasizes the rural and primarily white ranching population in the area the study took place.

part of a Black diasporic tradition. Castellanos and Castellanos (1992, 192), Leé Llosas (2005, 19), and Espírito Santo (2015, 37–8, 59) all describe Cuban Spiritism as Black, partly because of its close ties to Ocha and Palo and because of the predominance of African spirit guides: Taita José, Ta Francisco, Ta Lorenzo Lucumí, Juan Mandinga, El Gangá, El Macuá, etcetera. All these entities manifest in *misas espirituales* (a form of creole séance), even when they are presided over by white mediums who have no affiliation with Ocha or Palo. Since Spiritism and Santería are the religious systems that most directly inform *toques de violín*, I also argue that *violines* should be considered Afro-Cuban. My view aligns with that Beliso-De Jesús (2015, 7) in framing them as a form of devotion that manifests "blackened ontologies" and racialized conceptions of the spiritual world drawn heavily from the African diaspora.

The way in which *toques de violín* straddle the boundary between religious and secular expression forces us to question whether they should be viewed as religious per se or only tied to a broader notion of spirituality. The latter I define as concern with the human soul or spirit as opposed to involvement in organized religious institutions or activities. Clifford Geertz (1973, 90) famously defined religion as a system of symbols "that establish powerful and long-lasting moods and motivations" in those who ascribe to them, helping define their understanding of the supernatural and guiding many of their everyday actions. By these criteria, *violines* are clearly religious in that they dialogue with and are informed by broader understandings of the divine. The fact that secular, bawdy, and irreverent moments feature prominently in *violines* as well does not negate their strong religious valence. Additionally, participants in *violines* also tend to worship in other, more traditional contexts as well. Thus, the overarching conceptual frame surrounding *violines* is congruent with Afrodescendant religious practice and might be considered a more secular variant of it.

Some authors describe African-influenced religions as manifesting a greater openness to external influences and to change than most other belief systems; on that basis, might the very newness and nontraditional nature of *violines* tie them to diasporic culture? Mintz and Price (1992, 45–7, 51), as one example, underscore the "additive ethos" of West and Central African religions, an acceptance of difference, an allowance for personal creative embellishment, and an expectation of cultural change as core elements. They note that the perpetuation of African religions in something approaching their original form in the Americas represents the exception rather than the rule. Ochoa (2010, 8) comes to similar conclusions. And David Font-Navarrete also perceives a fluidity to Afro-Cuban religion that allows for movement from one setting, language, format, or ritual context to another.[22] The association of particular *orishas* with Catholic saints represents one aspect of such fluidity, as do perceived equivalencies between certain Palo and Ocha spirits, the relatively free movement of song repertoires between Ocha worship, the *misa espiritual*, and *cajón de muerto* celebrations (discussed in Chapter 2), and between all of these modalities and *violines*.

TERMS OF CULTURAL DISLOCATION

Questions of terminology arise when considering how to describe the many cultural fusions and inter-influences found in *toques de violín*; such decisions are made against a backdrop of shifting understandings of culture in the humanities and social sciences. For some time these disciplines have described culture as emergent, shifting, mutable, contested, and heterogeneous, and they emphasize that all cultural forms involve fusion and mixture (e.g., Rosaldo 1995, xv). This is especially true in an era of mass migration, international markets, global communication, and in a region such as the Caribbean long known for cultural forms incorporating diverse influences (Bilby 1985). To what extent, then, is it useful or appropriate to discuss the striking displays of cultural mixture in *toques de violín* as different from diverse cultural influences found in other expressive forms, and, if so, from what perspective and using which concepts? I argue that much existing terminology must be used cautiously, and that it should align with local experiences and cultural politics. In the following paragraphs I discuss a few of the most commonly employed terms for cultural mixture from this perspective, most of which have been championed by foreign scholars.

Syncretism has become a polemical construct when describing Latin American heritage, largely because of its ties to colonialist expansion. Most tellingly, Catholic Church officials adopted it in the seventeenth century to deride local religious forms in the Americas believed to be aberrant and to contrast them with "true" orthodox beliefs (Stewart 2009, 204). Melville Herskovits attempted a revival of the term among academics in the 1930s; later authors have reframed it further in relation to notions of dominance and hegemony (e.g., Aijmer 1995) and have even proposed the additional term "anti-syncretism" to describe a resistance to cultural adaptation and the perpetuation of established cultural boundaries (Stewart and

---

[22] Zoom conversation, March 30, 2021.

Shaw 1994). Opinions differ about whether the concept of syncretism is fundamentally flawed. Many present-day authors in and beyond Cuba avoid it, though it still appears in some publications.[23] Cuban historian Zoila Lapique Becali advocates adopting syncretism from a subaltern perspective to describe the subversion of imposed hegemonic norms.[24] Antonio Benítez-Rojo (1996) provides another perspective, describing syncretic culture as inherently unstable, fragmented, and heterogeneous – a condition he views as a metaphor for the Caribbean itself. In discussing the Caridad del Cobre as a complex sign, for example, he suggests she be viewed not as a synthesis or unified whole, but rather as an aggregate of signifiers "made of differences" (1996, 12). I find the term potentially useful when analyzing the cultural assemblages found in *toques de violín*, though I prefer the locally generated terminology discussed in this section.

Notions of hybridity have a contested history as well, though one that only spans a few decades. In part the popularization of the term is linked to the rise of globalization studies, neoliberalist economics, a recognition of the ever more rapid movement of culture and ideas internationally, and a sense that cultural expression is increasingly transitory and malleable. García Canclini's work in the 1990s first tied the notion of hybridity to Latin America; he described the region as caught between traditional belief systems (characterized problematically in his writings as "premodern") and those imposed first through colonial dominance and later the influence of cosmopolitan urban elites. García Canclini's emphasis on the interpenetration of the foreign and the local resonates with Paul Gilroy's (1993, 35) descriptions of Black Atlantic cultures as fragmented through colonial and postcolonial encounters. In subsequent years, numerous critiques have been leveled at hybridity scholarship: for instance, that it fails to sufficiently interrogate concepts such as "traditional culture" which represent the constitutive parts of hybrid forms, and that in certain respects it perpetuates outmoded and apolitical notions of *mestizaje* from the mid-twentieth century (Nederveen Pieterse 2001). In response, scholars have tended to frame their analyses of hybridity in more overtly political terms within overarching structures of dominance (Stokes 2004), and/or to analyze the strategic uses of hybrid cultural forms on the part of local communities. While recognizing

---

[23] E.g., Castellanos and Castellanos 1992, 195; Leé Llosas 2005, 22.

[24] In the documentary *El misterio de las aguas* (Sotto 2012), for instance, she states "El sincretismo fue la forma de enmascarar a las deidades ancestrales africanas con las deidades católicas ... Como decía una vieja ex-esclava que yo tuve la suerte de conocer con Lydia Cabrera, 'Mis orishas tienen un nombre en Yoruba, y tienen un nombre en español.'"

the limitations of the term, I do occasionally use it to draw attention to striking juxtapositions of musical style in *violines*. Of course, the notion of hybridity generally fails to capture a full sense of the dynamic and emergent cultural space *violín* performance creates, and does not address what such fusions mean to participants.

In my analysis I more typically adopt other terms of cultural mixture derived from the Caribbean itself, such as "transculturation," coined by Fernando Ortiz in the 1940s (Moore 2018b, 27–9) and "creolization," initially championed by Black literary theorists of the 1960s such as Eduard Glissant (Moore 2010, 19–21). Ortiz framed transculturation as an alternative to Herskovits's earlier concept of acculturation; Ortiz viewed the latter as more multilinear, less focused on the impact of dominant or Eurocentric culture on non-Western populations. And he attempted, with a series of related terms (deculturation, neoculturation, metastasis, metalepsis), to more clearly define some of the ways cultural forms move between classes, racial/ethnic groups, and others. Those who advocate the use of transculturation today (e.g., Palmié 2013, 97) note that it suggests constant adaptation on the part of multiple groups and, thus, endlessly shifting or transient cultural exchanges as a component of the Caribbean experience. Some describe this implicitly "centerless" model as a precursor to postmodernist thought (Benítez-Rojo 1996, 150ff.), though others question whether Ortiz's writings imply belief in what he perceived as "pure" cultural forms derived from Africa and elsewhere before their integration in the Americas (Pavez Ojeda 2016). While the notion of transculturation remains useful, the model as conceived by Ortiz does not necessarily interrogate the motivations for cultural adaptation, nor does it emphasize the agency of musicians or religious practitioners within the creative processes central to *violines*.

Creolization as theorized by Glissant experienced a renaissance of sorts in the new millennium and has been foregrounded in numerous publications (Buisseret 2000; Chaudenson 2001; Stewart 2007; Lionnet and Shih 2011). It has its origins in the Portuguese word *crioulo*, referring first to a slave raised in a master's house, and by extension to Africans displaced from their homeland in new surroundings (Stewart 2009, 201–2).[25] Its etymology thus speaks to physical and cultural dislocation, and, accordingly, the strategies of those subjected to such experiences. Later in the Spanish-speaking Americas, the parallel term *criollo* originally came to denote anything of European origin

---

[25] Lorraine Leu (personal communication) notes that the term *crioulo* has tremendously negative associations in modern Portuguese, being roughly equivalent with the "n-word."

transplanted to or re-established in the New World, especially white/peninsular immigrants. To colonial-era authors in Spain, white creole populations were often associated negatively with the loss of habits or established practices. But increasingly in the twentieth century, Caribbeanists have reconceived the concept to emphasize the creative fusion or blending of cultural elements over time and the fashioning of something new and unique out of them. In this way, creolization does foreground local agency on the part of Black or mixed-race populations and implicitly references broader patterns of dominance and resistance that have long characterized the region (Camal 2019). Creative processes of creolization have allowed Afrodescendent groups to survive the processes of cultural and psychological genocide initiated by the slave trade, as noted by Reynaldo Fernández Pavón.[26] Because of the term's grassroots resonance and transgressive associations, I find creolization one of the most useful ways of denoting processes of religious cultural fusion.

All of the concepts mentioned here can be useful in analyzing *violines*, yet I would argue that none is entirely satisfactory given the challenges to established practice that such performance represents. By their very nature *violines* subvert normative constructs of religion, even *orisha* worship, and blur the binary of sacred/secular. They create a performance space that does not allow for singular forms of expression of any kind. Music making across established boundaries becomes not only the norm but the only acceptable option; the world of *violín* performance forcefully rejects unilinear views of culture.

The multilayered nature Afro-Cuban religions makes any analysis of them a daunting task; this is especially true because of the many ways they have influenced one another since the earliest days of colonization (Mintz and Price 1992, 3). Contemporary ethnographies documenting the lives of practitioners underscore the extent of this interpenetration. Ochoa (2010, 55, 145; 2020, 78), for instance, describes rural Cuban devotion in which Palo and Ocha influences mix freely, and he notes that Palo Kimbisa and other Kongo-influenced traditions freely adopt Spiritist and other practices. Espírito Santo (2015, x) similarly describes Black Cuban religious domains (Lucumí, Palo, Spiritist) as intertwined, noting that her primary consultants were involved in all of them. Additional examples underscoring connections between Afrodiasporic religious spheres include the memoirs of Irna, as compiled by Feraudy Espino (1999), and the biographies of percussionist Felipe García Villamil (Vélez 2000), the religious figures Eva

[26] Personal email, November 19, 2023.

Fernández Bravo (Mikelsons 2005), Alfredo Calvo Cano (Beliso-De Jesús 2015), and others interviewed by José Millet (1993). These publications make the case that Black religious traditions must be viewed as a collective, rather than as distinct beliefs.

Brief discussion of the positionality of authors writing on Caribbean religions is appropriate here. With a few exceptions – Rómulo Lachatañeré, Rogelio Martínez Furé, Tomás Fernández Robaina – most prominent authors on Afro-Cuban religions (local and foreign) are white, and many are non-practitioners. Collectively, these scholars have been accused of intellectual theft, stealing secrets and mystical knowledge from their informants to further their own careers (see Beliso-De Jesús 2015, 33), as well as of sensationalizing aspects of devotion in their publications, such as the ritual sacrifice of animals or the invocation of *orisha* spirits. This was especially true in the mid-twentieth century. As a white researcher myself, and with no overt religious affiliations, I am forced to confront this uncomfortable legacy, something Martínez Furé describes as *jineterismo pseudocultural*[27] and that resonates with many recent critiques in anthropology, ethnomusicology, and related disciplines. David Font-Navarrete expresses concern with this aspect of religious scholarship that he believes implicates him as well (even as a Hispanic *santero*);[28] he notes that it speaks to the extent of white privilege in the Americas, to stark divisions between elites and communities of color, and, more broadly, to the importance of considering racial dynamics in all facets of academia. I have not resolved this issue to my satisfaction, but I have tried to foreground Black voices and perspectives throughout the book, following the pathbreaking scholarship of Tomás Fernández Robaina (2001), who was one of the first to allow believers a chance to express their opinions directly in print. I hope my work affords the religious community a small measure of additional representation, and that the project documents and legitimizes a form of expression they care deeply about. The only factor making a study of *violines* somewhat less problematic than other religious modalities is that they do not typically lead to possession. For that reason, receiving permission to film performances was often possible (drumming events cannot be filmed), and for the most part participants seemed genuinely interested in discussing in *violines* with Melena Francis Valdés, Rosy Bayona Mojena, and

---

[27] Feraudy Espino 1999, 14. *Jineterismo* derives from *jinete* or horseman. It refers to streetwise hustlers in present-day Cuba who find ways to make a living by "riding" tourists: providing them goods or services, or selling sex, in exchange for cash. Martínez Furé flips the association and makes foreign academics, especially, the focus of exploitative practices.

[28] Zoom conversation, March 30, 2021.

me. Melena was especially effective at conducting interviews because of her personal status as a professional musician and religious practitioner consecrated in Ocha as a daughter of Ochún. Some in the Cuban religious community continue to view *violín* worship as too "light" and/or too far removed from other forms of Black devotional practice (see Chapter 2 and the conclusion), but the fact that direct interaction with spirits and *orishas* is not the goal makes it a somewhat less contentious focus of study.

CHAPTER DESCRIPTIONS

Chapter 2 provides an overview of what is known of the development of the *violines* since their inception in the early twentieth century and the influences that gave rise to them. It describes *violín* ensembles and the repertoire they play in detail, the musical backgrounds of performers, and the motivations behind organizing such an event. It discusses the relationship of *violines* to other kinds of worship, such as the *cajón de muerto*, and the contested meanings of *violín* performance in present-day Cuba. Chapter 3 explores the close ties between *misas espirituales* and the *violín* tradition. It considers the ways in which the praise songs and *plegarias* of Spiritism, and, to an extent, the structure of the *misa* itself, have influenced *violines*. Later, the chapter examines music making in Spiritist-oriented *violines*, and how musicians elaborate *plegarias* and other praise songs through acts of devotion.

Chapter 4 explores the ways that *violines* have been incorporated into Regla de Ocha worship, with an emphasis on ceremonies dedicated to Ochún, which are by far the most common. It reflects on the importance of the Caridad del Cobre as a local mixed-race saint to notions of *cubanidad* beginning in the late nineteenth century, and her strong association with Ochún on the part of *santeros*. The chapter continues by examining typical repertoire in *violines de santo* and the ways musicians make musical offerings to the *orishas*. Chapter 5, on performance dynamics, begins by stressing the degree to which individual *violín* events differ from one another, stressing the elastic construct of the genre and the many modalities musicians choose from as they play. It continues by exploring spontaneity, improvisation, and verbal play in *violines* through a close analysis of several climactic sequences in particular devotional acts. Chapter 6 discusses the spread of *violines* outside of Cuba through its diaspora to Mexico City, Caracas, New York, Miami, and elsewhere, and how the tradition has changed in the process. It notes that the relatively loose notion of how to honor *orishas* and spirits in *violines* has allowed performers abroad to reimagine the practice as they see fit, often resulting in entirely new forms of worship. The Conclusion reflects further on the significance of *violines* to the history of Cuban and Afrodiasporic religions by comparing them with similar musical styles such as gospelypso in Trinidad, devotional samba in Brazil (Burdick 2013; Iyanga 2015, 2023), and recent fusions of Dominican sacred and secular repertoire in New York (Tallaj 2018).

2

Situating *Violines*

> A few years ago in the Havana temple on Salud street, I was surprised to hear the piece "La bella cubana" by José White played for the Caridad del Cobre. While the violinist performed, an *iyawó* prayed in front of her image. In this convergence of elegant colonial-era repertoire typical of a salon and the faith of an Ocha initiate ... I discovered a complex sign, a unique expression, singularly creative, a way of treating and experiencing the sacred that does not recognize hard differences and instead adds, mixes, interlinks.
>
> (Sarria 2012, 64)[1]

Chapter 2 provides contextual information surrounding *violines* so as to better understand their varied manifestations in Cuba and their broader social meanings. It discusses what is known of *violín* history and how the practice has changed since the 1970s. It describes the ensembles that perform them and the events themselves in greater detail. It devotes attention to the relationship between the *toque de violín* and *cajón de muerto*, the latter another under-researched form of religious devotion fusing elements of multiple religious practices and that shares musical repertoire with *violines*. Finally, the chapter considers the relationship of

---

[1] Hace unos años, en el templo habanero de la calle Salud, me sorprendió escuchar la música de 'La bella cubana' de José White, tocada para Ella. Mientras el violinista ejecutaba, un iyawó pedía ante su imagen. En esa conciliación de nuestra sonoridad colonial, de la elegancia de salón, con la fe del iniciado en Ocha ... descubría un complejo signo, una forma propia, singular y creadora, de tratar, de sentir lo sagrado, que no repara en diferenciaciones estrictas, que añade, mezcla, entrecruza.

The temple referred to here is apparently the Santuario Diocesano de Nuestra Señora de La Caridad on the corner of Salud and Manrique streets, known for devotional events dedicated to la Caridad del Cobre.

violín issues of class. *Violines* represent a marked shift in aesthetics relative to earlier events used to praise *orishas* and other spirit beings; for that reason they can appeal to individuals with "aspirational" sensibilities or those who feel more comfortable listening to string and harmony instruments rather than drums alone. A variety of opinions exist about *violines* and their appeal vis-à-vis traditional drumming and song. Some listeners prefer them, others view them as too much of a break with tradition.

VIOLINES AS PRACTICE

Violines have existed in something resembling their current form only since about the 1940s or 1950s. Initially they developed among the Black professional classes and involved preparing an altar, buying a cake or other pastries, getting the family together, inviting one's spiritual community, and playing or singing as a group, especially to Ochún. More than anything else, as mentioned, a *toque de violín* represents an act of homage, a gift, an offering.[2] It is not intended to displace other forms of worship, though its heightened visibility suggests that it may in time. Some in the religious community view *violines* as a way of refreshing the ambience of devotional gatherings after "heavier" or more emotionally intense drumming and spirit mounting,[3] or simply to make people happy by dancing and singing in more popular styles.[4] For these reasons, patrons may keep *violín* musicians around to play after a formal ceremony ends (either a *toque de violín* or other religious performance) simply to entertain their guests.[5] Devotees view *violines* as a natural extension of daily offerings or interactions of a less spectacular nature that they exchange with their *orishas* and other spirit guardians. *Santeros* and Spiritists typically maintain an altar both to their *orisha(s)* and to ancestors or spirit guides in their home, frequently cleaning them and replacing flowers, candles, or other gifts (Castellanos and Castellanos 1992, 195). They offer prayers to the dead and to *orishas* every day, and *violín* performance can be understood as an extension of the same tendency (Figure 2.1).

Violines are rarely offered spontaneously because of the expense involved; worshippers organize them because they feel indebted to an

---

[2] Zurbano interview, June 2018.
[3] Anonymous interview, April 2022.
[4] Fernández Díaz interview, January 2021.
[5] Anonymous interview, December 2020.

FIGURE 2.1 A *brindis* or toast in honor of the *orisha* Ochún, a climactic moment in many *violín* ceremonies (see Chapter 4). Photo courtesy of Rosy Bayona Mojena, 2018.

orisha or *muerto* (Martiatu 1998) or because such an event has been requested in a spiritual reading (*consulta*). They take place throughout the year, but most often from September to December, sometimes on a particular saint's day (for instance, on September 8th for La Caridad del Cobre),[6] or on the anniversary of the day a devotee completed their initiation. And they can be dedicated to a variety of *orishas* (especially Ochún, Yemayá, Oyá, and Obatalá) or spirits. Most Afrodiasporic religions share a belief that supernatural forces actively intervene in the lives of the living to solve personal problems (Gidal 2016, 3), but their help requires worshippers to demonstrate their dedication on a regular basis. This contractual relationship motivates ritual, and in fact the need to resolve an imminent personal crisis compels many believers to involve themselves in religion in the first place. As an example, some may organize a *violín* because their daughter is pregnant and they want the baby to be born healthy. Some may have a son or daughter in prison and seek divine intervention to shorten their confinement. Others may wish to travel, to request aid so that some other traveler reaches their destination safely, or

---

[6] Other important saints' days frequently associated with *violines* include September 7 (associated with the Virgin of Regla/Yemayá), September 24 (the day of Nuestra Señora de las Mercedes/Obatalá), December 4 (for Santa Bárbara/Changó), December 17 (for San Lázaro/Babalú Aye), and February 2 (for Santa Teresa/Oyá). See also Brown 2019, 305.

to ritually cleanse their home of an unfriendly spirit presence.[7] Musicians communicate with organizers prior to each event to see which spirit entities need to be praised and modify their repertoire accordingly.[8]

Divination often leads devotees to organize *violines*. *Babalawos* – trained ritual specialists in Ifá divination (an ancient Yoruba-derived system of seeking guidance from the *orisha* Orunla) – cast a divining chain to generate sets of numbers (with 256 possible *odu* or combinations) that correspond to distinct proverbs; the *babalawo* then interprets the proverbs for individuals based on their concerns and determines the best course of action for them. Certain proverbs may imply a deity is upset and needs to be placated: if that deity is Ochún, for instance, who enjoys *violines*, music making may be organized for her, along with other ritual offerings (the latter might involve placing honey and fresh water on an altar in one's home).[9] The specific nature of an offering may be determined through additional questions posed to Orunla by the *babalawo*: does Ochún (for instance) want a *tambor*? Does she want a *güiro*? Does she want a *violín*?[10] Though *violín* performances are open to all friends and neighbors, the motivations behind them are rarely discussed; they reference personal aspects of an individual's life that many prefer to keep to themselves.

Much as in the case of drumming events, a typical *violín* takes place in the afternoon and lasts about two hours. Most often they are held in a private home but also in churches, on the edge of a river, at the ocean, in the countryside, or in a cemetery (García Lacerra 2015, 45). Events frequently consist of public and private segments. The latter takes place before most guests arrive and may involve only the person(s) organizing the event and close friends or a spiritual guide.[11] This segment is relatively short and features slower repertoire: often a capella singing dedicated to the *orishas* and/or the spirit world, or instrumental pieces derived from music of the Catholic Church or classical concert works. Musicians perform these pieces in front of a carefully prepared altar, often featuring a selection of local sweets in front of it, especially if the event is held in honor of Ochún: *natilla* (a custard-like dish), *dulce de coco* (a shaved coconut treat), *torrejas* (a Cuban-style French toast, often

---

[7] Zurbano interview, June 2018.
[8] Duquesne Mora and Molina del Valle, interview, April 2022. The documentary film *Estampas de fe* (Ortega 2008) about devotion to La Caridad del Cobre provides additional examples of the importance of *promesas* (spiritual promises, oaths) in Cuban religious life.
[9] Anonymous interview, March 2021.
[10] Johnny Frías, personal email, January 20, 2023.
[11] Mesa interview, June 2018.

served with guava jam), etcetera.[12] At one time the audience for *violines* were majority Black or mixed race, but these days participants can be of any race. In terms of audience participation, events run the gamut: in some, organizers merely look on as the ensemble performs by itself, while others are highly interactive. In the latter case, participants sing along to boleros or popular music and they usually assume the part of a chorus in call–response alternation with the musical group's lead singer. Audiences may dance as well, moving to the music freely, often without set choreography. If traditional songs to the *orishas* are performed, participants may incorporate sacred or ritualistic choreography (see Figure 2.2). Or, at times, they may dance in the style of *son*/salsa music, even forming *ruedas de casino*.[13]

Violín musical repertoire varies widely, as mentioned, but tends to progress overall from slower to faster sequences, and from precomposed to at least partially improvised expression. In this sense, the aesthetic roughly parallels more traditional Black religious events (*tambores*). Intentionality ties together the many musical styles in a *violín*:

> It doesn't matter whether you're playing Bach, or a piece by the Trio Matamoros, or a ritual Kongo chant: in the context of a *violín* you are dedicating all of that to an *orisha*, or to the spirit of the dead, someone who died in the home, a famous *santera*, a family member, or a spirit that has accompanied you and resolved a problem for you.[14]

Though the composition of ensembles varies, most groups consist of between three and seven members and include at least one violinist, often two or three. Videos of *violín* performance/repertoire can be viewed on YouTube, with an array of different ensembles: everything from a single instrumentalist to an entire dance-style orchestra.[15] "Pickup" ensembles are most common, with a lead musician inviting others to take part in the show according to the budget of his or her patron and their musical preferences.

---

[12] González Siones interview, May 2018.
[13] Mesa interview, June 2018. A circle-style dance style in which all participants execute simultaneous moves and trading partners around the ring. The performance style developed in the 1960s; see Balbuena 2005; Moore 2010, 126–7).
[14] Zurbano interview, June 2018.
[15] Solo violin performances can be viewed on Yillian Orama's Facebook page: www.facebook.com/profile.php?id=100038284692274; based in Miami, she performs both traditional Lucumí chants instrumentally and Catholic/Spiritist repertoire. A medium-sized group with keyboard, maracas, violin, bell, and singers can be viewed at www.YouTube.com/watch?v=PCONdt_m_GA (accessed April 28, 2021). Footage of the even larger Orquesta Estrellas Cubanas recording *violín* repertoire for their CD appears here: www.YouTube.com/watch?v=XJzEXEmb88Y (accessed April 28, 2021).

FIGURE 2.2 A *violín* in the Cabildo de Santa Teresa, Matanzas, from 1989. Photo courtesy of David Brown.

Typically, a harmony instrument, a singer, and a percussionist accompany the violin(s), with instrumentalists sometimes doubling as singers or additional percussionists. Guitar or electric keyboard provide harmonic support, and the bongo, conga, *güiro*, *cajón*, bell, and maracas all commonly feature as percussion. A standard ensemble might consist of two violins, guitar, and bongo drum, for instance, with violinists doubling as singers or playing claves or maracas at times (see Figure 2.1). A flute occasionally provides a melodic counterpart to the violin, evoking the sound of *charanga* dance bands. Carlos Cortes (2016) even mentions a musical saw being used during a *violín*, perhaps incorporated because of its ethereal and otherworldly timbre. Other instruments found less frequently include the accordion, viola, and *tres*.

Many violinists in ritual contexts have formal musical training, including advanced degrees from national conservatories. Indeed, Balbuena Gutiérrez (2003, 113) credits such graduates with the proliferation of violin performance in new religious settings. One notices a split among performers between the self-taught with a background in popular and/or religious music and those with formal training who often have no direct ties to the religious community. Some formally trained performers use sheet music at shows, though they often find it necessary to learn some songs by ear anyway since much of the repertoire has never been transcribed or published. *Violín* performers often earn a salary higher than anything offered through government-sponsored employment. The 1990s and beyond have witnessed extended periods of economic hardship for the Cuban population, and thus the income such events provide motivates many instrumentalists regardless of their religious beliefs (García Lacerra 2015, 34) (see Figure 2.3).

Prominent *violín* ensembles of the early 2000s included a group formed by members of the Orquesta Estrellas Cubanas, led by Félix Reyna, and another organized by *charanga* flutist Richard Egües (Balbuena Gutiérrez 2003, 115). Women figure prominently as *violín* musicians (and among audience members), finding their niche in a world of Afro-Cuban religious music previously dominated by male drummers. Band leaders now print and distribute business cards and compete with one another for work in ways reminiscent of capitalist society that would have been unthinkable only a few decades ago. Virtually all aspects of Afro-Cuban religion and culture have been monetized in this way, reflecting widespread economic need (Hernández Reguant 2009, 14).

The price of hiring a *violín* ensemble continues to increase and is now beyond the reach of many devotees. In the 1950s ensembles charged 20–30 Cuban pesos for a performance, and 70–80 pesos in the 1970s and 1980s, the latter representing perhaps a third of an average person's monthly salary.[16] By contrast, groups in 2023 regularly charged 7,500 pesos for a performance – more than most workers earn in several months.[17] The

---

[16] Gómez Noguera interview, June 2018.
[17] These prices come from Melena Francis Valdés (personal communication, November 19, 2023). Beginning in the 1990s, Cuba used both a national peso-based currency and a "CUC" or convertible peso whose value was more closely tied to international market

FIGURE 2.3 The *violín* ensemble Los Águilas posing for a photo in Havana, 1993. Individuals depicted include director Pablo Águila (violin), Pedro Ibáñez (guitar), Juan Febles (*güiro*), Jorge Eliezer Perdomo (conga), Alfredo Saín-Ives (lead voice, claves), and Felipe Oliva (violin and bell). Ivor L. Miller Papers, Amherst College Archives and Special Collections, Amherst College Library.

value of Cuba's currency experienced radical change in 2021; state worker salaries increased roughly threefold, and the price of basic goods almost tenfold. For that reason, the exact cost of future performances is unclear, but will undoubtedly remain high.

The many intersecting religious influences in *violín* performance make it difficult to distinguish between rites oriented primarily toward *orishas* or other entities. Literature written about the tradition to date,[18] and many musicians themselves, distinguish between *violines de santo* (or *violines santorales*), dedicated to the *orishas*; *violines espirituales*, dedicated to the dead and/or ancestors; and *dones de gracia*, lighter events often associated with noninitiates. The latter frequently avoid songs with Lucumí texts and

---

rates. In early 2021 the government eliminated the CUC, creating a single national currency once again but adding to the population's economic woes in the process. See https://bit.ly/4hplKR0. See also Vidal and Luis 2024. Francis Valdés (personal communication, May 4, 2021) notes that the cost of *violín* with four performers essentially doubled in 2021 in comparison with those held earlier.

[18] For example, García Lacerra 2015.

instead foreground popular repertoire. Such distinctions are useful in many respects, but in practice they often blur. In an event documented by Rosy Bayona Mojena, for instance (Figure 3.1), the organizer explained she had requested a *don de gracia* in honor of one of her spirit guides (whom she referred to as "La Negra") because of an unspecified wish that the spirit had granted her. La Negra in life had been a child of Yemayá; for that reason the organizer, Ileana (who introduced herself at the event using her ritual initiation name in Ocha: Lama Siya Alabí Oggué), represented La Negra on the altar with a doll dressed in Yemayá's colors (see Figure 3.1); she asked for songs to be played in praise of that *orisha* as well as for the dead. Ileana described herself as a *santera* and child of Obatalá, even as she relied heavily for guidance and support on La Negra, a Kongo spirit. She explained what she hoped the *violín* would mean for other participants.

[La Negra asked for the ritual] so that everyone who came here would be given health and supported in spiritual growth, stability, and firmness of purpose. Everyone you see gathered here, when they leave they're going to feel revitalized. All the things that happened to them before in their lives, [La Negra] will release them from all of it ... The people here with me are those who love me wholeheartedly. I did this in order to help all of them at one time.[19]

Clearly this *don de gracia* had strong religious associations, and the repertoire performed at the event included music associated with Santería, Spiritism, and Palo in addition to commercial songs. This suggests the extent to which all systems of *violín* classification must be understood as porous.

Spirit beings occasionally possess participants in *violines*, and because this is unexpected it tends to result in less predictable behavior than in most other ceremonies. When members of the religious community organize drumming events for the *orishas*, they take pains to ensure that only *orishas* manifest in them; if a deceased family member or spirit guide begins to mount a participant, leaders intervene and break the trance, sending the spirit away. This is done in order to ensure that the focus of devotion remains on the *orisha* to whom the event is dedicated.[20] In a similar way, organizers of a creole séance (*misa*) or *cajón* in honor of spirits of the dead would not allow an *orisha* to appear. But in the case of *violines*, the performance may reference

---

[19] [La Negra pidió el ritual] para que todos los que vinieran aquí cogieran salud, desenvolvimiento, [estabilidad] y firmeza. Todas las personas que ves reunidas aquí, cuando salgan van a salir fortalecidas. Porque todas las cosas que tenían detrás en su vida, ella se lo va a quitar ... Todas la personas que estuvieron aquí conmigo eran personas que me querían a mí de corazón. Y que tenía yo hacer esto para poder ayudar a todo el mundo de una sola vez. Commentary in Ileana's *violín* video, July 2018.
[20] Nicolás Martínez Palacios interview, January 2021.

spirit guides or *orishas*, or both. Most typically, if possession occurs the deity appearing will be the one to whom the event is dedicated.[21] But occasionally other spirits may appear as well. Spirit mediums especially susceptible to trance may be triggered by *violín* worship, for instance.[22]

Some of those interviewed note that musicians can strongly influence when or whether possession takes place in *violines*. They generally prefer to perform most of their repertoire in Spanish rather than incorporate traditional chants with Lucumí texts; in this way, the music sounds less ceremonial and represents less of a direct call to the *orishas*. Ensemble members can often tell when energy is flowing in a given participant that may result in possession; they may facilitate it or not, depending on what the organizers prefer and/or what seems appropriate to the situation. Many tread carefully in this sense, knowing that since possession is not expected in *violines* religious leaders may not be available to guide younger believers who experience it. One bandleader[23] described playing at a ceremony when a new initiate started to be possessed by an incarnation of Obatalá, who manifests as a powerful male warrior. The woman didn't seem prepared for the transformation and her movements started to become unpredictable, so the group ended their praise sequence to Obatalá in order to calm her. The bandleader stressed that those experiencing trance need guidance and oversight from ritual specialists. Unsupervised, he has witnessed such individuals colliding with others in attendance, falling, and potentially hurting themselves, which he takes pains to avoid.

ORIGINS AND DEVELOPMENT OF VIOLINES

The entire history of the violin in Cuba is perhaps best understood as an ongoing process of creolization and blackening. Introduced by the Spanish and French in the eighteenth century alongside the piano, local performers (primarily Black and mixed-race) initially played violins in Catholic devotional contexts[24] but soon began incorporating them into dance ensembles such as *orquestas típicas*[25] and interpreting new creole

---

[21] Villas Junco interview, March 2021.
[22] Mesa interview, June 2018.
[23] Anonymous interview, December 2020.
[24] Afro-Cuban composer Esteban Salas y Castro (1725–1803) represents one prominent example of this tendency; he is known for *villancicos* and other church repertoire in a Baroque style written for the cathedral in Santiago.
[25] A dance band format featuring trombone, cornet, ophicleide, clarinet, violin, and *güiro*, among other instruments.

genres such as *contradanza*, *danza*, *habanera*, and *danzón*. By the 1920s, violins were played in *charanga* ensembles together with prominent Afro-Cuban percussion (the *güiro*, timbales, congas, bongo, claves), culminating in the mass popularity of the *danzón de nuevo ritmo* and *chachachá* (Madrid and Moore 2013, 22ff.). Despite the instrument's European origins and its associations with concert repertoire, some now question whether it is appropriate to view it as culturally "whiter" than a conga drum. Roberto Zurbano[26] sees cultural fusions similar to those in *violín* ensembles taking place in Africa itself and around the world, and notes that such transnational exchanges have always been central to Cuban music. Musicians freely combine all sorts of repertoire in religious and nonreligious contexts; experiments with *violines* represent only a small part of that process (see Figure 2.4).

Informal violin performances for *orishas* and/or spirits probably first took place on the western side of the island in urban areas, particularly Havana and Matanzas, organized by the Black middle classes.[27] Certainly Matanzas, known in the nineteenth century as the "Athens of Cuba," had

FIGURE 2.4 Percussionist Rafael Espinosa Casanova (left) performing in a *violín* ensemble consisting of bongo, electric keyboard, violin, and lead singer. Havana, June 2018. Photo by Rosy Bayona Mojena.

---

[26] Interview. June 2018.
[27] Livari's (2023, 118) informants mentioned that *violines* did not become common in eastern Cuba until the 1970s.

a strong tradition of elite musical performance in which Black performers featured prominently. All of the *orquesta típica* directors of the period were well trained in European traditions, and the Black middle class in the city was large. Though many experienced persecution, exile, or were killed during investigations associated with the Escalera Conspiracy in the 1840s (purportedly an attempted slave uprising; see Paquette 1988), the Black middle class re-emerged as a powerful cultural force following the Wars of Independence (1868–98). José White Laffite (1836–1918), one of the most famous Black Cuban violinists and composers of all time, was born in Matanzas, the son of a Spaniard father and an Afro-Cuban mother. His best-known composition, a concert-style *habanera* called "La bella cubana" ("The Lovely Cuban Woman"), is incorporated into many *violines*, especially those for Ochún. One interviewee recalled hearing that White played "La bella cubana" at a cultural event organized by José Martí for cigar workers; according to that story, Martí himself suggested it should be played for the Caridad del Cobre, and for that reason it was later incorporated into *violines* dedicated to her and to Ochún.[28] Miguel Faílde Pérez (1852–1921), another prominent mixed-race musician and early composer of the *danzón*, also lived in Matanzas. These individuals are emblematic of the relatively affluent, urban, mixed-race community in which creolized violin worship first developed. It is also possible that *violines* developed in Matanzas and Havana more or less simultaneously, since both represented prominent centers of music making and musicians traveled constantly between the two cities.[29]

Countless unsubstantiated stories tie early *orisha* devotion on the violin to prominent Black and mulatto violinists of the nineteenth century, such as Havana-born Claudio Brindis de Salas Garrido (1852–1911), known for his interpretation of European concert repertoire and international concert fame. Some recall that Brindis de Salas was born in a poor Black neighborhood in Havana (Jesús María), that his mother and other family members had been raised in slave barracks, and that as an adolescent he attended numerous drumming events and sometimes would play his violin there. Others mention that Brindis de Salas' godmother was a *santera* and child of Ochún, and that he would play in events dedicated to Ochún organized by her.[30] These accounts are difficult to verify, as the only extended study undertaken of the artist (Toledo 1981) focuses on his concert career and

---

[28] Betancourt Bejerano interview, March 2021.
[29] Rodríguez interview, June 2018.
[30] Anonymous interview, February 2021.

never mentions his childhood; the same is true of encyclopedia entries about him (Giro 2002, vol. 1, 161–2). Others are skeptical that anything like the *violín* celebrations of today existed in the nineteenth century. Isabel González Giró,[31] for instance, notes that both Brindis de Salas and José White spent most of their lives abroad, and that they couldn't have been too closely tied to local devotional practices for that reason. She believes it more likely that Brindis y Salsas Monte (1800–72), father of the famous concert performer and a prominent musician in his own right, might have had more sustained contact with Afrodiasporic religions. But if so, he would have had to undertake such devotion in utmost secrecy, given the heavy stigma associated with them at the time. Regardless of the truth of such accounts, they speak to a desire to tie *violines* to the Black community's long history of engagement with European concert music, and to its countless high-profile violinists of the nineteenth and early twentieth centuries (Reyes Fortún 2006, 93). In addition to the figures mentioned earlier, these include Tomás Buelta y Flores (1791–1844), Francisco de Paula Arango (1855–1939), and Virgilio Diago (1897–1941), and, of course, the many renowned *charanga* performers of the early twentieth century: Elizardo Aroche, Félix Reyna, Elio Valdés, Rafael Lay, Enrique Jorrín, and Miguel Barbón,[32] among others.

Cuban researchers and musicians told Ana Koprivica that members of the religious community first incorporated the violin into Spiritist practices and only thereafter into *orisha* worship.

According to some musicians I interviewed, an ensemble of five violins was primarily added to accompany the séance of spiritism, [performances] which in the beginning were only sung ... Gradually, other instruments such as guitars and some percussion instruments were added and [the ensemble] became known as a *toque de violín* ... these celebrations, used only in spiritism, have passed through a long period of syncretism among musical practices of *Santería* and to be finally

---

[31] Personal email, March 24, 2021.
[32] González Siones (interview, May 2018) mentions that Miguel "Brindis" Barbón, aside from being an influential *charanga* violinist, deserves mention as an innovator in the devotional *violín* tradition even though his ties to such performance is largely unrecognized. A virtuoso improvisor with classical training, Barbón became a model for many violinists of subsequent generations. He was a member of the Orquesta Melodías del 40 (founded in 1940), performed widely on radio stations of the period, and later in life was a featured soloist in the Afro-Cuban All-Stars (Giro 2002 vol. 3, 94). Barbón is one of the first Cuban violinists featured as an improviser in a *charanga*. One of his better-known early improvisations can be heard on the recording of "Esta melodía," available on YouTube: www.youtube.com/watch?v=oLN-e3aKSXM (accessed May 21, 2024).

representative of "crossed spiritism." (Koprivica 2010, 279; see also Balbuena Gutiérrez 2003, 112)

Most of the introductory songs associated with *violines* come from the Spiritist tradition, reinforcing the position of Koprivica and Balbuena Gutiérrez. Ieana Hodge Limonta also considers *violines* a primarily Spiritist form of devotion, describing them as the "most Cuban and contemporary modality of pleasing and refreshing the dead,"[33] even as she recognizes that *orishas* may be honored as well. Of course, the conceptual division between Santería and Spiritism itself is fraught since both involve spirit worship and since *orishas* are believed to be distant ancestors who have been transformed into abstract divinities over time (e.g., Espírito Santo 2015, 72). Kongo religions too involve communication with spirits. Participants seem to view *violín* devotion as a space especially welcoming of multiple religious modalities, a tendency Beliso-De Jesús (2015, 9–10) perceives in Black Cuban religions generally: "Afro-Cuban religions draw on multiple religious sites and different religious ontologies in the construction of their spiritual places and senses of being: French Kardecian spiritisms; Yoruba-Atlantic cosmologies; wild colonial "Africans" and "indians" in inhabitable Cuban forests; Catholic saintly avatars and holy water ... These complicated spaces of sensual presence embrace different frames of relationality."

The practice of hiring dedicated violin ensembles for religious events only became a widespread practice in the mid-twentieth century, and many suggest that Aurelia Crespo (1905 or 1909–77) of Corral Falso, Matanzas province helped to popularize that practice.[34] Facebook posts claim she had a dream as a child in which Ochún requested she hold a *violín* in her honor, and that she did so for the first time on September 12, 1941. An orphan and originally of limited means, Crespo was later nicknamed "the millionaire" (*la millonaria*) because of the lavish events she organized (including performances by large dance orchestras), made possible because of a romantic relationship with a prominent military officer.[35] Some of her *violines* ostensibly resulted in possession by Ochún, with the *orisha* offering advice and

---

[33] "[U]na modalidad más cubana, más contemporánea, de contentar, refrescar los muertos." Interview, February 2021.

[34] See, for instance, https://20deoctubrecom.wordpress.com/2019/03/02/el-primer-violin-para-ochun/ or www.facebook.com/yemaya0907/posts/1132189936864123/ (accessed May 24, 2024). Literary and religious studies scholar Arisbel López Andraca (personal email, September 30, 2019) notes that others insisted to him that the first *violín* took place in Havana, specifically in Marianao.

[35] Arisbel López Atraca, personal email, September 30, 2019.

pronouncements about the future (Cortes 2016). This account could imply ties to Spiritist mediumship as well, as many *orishas* are aligned with spirit guides. Some[36] credit Crespo with popularizing the tradition of requesting the presence of at least five devotees of Ochún at any given *violín* who present themselves collectively at her altar and toast to her health together the end of the night. Crespo is also said to have contracted groups of five violinists to play together for Ochún in many of her gatherings. This derives from the fact that Ochún's sacred number is five and because devotees associate her with five principal *caminos* or incarnations.[37]

Roy Vázquez[38] (Figure 2.5) believes that in the 1950s a vaguely standardized approach to *violines* slowly emerged out of the undoubtedly diverse formats that existed previously. Initially, all pieces offered in praise of *orishas* or spirits were performed instrumentally or with Spanish-language lyrics. But, over time, as musicians played for a wider public and collaborated with musicians from varied backgrounds, the repertoire expanded. Sung hymns from creole séances (*misas*) were incorporated and eventually

FIGURE 2.5 Roy Vázquez and María Teresa Gómez Noguera performing in East Havana, June 2018. Photo by the author.

---

[36] www.facebook.com/p/Centro-Yoruba-Oshun-Ibu-A%C3%B1a-100067490557284/ (accessed May 21, 2024).
[37] See http://santeriachurch.org/the-orishas/oshun/ (accessed May 3, 2021).
[38] Interview, June 2018.

harmonized and improvised upon. Songs with Lucumí texts appeared alongside concert repertoire, and popular tunes with religious overtones gained prominence. Livari (2023, 113) reports that Carmita Fernández, a *santera* from the Pogolotti neighborhood, was among the first to incorporate the violin into Ocha worship in Havana of the 1950s. Manuel de los Reyes Cajigal of Havana appears to have been one early bandleader to experiment with the inclusion of hand percussion in his ensembles during the same decade.[39] Early *violín* devotion for Ochún featured primarily concert works; many ensembles included only one to three violins with no harmonic support (Balbuena Gutiérrez 2003, 112). When the Orquesta Estrellas Cubanas began performing *violines* in the 1970s, it effectively shifted the focus of the repertoire further toward dance music, improvisational performance, and the "festive" ambience discussed by García Lacerra (2015, 35).

Some participants may still prefer to hear subdued solo violin repertoire in front of an altar, but most patrons now request a livelier sound.[40] In part, the emphasis on vocal and secular repertoire represents a "crowd-pleasing" imperative, part of an attempt to make *violines* attractive to audiences. As Danai Pérez Domínguez notes, "now it's like a competition, no one wants to be left behind,"[41] referencing a desire to connect to with and animate listeners. Others concur, noting that Cubans in general enjoy dancing and rhythmic music, and thus *violines* with such content tend to be well received. Many refer to modern, upbeat performances as *violines fusionados* (hybrid *violines*) to underscore the blending of slower sacred pieces common in past decades with rhythmic popular tunes. In a certain sense, danceable, call–response singing in a *violín* represents an equivalent of the *rumbitas de santo* heard in traditional drumming events: *rumbitas* foreground short, catchy, songs with Lucumí texts performed toward the end of a *tratado* (song sequence) in order to bring the event to a climax. Some interviewees nevertheless express ambivalence about the inclusion of so many diverse elements in present-day *violines*. Lázaro Pedroso, for instance, suggests that too much mixing of religious and nonreligious influences is inappropriate and that *violín* performers may experiment too aggressively with established practice.[42]

---

[39] Gómez Noguera interview, June 2018.
[40] Sivico Sulueta interview, January 2021.
[41] Pérez Domínguez interview, January 2021.
[42] Lázaro Pedroso, Facebook Messenger, August 1, 2022.

THE 1990S AND EXPANSION OF RELIGIOSITY

Elsewhere (Moore 2006, 197ff.), I have detailed the highly ambivalent views of the Cuban socialist government about all religious activity for many years, and especially African-influenced practices. The primarily white leaders of the socialist revolution inherited countless biases about Black religions from the colonial era that manifest themselves in formal and informal policies of persecution. The early 1960s represented a period of relative tolerance, but by the end of that decade officials pressured believers of all sorts (Catholics, Protestants, Jews, *santeros*, *espiritistas*, etc.) to distance themselves from religion and/or forced them to keep their devotion secret. Government agencies did all they could to discourage devotional activity, especially in the young. From about 1968 through the mid-1980s, academic and other publications on religion disappeared, as did recordings of music with religious content and even popular repertoire alluding to such topics. Secularized forms of religious drumming – incorporated into experimental jazz or used to accompany modern dance – could still be heard now and then, but religion per se was understood as false consciousness (Menéndez Vázquez 2005b, 342–3) and antithetical to the new socialist society.

Liliana González Moreno[43] suggests that during the years associated with the greatest repression of religious expression in Cuba, officials viewed *violín* performance more favorably than drumming and tended to regulate it less harshly. While some revolutionaries characterized drumming rites as atavistic superstition, *violín* performance seemed less threatening to them. González Moreno believes that the repression of drumming in its traditional form may have led members of the religious community to embrace *violín* ceremonies instead. Yunior Terry agrees with this; he emphasizes that, especially in the 1970s, *violines* offered a way of worshipping the *orishas* that created fewer risks for those in attendance. "In that way, you didn't draw the attention of your neighbors and you could just pretend you were organizing a serenata or other secular event." Terry suggests that playing less repertoire with Lucumí texts probably became standard practice for the same reason, as a way of not marking the event as so overtly African-sounding. Other interviewees suggest that the shift toward the use of violins for the same reasons date from the 1940s and 1950s.[44] These strategies align with the countless choices made by Black religious leaders since the early nineteenth century to innovate,

---

[43] Society for Ethnomusicology annual conference presentation, New Orleans, November 13, 2022.

[44] Ivor Miller (personal email, March 13, 2024) recalls that interviewees such as "China" (a *santera* from Cienfuegos) suggested the repression of Afro-Cuban religious drumming was

allowing their beliefs to persevere despite "relentless official efforts to coopt, control, and destroy them" (Brown 2019, 5–7, 10). Drawing on Bastide, Brown notes that Afrodiasporic religions have a long history of insinuating themselves into and then emerging from within new social and cultural frameworks, and of transforming practices according to areas of flexibility within existing constraints. Thus, practitioners frequently serve as "historically conscious, aesthetically concerned, reflective agents of change" (15).

Beginning in the mid-1980s, the government's position of intolerance toward religion and religious music began to soften. In the context of Perestroika and reflection on the mass migration of many dissatisfied citizens manifest in the Mariel exodus of 1980, officials gradually loosened restrictions. Fidel Castro himself initiated a series of conciliatory conversations with a Catholic priest which were later published as the book *Fidel and Religion*. At approximately the same time the government invited the supreme representative of Yoruba religion in Nigeria to Cuba for a visit (Matibag 1996, 232). In the academic realm, ethnographic recordings of traditional religious repertoire began to appear on government-controlled music labels such as the ten-volume LP collection released by CIDMUC[45] known as the *Antología de la música afrocubana*. The groups Síntesis (led by Carlos and Ele Alfonso) and Mezcla (led by Pablo Menéndez) began promoting harmonized and rockified versions of traditional Afro-Cuban religious chants in concert. Pope John Paul II's visit to the island and the Communist Party's Fourth Congress in 1991 helped usher in a new era more accepting of devotion. The revival that began thereafter should be viewed as part of broader changes in which Cuba began to celebrate its multicultural and multiracial heritage in new ways (Menéndez Vázquez 2005b, 340), and during which many practitioners felt emboldened to participate in religion publicly for the first time (Mikelsons 2005, 238).

The 1990s represents the most critical decade in the popularization of *toques de violín*, and the broader changes associated with those years had a profound effect on Cuban society. The breakup of the Soviet Union in 1989 and an end to longstanding economic ties with the Eastern Bloc led to a drastic drop in Cuba's GDP, ushering in the so-called Special Period in Times of Peace. Within a few years, shortages of food, electricity, gasoline,

---

a central determinant in the emergence of *violín* performance in the mid-twentieth century, well before the socialist period.

[45] Centro de Investigación y Desarrollo de la Música Cubana, one of Cuba's major music research centers, located in Havana. CIDMUC also began publishing academic studies of religious music in the 1990s.

water, and countless other basic goods led to tremendous hardship and new waves of emigration, often on rafts and in small boats. Economic desperation resulted in a sharp rise in robbery and assaults. The government's inability to provide for its citizens contributed to the rapid expansion of a black-market economy. An increasing reliance on foreign tourism to generate income resulted in the rise of prostitution and other social ills that had largely disappeared in the 1960s. This dire context, exacerbated by the simultaneous tightening of the US trade embargo, resulted in feelings of intense anxiety and contributed to religious revival (Perera and Pérez Cruz 2009, 138; Hagedorn 2002, 50–1). Cubans turned to religion for comfort, economic support (as many established churches provided food aid), as a response to the perceived moral decline in society (Basail Rodríguez and Castañeda Seijas, 1999, 180), and as a form of generating income, for instance through musical performance or by charging a fee to initiate tourists into Santería (García Lacerra 2015, 39; Hagedorn 2014).

All types of religion became much more visible by the mid-1990s, and especially Afrodescendant religions that had long been hidden. Participation in Protestant and Catholic devotion (about which more data are available) increased by roughly 300 percent as the public searched for new forms of community, the majority of younger individuals joining churches for the first time (Perera and Pérez Cruz 2009, 144; Basail Rodríguez and Castañeda Seijas, 1999, 180). Regla de Ocha's similar surge in popularity may relate to the fact that *orisha* worship is understood as a way to overcome problems in life and to obtain practical results, as mentioned. Initiates dressed in solid white became a common sight on the streets of Havana and elsewhere; others openly wore ritual *collares* (necklaces) or wrist bracelets, indicating their devotion to particular deities. The expanding ranks of *santeros* and the relative inexperience of many with traditional ceremonies may have made them receptive to new forms of expression such as *toques de violín*.

In other contexts, stage shows began to appear in tourist hotels featuring folkloric dancers, percussionists, and singers who performed Afro-Cuban religious repertoire, and prominent visual artists such as Salvador González Escalona (1948–2021) began working with related imagery, famously painting the walls of Havana's Callejón de Hámel with Ocha-inspired images and converting it into a major tourist attraction. In bookstores, publications on religious topics and new editions of classic works by Lydia Cabrera and Fernando Ortiz appeared. In this context, Afro-Cuban religious and cultural leaders continued their longstanding struggles for recognition; the Cuban government first permitted the establishment of a Yoruba Cultural Association in 1992 and officially recognized the United Abakuá Association in 1996 (Quiñones 2014, 273). Local residents created websites focused on religious communities and their concerns, part of what Basail Rodríguez and Castañeda Seijas (1999, 183) describe as "a flight to the sacred." For their part, government officials actively sought the support of religious leaders of Black religions as a base of ongoing support for the faltering revolution, and in the process gave them freedom to practice their faith in new ways (Hernández Reguant 2009, 15).

Somewhat paradoxically, the rise of religious innovations such as *cajón* and *violín* performance was paralleled by a contrasting desire among some to reconnect to African roots, and even calls to purge Afrodescendant religions of European influences. This "purist" impulse had roots in Nigeria and other parts of Africa itself, but attracted supporters in the Caribbean as well (Perera and Pérez Cruz 2009, 145–7). Such divergent tendencies in Cuba derive both from the greater religious freedoms described herein and more sustained national and international dialogues about religious orthodoxy. For instance, the Yoruba Cultural Association and Cuban Academy of Sciences organized an international conference in June 1992 – the "Primer Seminario Internacional Sobre los Problemas de la Cultura Yoruba" (First International Conference on the Problematics of Yoruba Culture) – that helped foster such connections (Rossbach de Olmos 2007, 135). A small but vocal group of participants in Cuba framed Santería as an exclusively Yoruba religion and characterized Catholic or other influences it had incorporated as colonialist impositions to be avoided (Watson 2009, 200). Most participants contested this view, desiring greater contact with religious leaders in Nigeria in order to foster dialogue but considering local leaders the ultimate authorities in determining the nature of their own religious practices. Cuba continued exchanges with the international religious community by hosting the eighth meeting of the Global Conference on Orisha Traditions and Culture (COMTOC) in 2003, with guests from Nigeria, Brazil, Spain, the United States, and elsewhere.[46] Of course, a desire to return to the roots of the Lucumí tradition, while a fascinating trend, raises countless thorny questions: Which African source(s) should be considered the model for Cuban practice? Should orthodoxy be derived from current or historical African traditions? In practical terms, how can Afro-Cuban religions be

---

[46] See www.afrocubaweb.com/8thworld.htm (accessed May 21, 2024) for additional information about the 2003 conference; it represents part of a series beginning with an initial meeting in Nigeria in the early 1980s.

divested of their rich and varied external influences? Would believers ever accept such changes?

Cuban musicians, for their part, continue to experiment with new formats and instrumental combinations without feeling terribly constrained by religious tradition. Some *violín* groups now incorporate *chekerés* or other percussion associated with older forms of *orisha* devotion, for instance.[47] Musicians in the Otura Di temple in Matanzas (apparently one of the first to ordain a female *babalawo*[48]) have used an ensemble of *batá* drums, violin, and a classically trained vocalist to accompany devotion to Ochún.[49] The 1990s also gave rise to *violín* recordings featuring the Orquesta Estrellas Cubanas and their elaborate three-part string and vocal arrangements of Lucumí chants (Oviedo and Pinelli 2011). *Violines* may well have emerged out of the Black religious community's desire to avoid persecution, but the situation has changed. Performers and audiences now seem comfortable blackening earlier modalities of European-derived performance as well as creating new musical forms.

PARALLEL MUSICAL TRENDS: CAJÓN DE MUERTO

No attempt to situate *violín* performance relative to other present-day cultural manifestations would be complete without discussing *cajón de muerto* ensembles,[50] given the parallels between the two. Information on *cajón* traditions is limited; my overview here draws heavily from Nolan Warden's (2006) masters thesis on the topic, a handful of publications by Cuban musicologists such as Bárbara Balbuena Gutiérrez (2003), the few events I have been able to observe personally, commercial recordings by Los Nani (Álvarez 1997) and Luca Brandoli y Grupo Barracón (Brandoli 2011), and comments by present-day performers. Like *violines*, *cajón* has developed a relatively standardized ensemble format only since the 1970s (Warden 2006, 81), though related practices have existed for many years,[51] and, like

---

[47] Zurbano interview, June 2018.
[48] See https://bit.ly/418T9Jo (accessed May 6, 2021).
[49] www.YouTube.com/watch?v=UIRcr7rC5vE (accessed May 6, 2021).
[50] Nolan Warden indicates that *cajón* events are sometimes referred to as *cajón pa' los muertos*, *cajón para muerto*, or *cajón al muerto*, but such terms tend to be less common now.
[51] Santiago "Chaguito" Garzón Rill, for instance, describes *cajón de muerto* rites as part of a longstanding practice in the Afro-Cuban religious community (Interview February 4, 2021 and WhatsApp communication April 26, 2024). He defines *cajón* performance dedicated to spirit guides as "a *misa espiritual* with instrumental accompaniment." He notes that it derives from a tradition of playing rumba for a *santero*'s birthday in Ocha, a *palero*'s *prenda*, or someone's *muerto* (ancestor). The *cajón* ensemble was established officially as a format in

them, *cajón* events take elements of secular music (such as rhythms from traditional rumba) and repurpose them in religious contexts. Many songs in both formats are sung in Spanish rather than in ritual languages, and both incorporate *plegarias* to spirit beings, though *cajón de muerto* foregrounds Palo songs more prominently, suggesting closer ties to that tradition (see Brandoli 2011).

According to Fernando Ortiz (1955 III, 148–9), resonant wooden boxes have been used as musical instruments for centuries by Afrodescendant communities throughout the Americas, for instance in Peru, Colombia, and also in New Orleans' Congo Square. Nineteenth-century dockworkers in Havana used the *cajón* frequently, especially in conjunction with rumba performance, and it is still used in rumba today. A typical *cajón* ensemble at present features two or three of the instruments in different sizes (substituting for the three conga drums of the standard rumba ensemble), often accompanied by claves, a hoe blade or bell, and singers. Ortiz describes the *cajón* as substituting for drums in religious contexts (including Kongo- and Yoruba-influenced practices), either because a community's drums had been confiscated[52] or because the organizers could not afford to hire consecrated *bataleros* (batá drummers). The practice of playing these instruments for *orishas* – in events known originally as *cajón de santo* and now more typically as a *rumba de santo* – dates back at least to the 1950s (Balbuena Gutiérrez 2003, 101, 128), and indeed appears to have even older roots. Much like Liliana González Moreno, Warden (2006, 81) believes that the increasing use of *cajón* ensembles (and perhaps, by extension, other secular instruments like the violin) to play sacred repertoire of various sorts in the 1970s may be linked to the suppression of traditional forms of religion and religious instruments in Cuban society. Balbuena Gutiérrez (2003, 106–8) notes that the modern approach to *cajón* ensemble performance derives from a style established in the Atarés neighborhood of Havana during the first decades of the revolution, but it soon spread more widely (see also Johnson and Palmié 2018, 463).

In terms of repertoire, many parallels are evident between *violín* and *cajón*. Like *violines*, the majority of *cajón* music in religious contexts is

---

Havana, but it has always had ties to ceremonial practice in Havana and other parts of Cuba. For that reason, many groups have different instrumentation. Some use conga drums and *cajón*, other include additional instruments.

[52] Ortiz (1955 III, 151) emphasizes the persecution of many Afrodescendant religious practices in the 1940s and 1950s and mentions that the three *cajones* he includes a picture of were impounded by the police when they were found being used in a Santería ceremony.

sung in Spanish,[53] but with some songs in ritual languages also. Both *violín* and *cajón* incorporate Catholic and Spiritist repertoire, especially early in the ceremony, with songs such as "A lo lejos se ve una gran claridad" (In the Distance a Bright Light Appears), "O venid protectores" (Oh Come Spirit Protectors; Figure 3.4), and "La luz redentora" (The Redeeming Light; Figure 3.3).[54] It is unclear what the events Ortiz heard in the 1940s sounded like, but contemporary *cajón* involves significant musical fusion. Following *plegarias* performed to the accompaniment of slower, secular *rumba yambú* or *guaguancó* patterns, one hears other praise songs over the same rhythms dedicated to Kongo and Indigenous spirits (Warden 2006, 99). Musicians accompany pieces dedicated to Elegguá and/or other *orishas* with rhythms in imitation of *batá* patterns such as *ñongo* or *chachalokafun* (also *ichachalekefun*; see Moore and Sayre 2006, 140–1). And, finally, the fastest climactic segments of *cajón* rites are usually accompanied by sacred Palo or Iyesá rhythms[55] or others associated with Kongo heritage. Both *cajón* and *violín* thus begin with Catholic hymns and *plegarias*. Both proceed generally from slower to faster repertoire, with the later sections of a given event foregrounding music chosen more freely by the musicians. Finally, both *violines* and *cajón* are conceived as a musical offering to the spirit world. Usually, believers organize a *cajón* to thank a spirit entity for a favor granted, or because the spirit itself requested a performance. To the outsider, the sound of *cajón* (especially early in the ceremonies) is similar to traditional rumba, as can be heard in numerous postings to YouTube.[56]

Multiple religious influences converge in *cajón* performance aside from those mentioned here, including Islam; greetings such as "Salamalecum"

---

[53] Songs performed in *cajón* events are unique in that many of them are written in broken *bozal*-style Spanish, such as might have been spoken by enslaved Cubans born in Africa. Sometimes songs in French patois (as spoken by the many Blacks who immigrated to Cuba from Haiti in the early nineteenth century) are incorporated as well.

[54] Johnny Frías (personal communication, February 6, 2023) also sees many parallels between *cajón* and *violín*, suggesting that *violín* might be viewed as a "pop version" of *cajón* with additional repertoire added. Members of Los Nani note their group was the first to release a CD consisting exclusively of Spiritist repertoire in the 1990s (Duquesne Mora interview, April 2022). They mention that singers such as Merceditas Valdés made earlier recordings of individual songs, but never a complete album.

[55] Iyesá music derives from the Iyesá (or Ijesha) people of West Africa, an ethnic minority of the Yoruba people with their own percussion instruments and rhythms used in religious contexts. Iyesá repertoire has been incorporated into Santería, particularly by *batá* players and ritual singers.

[56] Footage of a representative *cajón* in Matanzas is available at www.YouTube.com/watch?v=ea1ZnFwuGL4 (accessed May 7, 2021); many others are available as well.

are heard frequently in Palo and in *cajón* devotion (Warden 2006, 63), as one example, to salute Kongo or African spirits.[57] *Cajón* exists between religious modalities (as do *violines*), but it is most strongly influenced by *espiritismo cruzado* (discussed in Chapter 3). While recognizing the longstanding practice of playing rumba for spirits or *orishas*, interviewees characterize the use of a formal *cajón* ensemble and ceremony as a fairly recent practice.[58] Kongo ancestors feature prominently in *cajón* devotion and frequently possess participants. Abakuá spirits appear on occasion too, as do Haitians,[59] and all have their preferred musical repertoire. Most of these spirits prefer to be sung to in African dialects, but the repertoire dedicated to them can also extend into the realm of Western popular and concert music, aligning more closely with the sound of *violines*. "When Mama Chola [the Palo equivalent of Ochún] appears, you have to sing sweet, calm pieces for her. When [Madre de Agua the equivalent of Yemayá] comes, you sing pieces like "Marinero, marinero" (Mariner, Mariner; see Figure 3.8)."[60] And if the spirit of a particular Kongo spirit or deceased relative visits the event or if the event is dedicated to them, it may be appropriate to play popular or other repertoire they enjoyed in life (see Figure 2.6).

The use of rhythm and the overall progression of a *cajón* differs in particular ways from a *violín*, however. In the *cajón*, as in a more traditional *tambor*, the progression from slow to fast is steady. In a *violín*, by contrast, performers vary the intensity of their repertoire and take breaks between *orus* (song sequences). Even toward the end of a performance, *violín* musicians might include boleros or other romantic numbers to slow things down and provide musical contrast. This greater rhythmic and stylistic variation makes sense since the musicians' goal is not to induce possession. *Cajón* events, by contrast, generally lead to possession. Warden (2006, 99ff.) describes the creative ways in which *cajón* percussionists mix diverse rhythmic elements as they play, something he refers to as "cohesive acts"; they may combine a bell pattern from *makuta* drumming with a percussion

---

[57] Certain Northwest African ethnic groups (the Mandinga, Wolof, Fula, etc.) have been strongly influenced by Islam, and their descendants may have introduced the phrase in the Caribbean. "Salamalecum" is now used as a way of saluting Kongo and other African spirits more generally.
[58] Ethnomusicologist Johnny Frías (personal communication, February 6, 2023) views the *cajón* tradition in this way, as an adaptation in Havana and Matanzas of Spiritist repertoire from eastern Cuba that came to be accompanied by rumba and other percussion styles.
[59] Fernández Díaz interview, January 2021.
[60] Ibid.

FIGURE 2.6 The *cajón* ensemble San Cristóbal de Regla directed by Andres Jacinto Balaez-Chinicle, with lead singer Jorge Alberto Duquesne Mora. Other members include Reinier Omar Romero Chávez and Roberto Hernández Arrendage on *cajón*, Jesús Argüeyes Ruiz on *catá* (sticks and bamboo), and Maykel del Sol Gómez on claves and bell. They perform here in Luyanó, Havana, April 10, 2024. Photo by Melena Francis Valdés.

pattern inspired by the Iyesá tradition, for instance. Thus, the musical texture itself reflects the fusion of religious and nonreligious components. The relationship between this form of music making in *toques de violín* is complex. To the extent that similar cohesive acts take place in a *violín*, they tend to involve the fusion of traditional *plegarias* or Lucumí chants with rhythms (such as cowbell patterns), instruments (the bongo and guitar), melodic riffs (like violin *guajeos*), or styles of performance (such as *montuno*-style vamps) associated with popular dance repertoire. These tendencies will be examined in Chapters 4 and 5. *Violines* also incorporate a great deal of commercial music in its original form, such as boleros or *sones* that are not combined with other repertoires. Closing activities in a *cajón* closely align with those in a *misa espiritual*, with the singing of songs such as "Con el agua del río" (With Water from the River), which accompanies the ritual cleansing of the performance space with perfumed water mixed with flower petals and ground eggshell, and the later tossing of that water out into the street to usher away uninvited spirits (Warden 2006, 101). In a typical *violín*, by contrast, musicians may play a few songs dedicated to Elegguá, then simply thank the audience, pack up, and leave.

Cajón performance can be used to salute the *orishas*, as mentioned. As one example, the Grupo San Cristóbal de Regla directed by Andres Jacinto Balaez-Chinicle (Figure 2.6) performed an event in April 2022 that they described as a "*rumba para Ochún*," a variant of the *rumba de santo*. As in the case of *cajón espiritual*, much of the percussive base was inspired by secular rumba rhythms in duple meter. The instrumentation for this event consisted of two *cajones*, a *guataca* or hoe blade used as a bell, *chekeré* (played by an invited guest, not usually included), and *catá* (a round and resonant piece of wood struck with sticks). Unlike Spiritist-inspired events, the *rumba para Ochún* included relatively few *plegarias* and began directly with songs dedicated to Elegguá and other *orishas*. Still, percussionist and researcher Melena Francis Valdés[61] describes the ensemble's rhythmic style as in dialogue with other influences including Makuta, Palo, and Abakuá rhythms and melodies blended with traditional *rumba guaguancó*. When singing to Ochún, musicians incorporated refrains in Spanish such as "Baila, baila Cachita" (Dance, dance Cachita – a nickname for the Caridad del Cobre), as well as others that referenced her counterpart in Palo, Mama Chola Wengue (e.g., "*Mama e, Chola, Mama e Chola, Chola con tanta manilla y yo no tengo ninguna*" [Mama Chola with so many bracelets and me without any]).[62] The organizer of the event, Luis Manuel Leyro, emphasized that he personally did not like *violines* because he considered them too Westernized, therefore he decided to offer Ochún percussion-oriented *cajón* music instead.[63] Musician Jorge Alberto Duquesne Mora, a member of the San Cristóbal de Regla ensemble, is attracted to *cajón* ceremonies because they can include so many distinct religious referents at once, using rhythms and refrains influenced by rumba.

As may be evident, the relationship between *cajón* and *violín* worship is deserving of further study. Both ensembles are less expensive to hire than a *batá* trio and involve minimal additional preparation (no ritual feeding of instruments, for instance). Both are flexible formats that bring together diverse influences. In this sense they speak more directly to Cuba's transculturated reality than an ensemble dedicated to a single repertoire. Practitioners with less advanced ritual knowledge may also feel

---

[61] Email communication, July 23, 2022.
[62] Jorge Alberto Duquesne Mora, WhatsApp communication, March 11, 2024.
[63] Leyro interview, April 2022.

comfortable with the relatively accessible music such groups foreground, largely sung in Spanish. Both ensembles, in their own ways, manifest the fusion of sacred and secular elements, musically and given that drinking and/or socializing understood to be part of the experience (Warden 2006, 92). Of course, differences are evident as well. *Cajón* performance is heavily male dominated, whereas *violines* (like Spiritist devotion) foreground women more frequently. *Cajón* still uses traditional Afro-Cuban percussion together with voices, not Western melodic or harmonic instruments, and thus its overall sound is much more tied to older Afrodescendant religious practice. *Violines* incorporate more popular and concert repertoire; this constitutes the bulk of the music performed. Spirits manifest much less frequently in *violines*, as noted, whereas soliciting advice from the dead is the primary purpose of a *cajón*. Both types of event may be participatory, but *violines* are more often presentational. In general, and while exceptions exist, *cajón* events maintain more of a focus on direct communication with the divine, whereas the aesthetic of *violines* is more grounded in musical offerings.

CLASS AND AESTHETICS

The reasons for the popularity of *violines* undoubtedly derive from many factors, including their overall sound and the ways that they differ from traditional drumming. As mentioned, Afrodescendant religions were the subject of persecution for many decades; *violines* (and also Spiritist practices) had the advantage of circumventing such criticisms. This is especially true of mid-twentieth-century devotion featuring solo violins which were largely devoid of Black aesthetics as represented by drumming traditions; attending a *violín* in its early years was "like going to the theater or listening to an opera": sitting in silence, respectfully, discretely, without speaking.[64] Koprivica (2010, 280) includes commentary by one of her informants (Mirta González, a musician), who believed *violines* developed partly in response to the frequently racist depictions of Black heritage associated with the *afrocubanismo* movement (see Moore 1997). Dulce María Veiga Freyre, a violinist and former member of Cuba's National Symphony Orchestra, takes this argument further, suggesting that early violin-based devotion implied a rejection of Afrodescendant culture on the part of worshippers:

---

[64] Anonymous interview, November 2020.

When a white *santero* or a Black *santero* from high society needed to play for the saints, they would contract a group of violinists. They did this out of disdain for Blacks and because of pervasive racism. Instead of organizing a drumming event with *batás*, they would play an "Ave Maria" by Schubert or by Bach-Gounod,[65] or traditional Cuban songs dedicated to the Caridad del Cobre and the Virgin of Regla. In reality they were playing for the *orishas*, but it wasn't as obvious as in the case of Black drummers. In that way the Cuban bourgeoisie maintained appearances in society, because the violin does not exist in Africa.[66]

Veiga Freyre's interpretation is certainly provocative and may accurately describe the motivations behind much early *violín* devotion. It does not explore the possible origins of *violín* worship in Spiritism, however. Veiga Freyre's interpretation also does not accurately characterize the attitudes of most participants toward *toques de violín* today. Though a variety of attitudes about such events exist, they have clearly been accepted by most of the religious community as a legitimate form of worship, not as racist or "watered-down." And those who attend or organize *violines* in the present also attend drumming events of various sorts and practice *espiritismo*.

Still, among the attitudes about *violines* that have surfaced in interviews, some describe them as more refined or elegant than other forms of devotion, ideas that resonate to an extent with Veiga Freyre's interpretation. Warden (2006, 75) mentions a white landlord who chose to organize a *violín* instead of a *toque de santo* because he considered the former "prettier" (*más bonito*). Ortega (2008) includes footage of *santera* Maritza Morell in his video documentary; she says Ochún enjoys *tambores* and *güiros*, but that she likes *violines* even more because they are "delicate." *Santera* Yenny Bahi enjoys *violines* more than other kinds of ceremonies; she views them as more influenced by Spiritism, refined, calmer, and – to her – musically appealing (*más suave, mas pasivo, más fino, más de oído*).[67] She notes that she also enjoys drumming; her inclination toward *violines* represents

---

[65] This composition, published in 1853, represented Charles Gounot's reworking of Bach's "Prelude no. 1 in C Major" (BWV 846) from the *Well-Tempered Clavier* (1722). Gounot wrote a new melody for his version, but used Bach's Prelude as the basis of its harmonic accompaniment.

[66] Personal email, facilitated by Reynaldo Fernández Pavón, January 2, 2020.

Cuando algún santero blanco o negro pero de la alta sociedad necesitaba tocarle a un santo contrataban a grupos de violines, por desprecio hacia los negros y por el racismo imperante. En vez de dar un tambor con los batás, tocaban el Ave María de Schubert o de Bach-Gounot, o canciones tradicionales cubanas como Las dedicadas a la Virgen de la Caridad del Cobre y a la Virgen de Regla. En realidad le tocaban al santo, pero no era algo tan evidente como unos tambores tocados por negros. Así la burguesía cubana mantenía las apariencias ante la sociedad, porque en África no existía el violín.

[67] Bahi interview, April 2022.

a personal preference (she feels their sound and aesthetic align with her personality) and reflects the fact that Ochún enjoys them. These evaluations suggest that some listeners prefer attending a *violín* because they identify with its calmer and more contemplative aesthetic.

Another anonymous interviewee describes the sound of the guitar and bongo drum in *violines* as mellower (*más suave*), more pleasurable (*más rico*), and more refined (*más fino*) than drumming alone, and notes that the latter does not appeal to her as much.[68] The interviewee elaborates on her preferences, noting "I like *violín* better. I don't like *cajón* events, they are too intense" (*fuertes*),[69] apparently referring to the volume or intensity of the percussive sounds or possibly the social context in which they are performed. She adds:

> The bongo is smoother, more pleasurable, and the guitar too is a string instrument, the sound of it is very pretty as well, very refined ... You feel as if you're in a clean environment. That's what I like about the *violín* ... The people there are of a certain cultural level. The people who like drumming are from the underclasses [*gente del bajo mundo*]: the drums, the people, and all the screwing around [*la jodedera*].[70]

Clearly, this individual strongly associates *violines* with expression that is sophisticated. And even though she is mixed-race herself, the speaker's comments suggest that she associates Afro-Cuban drumming with a lack of decorum and/or education. Most of our interviewees contested this position vociferously, describing her views as biased, even racist. One commentator, for instance, noted that neighborhoods associated with vibrant drumming scenes are also home to countless educated professionals, and that the same public attending *violines* tends to enjoy *tambores* as well.

Regardless of their accuracy, the comments cited here speak to associations many perceive between *violines* and segments of the population with social aspirations. To Octavio Rodríguez, the music has always had special appeal not only to the highly educated but also to members of the working classes interested in "bettering themselves," in part through

---

[68] Anonymous interviewee, November 2020.
[69] "Me gusta más el violín. El cajón no me gusta, son muy fuertes."
[70] El bongo es más suave y más rico, y la guitarra también que es un instrumento de cuerdas, que suena muy linda también, muy fina. Me gusta con su bongo, con su guitarra y su violín ... A mí me gusta, porque es muy lindo, rico. Tú te sientes en un ambiente limpio. Eso es lo que me gusta a mí del violín, que representa un ambiente limpio. Son personas con otro tipo de cultura. La gente de los tambores son gente del bajo mundo; los tambores, y la gente, y la jodedera.

listening to or consuming new types of music. Roberto Zurbano agrees, describing *toques de violín* as being attractive to more educated and/or culturally cosmopolitan practitioners. He suggests that some worshippers like them because they sound more complex in terms of harmony and instrumentation, and thus more modern. To Zurbano, the *violín* creates a new aesthetic space and provides a uniquely contemporary, urban form of devotion that didn't exist before. The multiple tensions or oppositions in *violines* – African versus European aesthetics, sacred versus secular, noncommercial versus commercial, texts in Spanish versus Lucumí or Kongo, etcetera – create an amalgam that is understood differently by various segments of the public. But many find the ties between devotional repertoire and commercial or concert music attractive.

No hard data exists on how many *violines* are performed in Cuba and elsewhere today relative to other events, yet multiple interviewees stress that drumming remains the most popular form of Afro-Cuban religious worship. "Cubans live by the *cajón*, the *güiro*, and the drum more than the *violín*," noted Marcel Fernández Díaz,[71] and added that he really didn't like *violines* very much himself. Others agree, though they also recognize that the popularity of *violines* has increased.[72] Negative views of *violín* practice stem largely from the ways it is perceived to deviate from past forms of worship. Traditionalists prefer *tambores* because of their grounding in longstanding practices; they do not believe the aggressive cultural mixtures in *violines* represent a positive development.[73] Others describe the participatory ethos of *tambores* as attractive, such as the fact that everyone sings and dances throughout rather than merely observing instrumental or vocal performances by others.[74] One tendency of late which complicates these debates is to begin an evening's worship with drumming or a *güiro* group, but to ask a *violín* group to play later on. In such cases, *violinistas* foreground even less traditional music to the spirits or *orishas*, concentrating instead on popular repertoire so as to contrast with what has come before.[75]

---

[71] Interview, January 2021.
[72] Sivico Sulueta interview, January 2021.
[73] Anonymous interview, January 2021.
[74] Anonymous interview, November 2020.
[75] Johnny Frías (personal communication, February 6, 2023) notes that in Miami the religious community organizes *violines* almost exclusively for Ochún, and that such events often precede a *tambor* or *güiro*. *Santeros* there view the *violín* as an extra gift to her rather than as the primary religious event.

Neither the fans of *violines* nor the performers who play them express much concern about their frequent use of secular music, but Cuban researchers have been struck by the abrupt transitions between devotional and nondevotional songs in ritual contexts. Citing one performance she observed in which the bolero "Quizás, quizás, quizás" was played immediately after ritual songs to Obatalá, Maraima García Lacerra (2015, 26) suggested that the bolero appeared to represent "an interruption in the religious sequence" and diminished any sense of ritual.[76] Interviewees who preferred *tambores* to *violines* did not frame their objections in precisely these terms, but clearly they have misgivings about the relation of the latter to Afrodescendant tradition, and to popular culture as well. *Violín* players continue to experiment in stylistic terms and to transgress boundaries of various sorts. Initially they foregrounded Catholic elements and obscured Afrodescendant heritage, but popular religious melodies now play a central role in many performances. If past *violines* effectively whitened Black religious practice, contemporary events arguably blacken or creolize Eurodescendant music to the same extent, or alternate between it and songs with many Afrodiasporic elements. Chapters 3, 4, and 5 explore these issues further by examining particular performances in detail.

---

[76] "Suponiendo que se interpretase tras cantarle a Obatalá, significaría una interrupción en el discurso religioso que se estaba efectuando ... Ello implica el despliegue de lo festivo mediante el repliegue de lo ritual."

3

Spiritism and *Violines Espirituales*

Cuban Spiritism and its most common ritual manifestation, the *misa espiritual* or contemporary Cuban séance (Otero 2020, 69), have strongly influenced *violín* performance, yet no study currently exists that examines the relationship between the two. Few publications exist on any aspect of Spiritism in comparison to other popular religious practices, and even fewer on the vocal repertoire employed in *misas* by mediums and worshippers as they invoke and consult with the dead.[1] This chapter provides a brief overview of Spiritism, its history in Cuba, its fusion with other forms of religion, and the typical format of the *misa espiritual*. It then examines the devotional songs heard in *misas* and in *violines* derived from Spiritism, Catholicism, Palo, or other sources, and the differences between the two forms of expression. Popular repertoire features prominently in *violines espirituales*, for instance, and musicians elaborate or extend traditional repertoire in various ways, often by adding choruses and improvisatory vamp sections.

Music serves as a mediating force in the context of the *violín espiritual*. It fuses diverse forms of religious practice into a unified whole. It mediates between the spirit world and the physical world, between the living and the dead, the past and the present. In paying homage to spirits – primarily from Africa or Cuba – *violines* assume a transtemporal and trans-spatial dimension, recognizing interconnections between various planes of existence.

---

[1] One arguable exception is Nolan Warden's work (2006), given that *cajón de muerto* incorporates Spiritist repertoire as well. Warden's study includes many lyrical transcriptions of common songs, but little melodic transcription. Larduet Luaces's (2016) essay and publications by Axel Hesse (1975) also include a few transcriptions of well-known *plegarias*.

Individual and collective memories of the dead are manifest through ritual sound and movement, recreated and given aural/physical form. The malleable content of *violines* allows organizers to personalize their relationships with spirits by dedicating song sequences to them and in some cases catering to their individual tastes, the music they enjoyed in life. More broadly, the prominence of popular music in *violines* references the soundscapes of the everyday; it mixes with devotional repertoire, presenting both spheres as a composite whole. The complex religious amalgam associated with Spiritism thus has its musical corollary in the *violín espiritual*.

ESPIRITISMO IN THE AMERICAS

Authors define Cuban Spiritism (*espiritismo*) in the most general sense as a practice of healing and otherworldly guidance with roots in the United States, Europe, and Africa (Fernández Olmos and Paravisini-Gebert, 2011). In the Americas, European-derived Spiritism fused over time with influences from African and Indigenous religions, especially the former in the Caribbean, given the strong demographic presence of Africans and their descendants and their belief that spirits cohabitate and communicate regularly with humans (Leé Llosas 2005, 11). Like Santería, Spiritism offers practitioners the possibility of finding immediate solutions to physical, social, or emotional problems through rituals of purification and consultation. Also like Santería, Spiritism has no central leadership or set of orthodox practices and thus individual mediums approach their work in varied ways (Dos Ventos 2008, 14). Spiritism is potentially compatible with any religion, and for that reason many adherents also identify as Catholic, Jewish, Hindu, or Muslim (Guevara 2014, 70). Castellanos and Castellanos aptly describe *misas espirituales* as among the most eclectic forms of Caribbean popular religion, reflecting a diversity of influences.

Of European origin, believers celebrate [*misas*] with *orishas* and *ngangas*.[2] One finds crucifixes, cane liquor, and cigars. Both Spanish and pidgin *bozal* are spoken. An "Our Father" will be prayed along with hymns to spirit beings, all within a ceremony preceding the reception of the [African] goddess Ochún. The *aché*[3] of Lukumí and Kongo religions is added the power of the Catholic Church and the hidden forces of Spiritism. (Castellanos and Castellanos 1992, 202)[4]

---

[2] Also known as a *prenda*, *nganga* refers to a ritual iron pot used in Kongo-derived religions, filled with various ritual objects. It is used to control the spirits of the dead.

[3] A term for spiritual force or power.

[4] De origen europea, la celebran creyentes en orichas y ngangas. En ella hay crucifijos, aguardiente y tabacos. Se habla en español y en bozal. Se rezan Padre Nuestros, se cantan

Espiritismo cruzado is widespread in Cuba, apart from the areas surrounding the cities of Bayamo, Manzanillo, Las Tunas, and Holguín which are associated with European-derived Spiritist practices (Leé Llosas 2005, 19). The "mixed" Cuban model has also spread regionally – for instance, to Colombia, as documented by Castro Ramírez (2017) – and has its corollary in Venezuela, Mexico, and elsewhere. Spiritist beliefs share many commonalities with folk Catholicism in Latin America – the veneration of a pantheon of saints as minor deities, the belief in an active spirit world, the use of sacred charms and related objects, the use of ritual as a form of healing – which perhaps helps explain its warm reception and integration into other devotional systems (Fernández Olmos and Paravisini-Gebert 2011, 15). Interestingly, considerable tension exists between practitioners of European or Kardec-style Spiritism and of *espiritismo cruzado*, who often question each other's legitimacy (Espírito Santo 2015, 11).

Many practitioners of Santería and Spiritism view the two religious systems as linked because of the centrality of ancestor veneration to both. They describe *espiritismo cruzado* as a logical extension of Eurodescendant Spiritism, not an aberration or conflation of European and African concepts. To José del Pilar, for instance, "The spirits of the dead (the *egun*) come first, because without them *orishas* would not exist. Everything [about both belief systems] is spiritual, spirit."[5] Priest Obá Bi (in Beliso-De Jesús 2015, 2) concurs: "When we are made *lukumí* we are united with our past and present ... the *egun* and *orisha*. So you know, wherever we go, wherever we are, they are here." This last comment underscores the fact that *orishas* themselves are believed to be ancestors and thus a particular type of *egun*.

African descendants in the Americas have long been concerned with spirits; former slave Esteban Montejo discussed them extensively in his recollections of religious life in Black Cuban communities of the nineteenth century, for instance (Barnet 1994, 118–21). Societies dedicated to worship of the dead existed historically in Nigeria, and Kongo peoples farther to the south also practiced ancestor veneration; the spread of European-style Spiritism throughout the Americas in the nineteenth century appears to have allowed Afrodescendant groups to revive and extend

---

himnos a los 'seres', todo ello en una ceremonia que precede a la recepción de la diosa Ochún. Al *aché* de las religiones lucumí y congas se añade el de la Iglesia Católica y el de las fuerzas ocultas del espiritismo ...

[5] "Lo primero es *egun* porque si no hay *egun* no hay santo, no hay Ocha. Todo es lo espiritual, el espíritu." Interview, November 2021.

their traditional forms of devotion (Bastide 1971, 107–8, 118). *Misas espirituales* are a central part of all Santería worship and are required prior to any major ceremony involving initiation, as discussed in Chapter 4. Ocha and Palo initiates make frequent offerings to the dead, often on broken plates to symbolize the rupture between the physical and the spiritual worlds. And at the end of most *orisha* ceremonies, ritual leaders consult the *egun* to ensure that they are satisfied with the proceedings (Espírito Santo 2015, 72–7).

Black religious communities in Cuba are interconnected and practitioners move easily between them. Beliso-De Jesús (2015, 3) begins her study by discussing the spiritual life of Alfredo Calvo Cano, for instance, an individual not only conversant in Santería, Palo, and Abakuá traditions, but also a medium or *media unidad*[6] for his deceased grandfather and great-uncle, both Kongos. They often possessed and spoke through him. Similarly, *orishas* have a prominent place in many Spiritist events; as one example, some of the most frequently heard songs in mediumistic contexts reference Babalú Ayé and San Lázaro interchangeably. This makes sense given that Babalú is a healer and many *misas espirituales* events involve healing (Espírito Santo 2015, 278).

Visitors to a *misa* or *violín espiritual* frequently see altars to the *egun* featuring lit candles, glasses filled with water, crucifixes, pieces of coconut shell, fresh flowers, dolls or figurines dressed in ritual colors, and other objects associated with spirit mediumship (Figure 3.1). Some additional information about these items as well as the history of Spiritism in Cuba need to be included in order to appreciate the religious symbolism associated *violín* performance. It clarifies the close relationship between *misas* and *violines*, the religious views of participants, and the focus of particular song sequences.

Current Spiritist practices date from the mid-nineteenth century, when belief in the ability of mediums to communicate with the dead became fashionable in the Americas and Europe. The popularity of Spiritism among the Black and mixed-race population in Cuba is best understood as a strategy of resistance, the appropriation and transformation of these practices in accordance with African-derived beliefs (Larduet Luaces 2016, 78). Within the United States, communication with the dead became fashionable in the 1840s during the Great Awakening, including "spirit rapping" mediums such as the Fox Sisters. It later spread to Europe; Alain

---

[6] Literally "half a unit" or "half an entity," a common term for an individual able to channel spirits.

FIGURE 3.1 A Spiritist altar featuring water glasses, fresh flowers, perfume, carefully dressed dolls representing spirit guides, and a lit candle. Photo by Rosy Bayona Mojena.

Kardec (Hippolyte Léon Denizard Rivail, 1804–69) eventually refashioned the practice, codifying it as Spiritism per se and generating widespread international interest in the phenomenon in the 1850s–1860s (Castellanos and Castellanos 1992, 193). Kardecist Spiritism ascribes to belief in a single God and in countless spirit entities, all of whom aspire to evolve from a lower to a higher state of existence. This process of evolution can involve reincarnation. Spiritists also recognize enlightened spirit guides who no longer need to incarnate but continue their development by offering advice to the living (Dos Ventos 2008, 13). Kardecist practice does not involve possession, only communication with the spirit world, and singing has no role in devotion (Larduet Luaces 2016, 80). Some of Kardec's views were overtly racist, suggesting that many non-Europeans were incapable of full spiritual development (Warden 2006, 25).

Nevertheless, beginning in the 1850s, Kardec's writings about spirits had a strong impact in Cuba: first among elites, and later within the general population (Brandon 1993, 86–7). Interest in communication with the dead increased even more rapidly in subsequent decades with the onset of the Wars of Independence (1868–98). Catholic leaders' political conservatism and defense of Spanish rule led much of the population to abandon them and to explore new religions (Millet 1993, 8ff.). An astounding 80 percent of *mambises* (Cuban insurgents) are said to have practiced Spiritism; deceased Cuban patriots evoked in séances apparently exhorted even revolutionary exiles in New York to offensive action during the Ten Years War of the 1860s and 1870s (Bermúdez 1967, 7–9). To many elites, Spiritism offered an explanation of death that was both scientific and modern, resonating with philosophical views of the period such as positivism. It appeared "verifiable and efficacious" since believers could talk to spirits themselves, and because the spirits provided practical advice. Catholicism, by contrast, seemed to offer neither. To the Black and mixed-race population, as mentioned, Spiritism afforded direct access to the ancestors and provided new opportunities for healing, as well as protection from malevolent spirits (Brandon 1993, 87–9). Kardecist beliefs soon fused with notions of the *egun*, *muertos*, and the broader Afro-Cuban religious world (Mikelsons 2005, 225).

Multiple interrelated forms of Spiritism are now practiced in Cuba that continue to influence each other including *espiritismo de mesa*, *espiritismo de cordón*, and *espiritismo cruzado*.[7] *Espiritismo de mesa* or *de mesa blanca* (white table Spiritism, sometimes referred to as "scientific Spiritism") most closely resembles Kardec's practices. Adherents prepare a table covered with a white cloth, known as a *bóveda* (literally a vault or crypt) that features various ritual objects such as candles, water glasses, and flowers as the center of ritual activity. Practitioners combine sung hymns, readings of prayers from Kardec's books or Catholic sources, and poetry as a means of engaging enlightened spirit beings (*buenos seres*). Most other forms of Spiritism also use *bóvedas*. *Espiritismo de cordón* (cord or chain Spiritism)[8] is practiced most widely in eastern Cuba; its devotion in certain respects resembles ring shouts associated with the Black community in the United States and the ecstatic chanting associated with forms of Sufism. Ceremonies usually begin with the reading of Kardecist or Catholic prayers as participants form into circles. They hold each other by the hand, then begin singing and rhythmically moving their bodies, stamping the ground, swinging their arms, and moving slowly counterclockwise. Sessions of this sort with the objective of purification or healing often last for many hours (Mikelsons 2005, 227).

---

[7] Mikelsons (2005, 225) also recognizes another variant, *espiritismo caridad*, focused exclusively on ritual cleansing or purification.

[8] The notion of a *cordón* (cord) references hand-holding in circles, but even more importantly the notion of an ethereal cord representing both part of an individual's life-essence and their ties to the spirit world, and particularly their own spirit guides (Espírito Santo 2015, 38–45).

The practice first became popular during the Wars of Independence as a way of responding to the massive casualties inflicted on the local population (Dos Ventos 2008, 15). Documentaries featuring *cordón* events and the responsorial songs used are available on the internet.[9]

Espiritismo cruzado, the most widespread form, combines elements of Catholicism and Spiritism with Santería and Palo, and it has most directly influenced *misas espirituales* and *violines*. This devotion represents a "deep amalgam" (Dos Ventos 2008, 15) of religious systems in the sense that Santería's Changó, Palo's Siete Rayos, and Catholicism's Santa Bárbara are all considered manifestations of the same deity or spiritual force, as are Yemayá, Madre de Agua, and the Virgin of Regla; and Ochún, Mama Chola, the Virgin of Charity, etcetera. Individual spirit protectors play a prominent role in *espiritismo cruzado* and are consulted frequently in ritual contexts (Espírito Santo 2015, 55). Some believe the tradition originated in eastern Cuba, possibly in conjunction with saints' day celebrations for La Caridad, San Lázaro, Santa Bárbara, and La Merced. Distinctions between Santería and Palo are less well defined in that region of the country and the religious community frequently incorporates diverse influences into devotion.[10]

Every Spiritist is understood to have a unique *cuadro espiritual* or spiritual cadre of otherworldly beings who watch over them; devotees cultivate intimate relationships with these spirits. They share certain affinities with the living person in terms of personality and may include deceased relatives, but also Gypsies (*gitanas*), Indians (*indios*), Kongos (*congos*), or others. Spiritists feel the presence of their *cuadro* constantly. They receive communication from the dead in dreams or in other contexts entirely outside of formal *misas* such as advice on how to avoid complications in a pregnancy, appease an angry relative (dead or alive), resolve a problem at work, or avoid harm of other sorts. Spiritists sometimes see the dead sitting or standing near them.[11] Women predominate as mediums and participants

---

[9] See, for instance, segments of the documentary *Monte Oscuro: Chants de spiritisme de cordon*: www.YouTube.com/watch?v=Oa_fYa8c4SY and www.YouTube.com/watch?v=phhr8TSqBOo (accessed May 20, 2021). Most of the musical repertoire appears unique to the region, but the song heard at 3:00 in the first excerpt of the documentary is very similar to "Corre el agua," a *plegaria* heard in *violines* associated with Yemayá (see Figure 3.9). Ileana Hodge Limonta (interview, February 2021) notes that many of the most famous songs associated with *cordoneros* were written by Salustiano Olivera. Dodson (2008) and Millet (1993, 1996) include additional historical and contemporary information about Spiritist practices in Oriente.

[10] Hodge Limonta interview, February 2021.

[11] Anonymous interview, 2021.

in ceremonies, and perhaps for that reason it is particularly common for devotees to receive advice from *negras africanas* (some referred to as *madamas* or "mammies") who lived and died in the Caribbean as slaves. Female spirits are said to be especially powerful and carry out "the brunt of the Great Work" in ceremonies (Guevara 2014, 33–4). Male Kongos and their descendants represent a strong presence as well.[12] They are wise in the ways of the forest, nature, magic, and natural healing remedies (Fernández Olmos and Paravisini-Gebert 2011, 227). Indian spirits are described as fierce warriors who work tirelessly to protect their human wards (Espírito Santo 2015 228). They tend not to possess mediums directly but instead communicate through visions, sounds, touches, or smells (Guevara 2014, 34). Interestingly, most Indian spirits channeled in *misas* derive from North American plains tribes (Sioux, Apache, Cherokee, etc.), rather than from Indigenous Caribbean groups (Feraudy Espino 1999, 49). Gypsy spirits (usually female) often foretell the future; they may be beautiful and seductive, but were often the victims of racism or bigotry in life (Guevara 2014, 28–9). Michael Mason (quoted in Warden 2006, 48) describes them as having tremendous psychic powers and the ability to warn the living about impending troubles or treat difficult illnesses. Like Ochún, they enjoy sweet and refined things.[13] Haitian and Jamaican spirits are also invoked on occasion by mediums. Relatively few Spaniard spirit entities appear in *cuadros* or are sung to in ceremonies, underscoring the emphasis on subaltern lives and memories in the religion. The faithful represent spirit guides on altars with dolls of various sorts, as mentioned (see Figure 3.1), or with items as tarot cards, bows and arrows, cigars, and so on.

THE MISA ESPIRITUAL

Misas espirituales represent the focal point of ritual activity for Spiritists, and they are also the source of much musical repertoire incorporated into *violines*. Practitioners organize *misas* for various reasons: to develop one's self as a medium (these are known as *misas de desarrollo*); to receive blessings and anointment with oil or holy water (also referred to as a *santiguo*; see Guevara 2014, 53); to determine whether they need to

---

[12] Warden (2006, 29) mentions the strong impact of the José Movement led by Leocadia Pérez Herrero, a medium for a Kongo slave named José. This apparently is the origin of the "Ta José" spirit referenced in many Kongo songs in Spiritist contexts.
[13] The gitana has been immortalized in rumba compositions by the Muñequitos de Matanzas. See, for instance, www.YouTube.com/watch?v=79AhdmSCNsI (accessed May 24, 2021).

rid themselves of any negative energies that may cause problems in their life;[14] to learn more about their own spiritual cadre (*misas de investigación*); to collect and dispel negative influences (*misas de recogimiento*); to honor and "give light" to a particular being so that it can achieve a spiritual higher state (Dos Ventos 2008, 24); or to strengthen ties to one's *cuadro* in order to facilitate spiritual or physical well-being and enhance otherworldly communication (*misas de coronación*). Spiritual coronations and related celebrations also prepare *santeros* to receive their primary *orisha*, as discussed in Chapter 4.

Most *misas* are presided over by two established mediums who support each other throughout the event as needed, especially if one falls into trance.[15] Most take place at night; those present usually wear white[16] and cover their heads (Dos Ventos 2008, 25–6). The ceremony begins with selected spoken prayers taken from one of Kardec's prayer books and/or from Catholic traditions, as well as a spoken or sung version of the "Padrenuestro/Our Father" prayer[17] as participants ritually cleanse themselves with perfumed water, *cascarilla* (ground eggshells),[18] or ritual herbs such as anamu or *espantamuertos*[19] in front of an altar or *bóveda*.[20] After this, everyone segues into the singing of a series of a cappella *plegarias*

---

[14] One name alluding to ridding an individual of negative energies is *rompe zaraguey* (or *saraguey*), denoting the breaking of a jinx or curse. The phrase also refers to mixtures intended to resolve the same problem sold in *botánicas*; it was immortalized in Héctor Lavoe's song of the same name, available on Youtube; see www.YouTube.com/watch?v=Rg4aB78TixU (accessed May 26, 2021).

[15] Solimar Otero (personal email, May 17, 2024) notes that a stenographer or note-taker usually participates as well, keeping track of statements made by the spirits after they arrive.

[16] The color white enables mediums to more quickly evaluate the spiritual condition of participants (Guevara 2014, 25), sometimes by reading their aura. The color is also appropriate because it is associated with the dead in many parts of Africa (Dos Ventos 2008 18), and with purity and holiness among Catholics.

[17] Leé Llosas (2005, 21) mentions that the "Padrenuestro" prayer is intended at least in part to placate those spirits who have not yet achieved full development/evolution and might choose to disrupt a *misa*. It helps them shed the *arrastre* or spiritual "drag" developed during life as the result of negative thoughts or actions. A transcription of the sung version of the "Padrenuestro" is provided in Figure 3.15. Castellanos and Castellanos (1992, 197–8) list other common verbal prayers initiating ceremonies, including "Ave María" and the "Plegaria al náufrago" (Hymn to Lost Souls).

[18] *Cascarilla* is known for its ability to break up negative spiritual energy; sometimes it is scattered around the *bóveda*, as well as rubbed onto the bodies of participants (Espírito Santo 2015, 214).

[19] *Espantamuertos* is known in English as false daisy; its scientific name is *eclipta prostrata*.

[20] Altars are more typically associated with *violines santorales* and *bóvedas* with Spiritist rites.

(Spiritualist hymns, also known as *transmisiones* to emphasize the way they call to the dead). Songs serve as the basis of devotion, interspersed with spoken pronouncements from mediums sensing spirit messages during the session. Events usually last a couple of hours in total (Espírito Santo 2015, 220). After initial prayers and songs, those desirous of advice or cleansing are asked to come forward; mediums discuss what they sense about the individual, their aura, and their *cuadro*. Mediums convey advice from their own spirits and attempt to lift any negativity they sense (Guevara 2014, 11–12). This continues until everyone has been attended to. Mediumship involves two sorts of otherworldly communication: direct and indirect. Much of the advice provided by spirits can be channeled through mediums indirectly without any need of trance, based only on feelings or impressions. But, of course, mediums can also allow themselves to fall into trance and let the spirit communicate directly through them (Castellanos and Castellanos 1992, 199).

The *bóveda* or *control* is a key ritual element of the *misa espiritual*, and is also part of many *violines espirituales*; performers often play alongside the shrine or in the same room (Figure 3.1). Typical items found on a *bóveda* include candles, glasses of water, a crucifix, a rosary, incense or perfumes, pictures of deceased family members, bottles of rum, cigars, and statuettes or dolls representing prominent spirit guides in one's cadre or items they enjoyed in life. Glasses of water feature prominently, usually seven or nine in number; they represent the primary *comisiones* or spirit groupings associated with a given practitioner (Balbuena Gutiérrez 2003, 46). Sometimes the glasses are positioned in "V" shapes with the most important spirits at the apex; this is meant to focus the energies of the dead and exhort them to "labor" (*laborar*) or perform tasks (Dos Ventos 2008, 21). A crucifix often sits in a central glass, evoking the presence of God and Olorun (the supreme deity of the Santería pantheon), the Most Holy (El Santísimo), driving away evil thoughts (Leé Llosas 2005, 21). Water symbolizes clarity and spiritual progress; it cools and refreshes the dead (Ochoa 2020, 48). Its presence links to Kardecist notions of how to attract the energy of the departed, but may also reflect the Kongo belief that the worlds of the living and the dead are separated by a body of water (Garoutte and Wambaugh, in Espírito Santo 2015, 247). Behind or within each glass are flowers representing various spirits: white flowers such as lilies for the Santísimo, dark roses for the *congos*, sunflowers for the Indian spirits, etcetera (Balbuena Gutiérrez 2003, 46). Perfume and incense are used to cleanse the ritual space, as sweet smells are believed to attract good spirits (Larduet Luaces 2016, 85). Candles serve as a homing beacon to guide the dead. Offerings of food and drink correspond to the preferences of ancestors or other spirit entities. While they take on special ritual importance in the context of a *misa*, *bóvedas* are a site of daily activity in the homes of Spiritists as they honor and consult with their *cuadro*.

MUSIC OF THE MISA ESPIRITUAL

Initial devotional songs in *misas* reference Catholic liturgy, offer praise to spirit guides collectively, or reference a mother's love for her children. Songs about mothers implicitly or explicitly allude to the Virgin Mary, other prominent Catholic saints such as the Caridad del Cobre, and, by extension, all female spirits and ancestors. These pieces ritually purify the meeting space; they do not typically result in trance. Many were recorded commercially by Merceditas Valdés (1949–96) in collaboration with Yoruba Andabo as part of a potpourri arrangement called "Espirituales cubanos," one of the final recordings Valdés made before her death.[21] The recording is noteworthy in that it harmonizes the hymns with guitar and percussion; such accompaniment would never be heard in the context of a *misa*, but it is common in a *violín*.[22] See the transcriptions presented in Figures 3.2, 3.3, and 3.4 for a sense of the melodies associated with initial sung Spiritist prayers. Some of them (e.g., "Sea el Santísimo," "La luz redentora") are performed out of time, perhaps to underscore their ethereal qualities. In the absence of a set rhythm, the lead singer guides other participants through successive melodic phrases. Other *plegarias* (e.g., "O venid protectores") are sung in moderate duple or triple meter. All have a clear tonal center and simple melodies. They often foreground responsorial alternations and thus participation by a group; some songs alternate phrases between a leader and chorus, while others are recited in full by the lead, then by the chorus. Lead singers can improvise, but everyone else sings the same response in order to generate spiritual energy and set the tone for the gathering.[23]

---

[21] Yoruba Andabo is a prominent rumba ensemble. The Spiritist potpourri they recorded in 1995 is available as a digital download on various sites, and on YouTube: www.YouTube.com/watch?v=9RVa1RGTXi8 (accessed May 21, 2021). All three *plegarias* discussed here are included. "La luz redentora" begins the sequence, "O venid protectores" can be heard at 4:00, and "Sea el Santísimo" at 4:47.

[22] Although instruments are not used in *misas*, some Spiritists in Eastern Cuba employ them in music and dance events following formal services; see Millet 1993, 32.

[23] Fernández Miranda interview, March 2021.

"Sea el Santísimo"/Praise to the Most Holy

Sea el Santísimo (chorus: *Sea*)	Praise to the Most Holy (*May it be praised*)
Sea el Santísimo (*Sea*)	Praise to the Most Holy (*May it be praised*)
Madre mía de la Caridad	My Mother of Charity
Ayúdanos, ampáranos	Help us, shelter us
En el nombre de Dios, ¡Ay, Dios!	In the name of God, Oh God![24]

FIGURE 3.2 "Sea el Santísimo."

This short piece is the first performed in many *misas*, *cajones*, and *violines*. The phrase "Sea el Santísimo" often appears in prayers referencing the holy sacrament in Catholic services; however, Warden (2006, 99) notes that it is simultaneously understood to reference Obatalá and the Spiritist altar or *bóveda* itself. One of his informants associated it with the creation of the world (Obatalá and Oduduwa are both creators) and thus considered it a fitting piece to begin worship services. The reference "my Mother of Charity" is similarly multivalent; it could be read as referencing the Virgin Mary, the Caridad del Cobre, or other saints/spirits, though Alira Ashvo-Muñoz confirms its associations in Cuba with the Caridad.[25] The lyrical ambivalence of "Sea el Santísimo," simultaneously alluding to spirituality generally and to multiple specific religions, contributes to its appeal.

---

[24] The key center chosen for the following transcriptions is arbitrary; it only provides a sense of the melody in question.
[25] Personal email, January 19, 2021.

"La luz redentora"/The Redeeming Light

Si la luz redentora te llama, buen ser	If the redeeming light calls you, good spirit
Y te llama con amor a la tierra	And it calls you lovingly to earth
Yo quisiera ver a ese ser	I would like to see that being
Cantándole gloria al Divino Manuel	Singing praises to the Lord Jesus/Oduduwa
Oye, buen ser, avanza y ven	Listen, good spirit, advance and come to us
Que el coro te llama y te dice "ven"	The chorus calls to you and tells you "come"
Oye, buen ser, avanza y ven	Listen, good spirit, advance and come to us
Que el coro te llama y te dice "ven"	The chorus calls to you and tells you "come"[26]

The lyrics of "La luz redentora" tack between implicit references to Spiritism, Catholicism, and Santería. Spaniards traditionally use the phrase "Divino Manuel" to refer to the baby Jesus; this may derive from the fact that "Emmanuel" is a Hebrew name meaning "God is with us" and suggests the appearance of a divine being. Older Spanish *villancicos* performed during the Christmas season incorporate both the names Jesus and Emmanuel (e.g., Domínguez Encinas 1958), implying that the baby represents the arrival of God. The verb *venid* (a second-person plural conjugation, uncommon in the Caribbean) references the song's Spanish origins. In Cuba, associations between "Divino Manuel" and the baby Jesus are no longer recognized; the religious community understands San Manuel as closely associated with Oduduwa, *orisha* of the dead (Balbuena Gutiérrez 2003, 34). The discussion of light and enlightenment found in "La luz redentora" is typical of Spiritist songs; candles are central ritual objects, as mentioned, as they focus mediumistic activities and attract the dead. Light represents truth and spiritual development more broadly, to such an extent that exclamations of "*luz*" (light), "*luz para ese espíritu*" (light for that spirit), or "*luz y progreso, buen ser*" (light and progress, good spirit) represent the most common forms of acknowledging wisdom shared by spirits in the context of a *misa* (Castellanos and Castellanos 1992, 201).

"O venid protectores" may be sung as part of the initial series of hymns intended to purify the ritual space of a *misa*, but it is also used in the context of *misas de coronación* to celebrate the establishment of

---

[26] Many performers follow "La luz redentora" with the following chorus in alternation with improvised passages: "Ay buen ser, avanza y ven, que el coro te llama y te dice ven."

FIGURE 3.3 "La luz redentora."

permanent ties between a living person and their spirit guides. In the latter case, a new medium typically kneels as other members stand around them, draping a white cloth over their head. They consecrate the top of the initiate's head above the cloth with flowers, water, crucifixes, or other objects while singing. Spiritual coronations of this sort can be viewed on the internet.[27]

"O venid protectores"/O Come, Protectors (also known as "Para la coronación espiritual"; see Crookes 2012)[28]

O, venid protectores, oh venid	Oh come, protectors, oh come
Seres guías de nuestra misión	Spirit guides of our [spiritual] mission
O, venid protectores a esta tierra	O come, protectors, down to earth
A esta linda coronación	To this lovely coronation
En coronación, en coronación	In coronation, in coronation
Bajan los seres	The spirits come down
En coronación, en coronación	In coronation, in coronation
Bajan los seres	The spirits come down

---

[27] See, for instance, www.YouTube.com/watch?v=tMEE2sRJohA, starting at 25:40 (accessed May 25, 2021).
[28] All *plegarias* exist in oral tradition in multiple forms. This version of the text comes from Crookes 2012; the version sung by Merceditas Valdés varies slightly.

FIGURE 3.4 "O venid protectores."

Little research has been conducted on the origins of Spiritist musical repertoire. As should be evident, *plegarias* or *transmisiones* are fundamental to spiritual communication and help regulate ritual acts. They can invoke, salute, and dismiss spirits from *misas*; later songs, especially, lead to possession and contribute to the *fluido* or spiritual fluid/energy mediums require (Hesse 1975, 69), the Spiritist equivalent of Santería's *aché*. Music in this sense assumes a role similar to that of the *pontos cantados* or "bridging songs" employed in Brazil (e.g., Gidal 2016, 9), with the caveat that *plegarias* are sung unaccompanied whereas Umbanda repertoire is supported by drumming. Only in Latin America has Spiritist musical repertoire become so elaborate; elsewhere, spoken prayers predominate in spirit mediumship. Hesse (1975, 69) divides *plegarias* into at least three categories: (1) those originating outside of Cuba, for instance in the folk Catholicism of Spain, including Andalucía's *cruces de mayo* celebrations; (2) melodies created in Cuba but not originally associated with Spiritism, such as the *Altares de cruz* repertoire and that of patron saint festivals,[29] Palo songs,[30] Franco-Haitian repertoire from *tumba francesa* performance,[31]

---

[29] See Moore 2006, 203–4, for additional background information on *Altares de cruz* traditions.

[30] Hesse 1971, 209ff. lists many common Palo songs heard in Spiritist contexts.

[31] Songs, drumming, and dance traditions brought to eastern Cuba by the Black Haitian population that emigrated following the Haitian revolution of the 1790s.

*cabildo*³² songs, work songs, songs from the revolutionary wars against Spain, and songs derived from the *espiritismo de cordón* tradition or created by setting Catholic texts to music (see also Larduet Luaces 2016, 80); and (3) songs specifically created for Spiritist worship by mediums or others, since many compose songs for their guiding spirits or are given songs directly by them in dreams or trance.³³ Spiritist songs emerged as a distinct corpus during the Wars of Independence (1868–98) or shortly thereafter and have been passed down through oral/aural tradition in the religious community.³⁴ Many of the best-known pieces are more than a century old, some apparently having been collected by William Crookes (1832–1919), a British chemist who developed a strong interest in Spiritism.³⁵

Most Cuban *plegarias* have Spanish lyrics, including not only those dedicated to Catholic saints but most others dedicated to Africans, *orishas*, or other spirit beings. *Misa* songs thus eschew "the esoteric traditionalism of an unknown language" (Warden 2006, 106) in favor of one that is easily understood. The shift from prayers to Afrodescendant deities in African-derived languages (as is typical in Santería and Palo) to Spanish creates a more accessible environment, one that requires less preparation or ritual training.

Mediums in charge of a given event choose pieces to sing in honor of spirit groups and lead participants through them in a prescribed order. On occasion, others may request permission to lead a song if their spirit guides tell them it would be advisable.³⁶ The overall sequence of devotional repertoire begins with songs in praise all spirits, then continues with others devoted to Catholic saints. These may mention Christ directly or reference the Virgin Mary (in songs such as "Misericordia" or "O María/Ave María"; Figure 3.5); they may focus on other figures such as San Miguel/St. Michael or the Caridad del Cobre, or reference the Holy Spirit with the imagery of a white dove (as in "Paloma blanca mensajera"; see Figure 4.5). Spiritist rites seem to foreground hymns open to multiple interpretations rather than those that are explicitly Christian.

---

³² Black social organizations dating from colonial times and organized by African ethnic groups or tribes.
³³ Diana Espírito Santo, personal email, March 9, 2021.
³⁴ Fernández Díaz interview, January 2021.
³⁵ Some collections of song lyrics available in Spanish online (Crookes 2012) cite him as their source, for instance.
³⁶ Fernández Miranda interview, March 2021.

After songs referencing Catholic saints come others dedicated to selected *orishas*; their inclusion suggests the extent to which Ocha and Spiritist beliefs have intertwined. Songs to San Lázaro/Babalú Ayé feature prominently, as well as others dedicated to the Virgin of Regla/Yemayá. Additional *orishas* may be invoked as well. Finally, the focus turns to songs devoted to spirit *comisiones*, especially Afrodescendant ancestors and/or spirits associated with Palo. I discuss all this repertoire in greater detail throughout the remainder of this chapter and provide transcribed examples. Song sequences devoted to spirit groups are of course broken up by with spoken prayers, mediumistic commentary, and other events (including trance/possession). But singing is nevertheless the most important part of the *misa* because it represents the primary way in which spirits are summoned.[37]

Songs not only help define a sanctified space but directly facilitate divine communication. They can trigger trance either because they reference one's *cuadro espiritual* in a general way or because the spirit in life enjoyed listening to a particular piece and is attracted to it.[38] Songs can also be used to determine what sort of spirit is present in a gathering, assuming one appears who hasn't been identified previously:

When spirits haven't been identified, you have to sing songs of all types to them because you don't know which correspond to them. So you sing many, many songs until you find one that the spirit likes. Because there are spirits that wait for a particular song, they have one in mind and say to themselves "Fine, until they sing that one for me I'm not going to appear."[39]

Often this approach is effective in identifying the spirit. If not, a medium in trance may use one of their own spirit guardians to "pull" (*jalar*) the unidentified being into the physical realm and possess another member of the group. Breaking down barriers between the physical and spiritual realms is a primary focus of *misas*, and music helps this take place. Other techniques employed to the same end include rites of purification (*despojos*), such as breaking coconut shells near the body

---

[37] Diana Espírito Santo, personal email, March 1, 2021.
[38] Fernández Miranda interview, March 2021.
[39] Los espíritus cuando no están definidos, tienes que cantarles todo tipo de canciones, porque tú no sabes cuál es. Entonces, se inspiran, se levantan distintas canciones, distintas canciones, hasta que llega a una canción que es la que le gusta al espíritu. Porque hay espíritus que esperan una canción, que tienen esa y dicen: "Bueno, hasta que no me canten mi canción, yo no voy bajar. (Fernández Miranda interview)

of a participant or the passing of whole coconuts around them, blowing smoke on them (smoke being a manifestation of both the tangible and the intangible), physically shaking them, or spraying cane alcohol on them – all in an effort to help the new medium transition from consciousness and make way for their spirit guides.[40]

A folk song of praise to the Virgin Mary, known as "O María" or "Ave María" (Figure 3.5), often features in musical invocations within the *misa*. Its use of verb conjugations such as *amparadnos* (as before, second-person plural, uncommon in Latin American Spanish) suggest it is older than other hymns.[41] As a means of emphasizing a Spiritist focus, singers often discuss the Virgin Mary as the *comisión María*. Sometimes the following lines are sung after the "Sea el Santísimo" chant discussed earlier, for instance: "*Estoy llamando a la comisión, la comisión María, estoy llamando a la comisión de protectores y guías*" (I am calling the commission of Mary, I am calling to the commission of protectors and guides). This recognizes ties between Mary and related spirit families, framing the Catholic pantheon as simply another group of beings who can be petitioned for advice or exhorted to intervene in daily problems.

"O María" (or "Ave María")

Del cielo ha bajado la madre de Dios	From Heaven the mother of God has descended
Cantemos un Ave a su protección	Let us sing praises for her protection
Ave, Ave, Ave María	Hail, hail, hail to Mary
Ave, Ave, Ave María	Hail, hail, hail to Mary
O María, madre mía	Oh Mary, my mother
O consuelo celestial	Oh celestial comfort
Amparadnos y guiadnos	Shelter and guide us
A la patria celestial	To our celestial home
Con el nombre de María	With the name María
Su grandeza espiritual	Her spiritual grandeur
Amparadnos y guiadnos	Shelter and guide us
A la patria celestial	To our celestial home

---

[40] Fernández Miranda interview, March 2021.
[41] Argeliers León and Armando Bermúdez (cited in Hesse 1971, 318) suggest the song was composed in the nineteenth century by Manuel Muñoz Sedeño and was originally called "Ave María," though now performers refer to it as "O María"; see www.ecured.cu/Manuel_Mu%C3%B1oz_Cede%C3%B1o (accessed July 18, 2023).

FIGURE 3.5 "O María" (or "Ave María"), initial melody.

Alongside the Virgin Mary, Spiritists often sing *plegarias* to Saint Michael/San Miguel early in their services, invoking his fierceness and his ability to ward off evil (see Figure 3.6). They use images of St. Michael to guard homes as well, placing them behind their front door. Pictures tend to show him mounted on a horse with a flag and a sword raised; this references stories in the Book of Revelation (12: 7–9) about St. Michael leading troops to victory against Lucifer (Larduet Luaces 2016, 83). The foregrounding of St. Michael may derive from prayers dedicated to him that appear in Kardec's publications. As mentioned, the saint has certain correspondences in Santería, though not as overtly as in the case of other Catholic figures. Practitioners I consulted had varied views on his Afrodiasporic counterparts. Some believed he had no ties to any *orisha*.[42] Others associated him with Obatalá[43] or Ogún. Regarding the latter, Lydia Cabrera in *El monte* (1989, 607) mentions that a plant called *palo negro* is "used by Ogún Achibiri Ki, who is San Miguel Archangel."[44] Clearly, St. Michael represents a multivalent construct whom the Cuban religious community associates with numerous belief systems and incarnations of specific *orishas*; this is a valued quality in such a thoroughly transculturated context. Note that

---

[42] Yeimer Arango, *santero*, *babalawo*, *palero* and *espiritista*, personal email, March 7, 2021. Alira Ashvo-Muñoz (personal email, April 5, 2021) similarly notes that Cubans consider San Miguel a son of God and one of the fiercest defenders of mankind, but not necessarily an *orisha*.

[43] Betancourt Bejerano interview, May 2021.

[44] Thanks to David Font-Navarrete for bringing the Cabrera reference to my attention.

although songs to Catholic saints usually appear early on, if a particular spirit had a close affinity to a saint in life, songs related to it might appear later in conjunction with more focused devotion.⁴⁵ In the *plegaria* presented below, the short initial melody to San Miguel is typically sung first by the lead singer alone; it can be repeated by the entire group, or the leader can segue directly into the final call–response chorus.

"San Miguel bendito"/Blessed Saint Michael

San Miguel, San Miguel bendito	Saint Michael, blessed Saint Michael
San Miguel, San Miguel bendito	Saint Michael, blessed Saint Michael
Préstame tu espada, ay Dios	Lend your sword to me, oh God
Que quiero vencer	I want to be victorious
Préstame tu espada, ay Dios	Lend your sword to me, oh God
Que quiero vencer	I want to be victorious

Semi-improvised call–response coda to "San Miguel bendito"

Guía: Yo venzo uno, yo venzo dos	Lead: You conquer one thing, I conquer two
Coro: *Vamo' a vencer, buen ser*	Chorus: *We will be victorious, good spirit*
Guía: Vamo a vencer la dificultad	Lead: We will conquer all difficulty
Coro: *Vamo' a vencer, buen ser*	Chorus: *We will be victorious, good spirit*
Guía: Vamo' a vencer la dificultad	Lead: We will conquer all difficulty
Coro: *Vamo' a vencer, buen ser*, etc.	Chorus: *We will be victorious, good spirit*, etc.

FIGURE 3.6 "San Miguel bendito."

⁴⁵ Ana Stela Cunha, personal WhatsApp communication, May 27, 2021.

An alternate song beginning with the phrase "San Miguel venció" often precedes the call–response segment as well. It is typically performed out of time.

"San Miguel venció"/Saint Michael the Victorious

San Miguel venció	Saint Michael was victorious
San Miguel venció	Saint Michael was victorious
San Miguel venció a su enemigo	Saint Michael defeated his enemy
Con el poder de Dios	With the power of God

Some spirit guides have especially close ties to *orishas* and blur distinctions between the two, as in the case of "La Negra" mentioned in Chapter 2. Joaquín Fernández Miranda explains that one's primary spiritual guides are often aligned with *orishas*, and that what appears to be possession by an *orisha* in the context of Santería devotion can also be viewed as a manifestation of a guiding spirit. This belief, while contested by some, is fairly widespread (e.g., Millet 1993, 44) and underscores yet again the interpenetrated nature of religious spheres often conceived as distinct. Whether one views *orisha* possession as the presence of an "actual" *orisha* or the "spiritual essence" of an *orisha* in another form, the distinction makes little difference to the religious community:

Let's suppose I'm a man and ... my spirit guide is also a man aligned with Santa Barbara and Siete Rayos ... When I try to make my saint, Changó comes. I'm not going to be possessed by Siete Rayos, because he is from Palo ... Even if the *muerto* [spirit] doesn't manifest through you, it is still there but transformed into an *orisha* [santo], representing it ... An *orisha*, a real *orisha*, never takes over an initiate. It is impossible to put all that in your head. What appears instead is your spirit guide manifesting as an *orisha*. The Yemayá that you see in church, you can't seat that on your head, it is too big, it will burst you ... What comes over you is your guardian spirit guide.[46]

From this perspective, it makes sense to include songs of praise to spirits alongside others to *orishas* since many view them as linked. Palo

---

[46] Por ejemplo, yo soy hombre y ... el guía espiritual mío es un hombre, es un espíritu que tiene que ver con Santa Bárbara, con Siete Rayos. Pero cuando yo me vaya a hacer santo, yo me hago Changó. Yo no me voy a hacer Siete Rayos, que es Palo ... Si no baja el muerto, pasa el mismo espíritu pero transformado en santo, representando al santo. El santo, realmente el santo, nunca baja. Es imposible bajar un santo y ponérselo en la cabeza. Lo que baja es el espíritu ya concretado en el Santo. La Yemayá que tú ves en la iglesia, esa tú no la puedes montar en la cabeza, es muy grande, te revienta ... Imposible que ese santo grandísimo tú lo puedas aguantar en la cabeza. Lo que estás coronando es el espíritu tuyo que es tu ángel de la guardia. (Fernández Miranda interview, March 2021)

deities have similar ties to *orishas* and broader notions of religiosity: Sarabanda is Palo's Ogún as well as St. Peter; Siete Rayos is Changó or St. Barbara; Lucero Mundo is Elegguá and the Niño de Atocha; Mama Chola or Mama Wengue is Ochún or the Virgin of Charity; Centella is Oyá or Santa Teresa; Tiembla Tierra is Obatalá or el Santísimo, etcetera (Warden 2006, 36–7).

While Ocha devotees perform extended song sequences (*orus*) to the *orishas* in a prescribed order, most *orisha* songs in *misas* follow no fixed order[47] and are incorporated based on perceived similarities between *orishas* and spirits. *Misa* participants sing *orisha* songs not to praise them individually, but rather because they are understood to be part of broader spiritual currents that tie them to other forces being honored.[48] For instance, an organizer's spirit guide may manifest in a form similar to San Lázaro/Babalú Ayé because they walk with a limp, or because they are interested in matters of physical or spiritual healing. In that case, the spirit and Babalú would be considered aligned in important respects and part of the same *corriente* (spiritual path or current). Health and purification represent a central focus of both *misas* and *orisha* worship, as mentioned; because St. Lazarus and Babalú Ayé share that interest, singing songs dedicated to them (see Figure 3.8) can serve as a means of praising guardian spirits too, and of encouraging them to manifest. In the same way, the spirits to whom a *misa* is dedicated may be women and mothers, or they may have been *santeras* in life whose principal *orisha* was Yemayá. For these reasons, singing songs of praise to Yemayá (Figure 3.9) and mothers may be appropriate. Similarly, fierce Kongo or Indian spirits associated with the rage of slavery and oppression share characteristics with *orishas* like Changó or Ogún and might be evoked or praised using the same songs.

"Canción a San Lázaro"/Song to Saint Lazarus

Siete días con siete noches	Seven days and seven nights
Por el mundo caminando	Through the world I walk
Y no encuentro una limosna	And I canta find any alms
Pa' mi viejo Babalú Ayé	For old Babalú Ayé
Tanto como yo trabajo	As much as I work
Tanto como yo camino	As much as I walk

---

[47] One exception might be songs sometimes performed early to Elegguá as a means of initiating *orisha* worship.
[48] Diana Espírito Santo, personal WhatsApp message, June 1, 2021.

Y no encuentro esa limosna
Pa' mi viejo Babalú Ayé

And I can't find any alms
For old Babalú Ayé

Ay, San Lázaro bendito
Santo de mi devoción
Si me das lo que te pido
Te haré una coronación[49]

Ay, blessed St. Lazarus
Saint of my devotion
If you give me what I ask
I will coronate you[50]

FIGURE 3.7 "Canción a San Lázaro," used in praise of all spirits of healing.

"Marinero, marinero"/Mariner, Mariner

Marinero, marinero
Marinero de alta mar
Préstame tu barquillita
Para irme a navegar, ay Dios

Mariner, mariner
Mariner of the high seas
Lend me your little boat
So I can navigate, oh God

Si yo fuera marinero
Marinero de verdad
Te prestaría mi barquilla
Para irme a navegar

If I were a mariner
A true mariner
I'd lend you my little boat
And head off sailing

---

[49] These songs exist in many versions. The lyrics to the last verse of the "Canción a San Lázaro" collected by Diana Espírito Santo give some sense of the extent to which texts vary: "Ay, San Lázaro bendito, padre de mi devoción/ Yo te pido, padre mío, misericordia y amor."

[50] Abilio Betancourt Bejerano (personal communication) notes that this song is often followed by a *montuno* or chorus taken from Margarita Lecuona's song "Babalú," with the lyrics "Babalú Ayé, Babalú, Aye." For a transcription of that *montuno*, see Figure 4.4.

FIGURE 3.8 Transcription of "Marinero, marinero," a children's song often incorporated into *misas* and *violines* in praise of Yemayá and related beings. Many additional verses may alternate with the chorus.

Other songs frequently sung in praise of Yemayá and other spirit beings associated with the water include "A remar" (Lets Row; Figure 5.12), a piece which often follows "Marinero, marinero" (Figure 3.8) in performances, and "Corre el agua" (The Water Flows; Figure 3.9).

"A remar"/Let's Row

A remar, a remar, a remar	Let's row, let's row, let's row
A remar, a remar, a remar	Let's row, let's row, let's row
A remar, a remar, a remar	Let's row, let's row, let's row
La Virgen de Regla nos va a acompañar	The Virgin of Regla will accompany us

"Corre el agua" (The Water Flows)

Corre el agua, corre el agua	The water flows, the water flows
Corre el agua Yemayá	The water flows, Yemayá
Corre el agua, corre el agua	The water flows, the water flows
Ay, con corriente espiritual	Ay, with a spiritual current/flow

FIGURE 3.9 "Corre el agua."

As should be evident, Spiritism is a conceptually open-ended religious practice. Beyond the standard conventions of purification and prayer that begin and end *misas*, their organization varies greatly depending on the mediums overseeing the event, the participants' individual needs, and the *cuadro espiritual* associated with each. For these reasons it is difficult to say which songs will be heard at any given time. But, typically, following the invocation of Catholic forces, songs dedicated to the *comisión india* or *gitana* may be sung (Figures 3.10 and 3.11). *Indios*, like Kongo spirits, are understood to be tenacious fighters, loyal but also wild and unpredictable, in need of oversight. Some songs align them with Kongos, suggesting that they adopt each other's personas as they manifest on the physical plane, with lyrics such as "I have an Indian spirit who appears as a Kongo, I have a Kongo who appears as an Indian."[51]

Gitanas for their part are often likened to Ochún in terms of overall temperament, given their sensual allure,[52] or with Oyá. But they can appear in multiple forms (as the Kongo Centenella, for instance, or even as a Spanish nun; see Otero 2020, 82) and in that sense are more mutable than an *orisha*. A *gitana* also may appear to mediums bearing objects or images that suggest the need for ritual action on the part of an individual; these might include making offerings to another spirit or pursuing initiation into Ocha or Palo. Alternately, a *gitana* may appear as Ochún herself, channeling the *orisha*'s *corriente* as a way of indicating that a devotee should focus their spiritual development or attention to matters of love.[53] Rather than representing a "whitening" of Afro-Latin, spirituality, Otero (2020, 83) suggests that *gitanas*

---

[51] "Yo tengo un indio que viste de congo, yo tengo un congo que viste de indio." As sung by Roy Vázquez, interview, July 2018. Otero (2020, 85) similarly describes a *misa* she attended in which the spirit of a Kongo priest (*ngangulero*) appeared in tandem with that of an Indian. See also Dodson (2008, 26) for visual documentation of the phenomenon in eastern Cuba.

[52] Vázquez interview, July 2018.

[53] Diana Espírito Santo, personal WhatsApp message, June 1, 2021.

reference Black Atlantic heritage as a nomadic and persecuted European minority that is racially coded as dark skinned.[54]

Indios, *gitanas*, and other spirit *comisiones* are each associated with dozens of *plegarias*; the transcriptions included here are far from comprehensive and are only intended to provide a sense of what the repertoire is like.

"La gitana"/The Gypsy Woman," lyric excerpt[55]

Hermana Rita, gitana mía	Sister Rita, my gypsy
Hermana Rita dame bondad	Sister Rita, show me kindness
Llévame a tu santuario	Take me to your sanctuary
A buscar la caridad	In search of charity
Gitana, gitana pura	Gypsy, pure gypsy
Gitana, gitana inmensa	Gypsy, immense gypsy
Líbrame de inquietudes	Free me from my concerns
Líbrame de los lamentos	Free me from lamentation
Cinco flores yo te ofrezco	Five flowers I offer you
Cinco flores de humildad	Five flowers of humility
Buscando que tú me brindes	With the intent that you will offer me
Esperanza y caridad	Hope and charity

FIGURE 3.10 "La gitana," selected verses.

---

[54] Sonia Seeman (2019, 33–9 and 255–311) has done fascinating work on the ways that Romani peoples are represented sonically in the music of countless others through acts of mimesis. Her work has much to offer Latin Americanists, given the prominence of "Gypsy" spirits to multiple religious and musical traditions.

[55] This piece was written by Emir Molina del Valle in 1995 in praise of a specific Gypsy spirit named Rita that guides his sister. He originally accompanied it with a *cajón* ensemble and recorded it on the CD *Los Nani: Espiritistas ¡a cantar!* (Álvarez 1997). See www.YouTube.com/watch?v=G_uOW2hUmyc (accessed June 2, 2021); it has since become popular in *violines* as well. In some live *violín* performances by others, I have heard lyrics from the *plegaria* "Misericordia" mixed with Molina del Valle's lyrics and melody. They begin "Misericordia, misericordia ay Dios, misericordia, poder divino. Misericordia, misericordia, ay Dios, sea derramada en el nombre de Dios."

"Canto al indio"/Song, to the Indian[56]

Ven, ven, indio te espero	Come, come, Indian I wait for you
Ven, ven, indio de mi amor	Come, come, my beloved Indian
Mira, que si tú no vienes	Look, if you don't come
Se muere mi corazón	My heart will break
Indio bravo, se muere mi corazón	Angry Indian, my heart dies
Por la pena entonces sea mejor	I feel such pain, that might be best
Ven, ven, indio te espero	Come, come, Indian I wait for you
Ven, ven indio te laboro	Come, come, I labor for you
Mira, que si tú no vienes	Look, if you don't come
Se muere el corazón	My heart will break
Indio rojo, indio bravo	Red Indian, angry Indian
Yo te llamo con amor	I call to you with love
Indio rojo, indio caribe	Red Indian, Caribbean Indian
Ven conmigo a laborar	Come with me to labor
Tú traes la fuerza, traes la trabuca[57]	You carry the force, you carry an explosion
En tu mero corazón	In your very heart
Somos la tribu de tus hermanos	We are the tribe of your brothers
Te invitamos a laborar	We invite you to labor

FIGURE 3.11 "Canto al indio" as performed by Roy Vázquez.

[56] Thanks to Abilio Betancourt Bejerano for his insights into these and other Spiritist lyrics reproduced in the chapter.
[57] Literally, a small firecracker much like the Fourth of July "poppers" that explode when thrown to the ground. Thanks to Agustín González García for clarification of this term.

Later sections of *misas* foreground interactions with the spirits of former African slaves (often referred to generically as *congos*). Participants consider these the most "intense" parts of the ritual, and they are the most likely to result in trance or possession. This may manifest in any participant, including the lead medium. If the lead medium falls into trance, the second medium takes charge of activities for a time. As possession occurs, singing typically stops and the spirit interacts with those in attendance; it may perform acts of purification, bring messages, or offer advice. Only after the spirit has fulfilled its mission and left the gathering does singing begin again.[58]

Kongo spirits figure more prominently than any other group in *misas espirituales* (Castellanos and Castellanos 1992, 200), both in Cuba, where they are known by names such as Ta José, Ta Julián, Ña (or Ma) Francisca,[59] Ta José, or Ta Lorenzo Lucumí (Cabrera 1989, 86; Otero 2020, 84),[60] and in Brazil, where common names for them include Velho João, Velho Joaquim, (Bastide 1971, 107–8), or Mae Xica.[61] "Ta" represents a shortened version of "Tata" or "Taita," meaning father or grandfather in Kikongo. The abbreviated pronunciation of the word suggests how it might have been spoken by the Black population in the nineteenth century with little formal education, or by recently arrived Africans still learning Spanish (a form of speech known as *bozal*).[62] Describing the spirits of African slaves generically as *congos* makes sense given that Bantu/Kongo peoples were the most prominently represented among slave populations throughout the Americas. In Cuba of the 1850s, for instance, more than 34 percent of Africans came from the Kongo "meta-ethnic group"; the next largest group, the Yoruba or Lucumí, comprised only 23 percent (Eli Rodríguez et al. 1997 vol. 1, 23).

Cane workers figure prominently among Kongo spirits who manifest in *misas*; they share a love of sweet black coffee and white rum or *aguardiente*, as well as cigars. Individuals intending to channel a *congo* may be

---

[58] Diana Espírito Santo, personal email, March 31, 2021.
[59] "Ña" appears to be a shortened version of "doña" or "lady." References to Ma Francisca have multiple associations; they can denote female Kongo ancestors, or the Kongo equivalent of Yemayá (Francisca or Madre Agua), or both.
[60] Cuban Spiritists today note that while the names ta José, ta Julián, or ma Francisca remain common in *misas*, others listed by Cabrera no longer are typically referenced.
[61] Ana Stela Cunha, personal WhatsApp communication, June 3, 2021.
[62] *Bozal* speech has many distinct uses and associations and clearly holds important meanings for the Afro-Cuban religious community today. It is incorporated into Palo liturgy alongside Kikongo terms, for instance, and also in Ocha ritual at times entirely aside from the Spiritist contexts discussed here. Historically it was used by elite authors to ridicule the African population as well, for instance in the *bufos* or comic theater.

ritually attuned beforehand by passing a machete near their body, since it was such common work tool in the nineteenth century (Guevara 2014, 71–2). As in the case of *indios*, *congos* are understood to be powerful and strong willed, good at guiding the living through hostile situations (Michael Mason in Warden 2006, 48). But they can also be brutal and aggressive, channeling the rage of the oppressed.

> You have to set limits on those spirits ... calm them, you see? Because those spirit protectors, [some of them] are beasts. They stick close to you, they are your defenders but they'll lead you into the abyss because they are brutish, ignorant. At that time [in the days of slavery] they lived like savages. There was no justice, nothing like that. Say Ta Julián is with you ... They [might have] killed him in prison, [maybe] he was a murderer ... He comes to keep you safe, but he comes in a form that isn't in your best interests ... he loves you terribly but he ends up ruining everything, you see?[63]

Spiritists use least two distinct types of song repertoire dedicated to Kongos: songs in Spanish calling to Cuban-born spirits (Figs. 3.12, 3.13), and songs in pidgin/*bozal* Spanish and/or fragmented Kongo languages derived from Palo religions (Figure 3.14). Palo songs appear less frequently in *violines* than those to Cuban-born spirits, but they are found in both *misas* and *cajón de muerto* devotion (Warden 2006, 36–7).

During *misas*, devotees sometimes accompany songs to Kongo spirits by clapping or rhythmic tapping on their chair or bench; these are the only songs with any accompaniment. The tapping can mark *clave* or simply keep the beat as a means of adding intensity to mediumistic activity.[64] One common melody evoking Kongo spirits is "Mamá Francisca," also referred to at times as "Siento una voz" (I Feel a Voice; Figure 3.12) whose lyrics reference both the ability of mediums to communicate with the spirit world and broader notions of West African cosmology in terms of the centrality of water and the sea. Cuban Spiritists view water as the home of the *comisión marina* as well as all water spirits, in the same way that the *comisión de ángeles* lives in the heavens (Larduet Luaces 2016, 82). Water is also the

---

[63] Esos espíritus tienes que darle un control ... pa' calmar a esos espíritus, ¿ya entiendes? Porque ... hay espíritus protectores que son unas bestias. Se te pegan arriba, y son protectores tuyos y te llevan al abismo porque son protectores muy brutos. En ese tiempo acuérdate que se vivía como salvajes. No había justicia, no había nada ... Y Ta Julián está contigo, no es un espíritu familiar. A él lo mataron en una prisión, es un asesino ... Y viene a cuidarte porque son familiares pero que viene con una forma que no te conviene a tí, lo que hace es desgraciarte. Te quiere tanto que te embarca, ¿me entiende? Fernández Miranda interview, March 2021.

[64] Fernández Miranda interview, March 2021.

realm of Olokun, *orisha* of the deep ocean, a realm also associated with the dead and thus central to Spiritist belief. "Mi madre" in this case could reference the Virgin Mary, the *comisión María*, or the medium's actual mother, in addition to Mamá Francisca herself.

"Mamá Francisca"

Siento una voz que me llama	I hear a voice that calls to me
De lo profundo del mar	From the depths of the sea
Es la voz de una africana	It is the voice of an African woman
Que me viene a saludar	Who comes to salute me
Llamo a mamá y no viene	I call to my mother but she doesn't come
Llamo a papá y tampoco	I call to dad, no response either
Yo llamo a mis seres guías	I call for my guiding spirits
Que vengan poquito a poco	As they arrive little by little
Mamá Francisca, te estoy llamando	Mamá Francisca, I am calling you
Mamá Francisca, no me respondes	Mamá Francisca, you don't reply
Reina africana, te estoy llamando	African queen, I am calling you
Te estoy llamando a laborar	I'm calling you to labor

FIGURE 3.12 "Mamá Francisca," initial melody, repeated in subsequent verses.

Most songs to the *comisión africana* are generic rather than mentioning a specific spirit. Aside from "Mamá Francisca," they include "Congo de Guinea soy" (I am a Kongo from Guinea) with its *montuno* "Congo, conguito" (Kongo, Dear Kongo; see Figure 3.13), "¿Pa' qué tú me llamas? (Why Do You Call Me?), and "Yo vine pa' ver" (I Came to See [a Kongo]). As an aside, hip hop artists such as the female duo Instinto have begun using fragments of these Spiritist melodies in pop repertoire.[65] Other

---

[65] See, for instance, this release, which begins with "¿Pa' qué tú me llamas?" and continues with "Lumbe, lumbe" (Figure 3.14): www.YouTube.com/watch?v=wd_Xeu9Tx-E (accessed June 23, 2021).

devotional songs to African spirits mention names such as "Ma Francisca" (the "Ma" here meaning mother or grandmother) or "Yo me llamo Ta José." Their lyrics include lines such as "Ma Francisca says not to be afraid, she can work with any handkerchief"[66] or "What am I called? My name is Ta José."[67]

"Congo de Guinea soy"/I am a Kongo from Guinea

Congo de Guinea soy	I am a Kongo from Guinea
Buena' noche' criollo'	Good evening to the Cuban-born
Yo deja mi hueso allá	I leave my bones over there
Yo vengo a hacer caridad	I have come to offer charity

Montuno

Congo, conguito, congo de verdad	Little Kongo, real Kongo
Yo vengo a la tierra a hacer caridad	I come to earth to offer charity

FIGURE 3.13 "Congo de Guinea soy," initial melody and *montuno*.

Songs derived directly from Palo ceremony tend to include less Spanish and more Kikongo or *bozal* terminology; the meaning of such lyrics is far from straightforward and may be disputed even among those familiar

---

[66] "Dice Ma Francisca que no tenga miedo, que ella trabaja con cualquier pañuelo." The kerchief in this case metaphorically alludes to distinct spirits or *corrientes*. A white cloth in a ceremony might obliquely reference Obatalá, or a yellow one Ochún/Mama Chola, etc. The song's lyrics suggest the way that references to Ma Francisca can both denote a particular Kongo spirit and allude to a broader array of related powers that transcend it.

[67] "¿Cómo me llamo yo? Yo me llamo Ta José" (Warden 2006, 182).

with ritual practice. One such piece heard frequently in *misas* and in *violines* is "Lumbe lumbe" (Figure 3.14), available on YouTube as recorded by the folkloric group Abbilona.[68] Worshippers use this piece to reference a series of Palo deities by substituting the name "Sarabanda" (the equivalent of Ogún) with Siete Rayos, Madre Agua, or others as they repeat the same melody. Anthropologist Ana Stela Cunha[69] describes *lumbe* as a Kikongo greeting, a salutation to the spirit world, while Hesse (1971, 396) suggests *lumbe* is a local Black adaptation of the Spanish *alumbra* (to illuminate). Both meanings seem to complement one another. *Tá* here is a local Black version of *está*, and "*sere sere*" means "good" or "well." The mention of a cave alludes to the fact that Palo practitioners often keep their *nganga* in a hole in the earth, or even buried; this is especially common of the *kindiambo* or *nganga judía*, those *prendas* created to inflict harm on enemies (Cabrera 2001, 198). The cave reference also underscores the sacred nature of the earth in Palo practice more broadly. The spelling of particular Kikongo terms in the following example is somewhat arbitrary since they are written and pronounced in multiple ways.

"Lumbe lumbe"/Welcome, Welcome

Lumbe, lumbe, lumbe	Welcome, welcome, give light
Lumbe la cueva en nganga	Welcome to the sacred *nganga* cave
Si Sarabanda tá sere sere	If Sarabanda is well
Palo Kindiambo ace agüe	The *nganga* will open a path

As indicated in measures 15–18 of Figure 3.14, the "Lumbe lumbe" invocation is usually followed by a faster, rhythmic call–response segment incorporating the phrase *salamalecum* that underscores both how the term *lumbe* can be used as a salutation and the many ties between Kongo practice in Cuba and other Afrodiasporic cultures. Influences from Islam into the Kongo religion seem to derive from the period of the slave trade and its immediate aftermath, one in which inter-African cultural influences spread among various groups; "*salamalecum*" (or *salaam alaikum*) has become so localized that many Palo practitioners no longer recognize its origins in the Arab world and only associate it with Kongo heritage.

Lumbe, lumbe	Welcome, light for the spirits
Yo salamalecum congo	May peace be with you, Kongo

---

[68] www.youtube.com/watch?v=EDaZM0DZRuc (accessed May 22, 2024).
[69] Personal WhatsApp communication, June 22, 2021.

FIGURE 3.14 "Lumbe lumbe," a Palo melody.

Following this climactic segment of the *misa* involving African spirits, worship concludes with a series of prayers, songs, and ritual cleansing. Usually, participants take the perfumed water bowl they have been using outside the house at this point and empty it to disperse any negative energies it may have collected in it (Dos Ventos 2008, 26–7), along with the flowers from the altar. Many *misas* end with participants standing to recite an "Our Father" or "Ave María" together. They may read a final spoken prayer and then sing "Se van los seres" (The Beings Are Leaving).[70] Following the event, refreshments are usually served before everyone heads home (Guevara 2014, 17).

Violines Espirituales

The previous section described the music of *misas espirituales* in detail because much *violín* repertoire derives directly from *misas* and because *misas* serve as a reference that helps organize much of their content and structure. Songs and prayers to the spirit world begin almost every *violín*, and the influence of Spiritist music in *violines* appears to be growing, as noted by performers who attended them in the 1990s.[71]

---

[70] For a recorded version of this *plegaria* in *cajón* format, see www.YouTube.com/watch?v=Pt7-6EcWpDo (accessed June 22, 2021).

[71] Pepe Reyes Jr., member of the Orquesta Estrellas Cubanas, personal WhatsApp message, March 31, 2021.

3 *Spiritism and* Violines Espirituales

The primary difference between *misas* and *violines* devoted to spirits is conceptual. Instead of attempting to interact with spirits directly, channel them, or ask them particular questions as would be common in a *misa*, the intent of a *violín* is simply to offer the spirits music that they enjoy. For this reason, Ileana Hodge Limonta refers to *violines* as "propitiatory acts": "Through propitiation you strive for good fortune. You want to do right by your ancestors, your dead, your *orisha*."[72] She notes that *misas* can also be organized to propitiate the spirit world rather than seek advice or guidance. Diana Espírito Santo also describes *violines espirituales* as a *"don de gracia* for your spirits" and mentions that Gypsies in one's *cordón* are especially pleased to have *violines* dedicated to them,[73] perhaps because the sound of the violin has historical ties to Gypsy/Roma heritage. In a *violín*, one offers music to the dead without expecting them to respond, unless they choose to. This alters the frame of activity considerably, opens it to more varied forms of performance, and allows for the diversification of its content. Hodge Limonta emphasizes that in *violines*

> You can sing anything from a Spiritist *transmisión* from the eastern part of the country to a somewhat more contemporary song that has something to do with religious beliefs, even if it isn't overtly religious. Everything is played there ... People sing, they have fun, they have a shot of rum. They know what they're up to, that they're involved in a propitiatory act ... The event becomes a kind of party.[74]

Initially, *violines espirituales* begin with instrumental music, usually slower works derived from Catholicism or the classical concert stage; performers later interweave *plegarias*, boleros, or other popular melodies, as well as devotional songs derived from Santería or Palo if desired. The musicians' interpretation of the music frequently alters its traditional sound. In some cases they may play songs instrumentally rather than vocally. In others, *plegarias* may be played at a faster tempo, harmonized, or formally arranged by the group to emphasize aesthetic enjoyment (by spirits and humans) rather than maximizing the chances that such music will induce trance. Yet despite the aesthetically oriented

---

[72] "Estás propiciando la buenaventura, tú quieres quedar bien con tus ancestros, con tus muertos, con tu santo." Hodge Limonta interview, March 2021.
[73] Personal email, February 3, 2021.
[74] Tú puedes cantar desde una transmisión espiritista que viene de la zona oriental, ya?, hasta una canción un poco más contemporánea que tenga algo que ver con la religión, aunque no sea de religión. Todo eso se toca ahí ... La gente canta, se divierte, se toma su traguito de ron. Saben en qué están, que están haciendo esa actividad propiciatoria ... y entonces se forma como una guarachita.
Hodge Limonta interview, March 2021.

and presentational nature of *violines*, performers recognize their spiritual nature. Most ritually cleanse themselves prior to performance using hibiscus flowers (*mar pacífico*), *cascarilla* (ground eggshells), and/or perfumes, and they wear white clothing out of respect for the dead, as do the spectators. Musicians often present their instruments to the altar before they begin; the organizer or medium overseeing the *violín* may bless them, making the sign of the cross on the bodies of performers and passing a glass of water over them from head to toe. Musicians often take a drink of *aguardiente* or rum, and offer a splash to the altar and/or performance space as well out of deference to the dead.[75]

Some performers believe that every *violín* should begin with a performance of "Our Father" (Padrenuestro) – either the standard spoken prayer or a particular musicalized version recognized as a "Spiritualist Hymn" and played instrumentally (Figure 3.15). The melody of this piece is anonymous, but its lyrics (when sung) were written by Puerto Rican poet Ramón Negrón Flores (1868–1945) and can be viewed in their entirety online.[76] The verses mirror many aspects of the spoken "Our Father" prayer, but the Negrón Flores adaptation includes lines that allude to Spiritist practices by discussing God alongside science and the creation of altars, and by foregrounding metaphorical references to light and darkness. Representative stanzas of the text are reproduced here.

Padre nuestro que estás en los cielos	Our Father who art in heaven
Circundado de gloria inmortal	Surrounded by immortal glory
Esperanza del alma que eleva	Hope of the soul that raises
al amor y a la ciencia un altar	An altar to love and science
Deja, deja que en nuestros hogares	May our homes never lack
nunca falten, ¡oh, Dios de bondad!	O God of generosity
Una chispa de luz para el alma	A spark of light for the soul
Para el cuerpo un pedazo de pan	For the body a piece of bread
No nos dejes caer en la noche	Do not let tus fall into the nighttime
Del pecado; en la sima del mal	Of sin; into the chasm of evil
Porque brille tu fe en la conciencia	In your consciousness shines faith
Como un faro de la eternidad	Like a beacon of eternity

---

[75] María Teresa Gómez Noguera, interview, June 2018.
[76] See www.tainoworld.com/rnflores.html (accessed July 19, 2021). A sung version of the piece can also be accessed on YouTube: www.YouTube.com/watch?v=7RcBSkiMQHA (accessed July 20, 2021).

FIGURE 3.15 A musical rendition of the Spiritist Padrenuestro by Ramón Negrón Flores.

Early segments of *violín espiritual* ceremonies vary least from event to event. Most often, the "Padrenuestro" is followed by an instrumental rendition of "Ave María" by Schubert or Bach/Gounoud, and then approximately four *plegarias* dedicated to all spirits beings, played either instrumentally or with voices and instruments together. As in the case of *misas*, some reference Catholic saints or deities (the Almighty, Jesus, and Mary). They typically include "Sea el Santísimo" (Figure 3.2), "La luz redentora" (Figure 3.3), "Misericordia" (with the melody depicted in Figure 3.10), and the folkloric version of "O/Ave María" discussed earlier (Figure 3.5), again in a much more polished and elaborated form than in a *misa espiritual*. Roy Vázquez[77] conceives of this first segment as an *oru* of sorts, a sequence of songs paying homage to the dead generally that sets the stage for more varied musical content later. Early segments frequently reference Eleguá or his Catholic counterpart, el Niño de Atocha, as well.

Later song sequences still roughly follow the order of sung prayers in *misas*, although they include additional repertoire. Song sequences follow a *tratado*-like organization in the sense that performers group multiple

[77] Interview, June 2018.

pieces devoted to a given spirit entity or *comisión* together, then pause before initiating a new series to a different entity or group. Musicians often separate these groupings further by interspersing boleros or popular songs between them, an alternative and more generic form of musical offering. One would expect to hear song sequences to Gypsy, Indian, and Kongo spirits at some point in the service, as well as others to figures such as San Miguel or San Lázaro/Babalú Aye. But, as in *misas*, major deities of Santería tend also to be praised. Beyond Elegguá and Babalú, the most commonly recognized *orishas* include Yemayá, Ochún, Obatalá, Oyá, and Changó (and/or their Palo counterparts). The centrality of the violin to the interpretation of these pieces varies, as mentioned; the instrument is foregrounded during concert repertoire or softer pieces such as boleros, but is overshadowed during danceable or more percussive segments. At the conclusion of the *violín*, verbal prayers or expressions of thanks are typically offered to the spirits; additional songs to Elegguá may be performed, and closing melodies such as "Se van los seres."

As noted, pieces originally associated with secular entertainment have become a prominent part of *violín* worship. One commonly hears Johann Strauss' "Blue Danube" in sequences dedicated to the Virgin of Regla/Yemayá/Madre de Agua because of its associations with water, for instance, or the Waldteufel waltz "Dolores" as a form of homage to Santa Teresa/Oyá/Centella. Instrumental renditions of *zarzuela* arias such as "Leyenda de un beso" (Legend of a Kiss, from the Spanish production of the same name) are also common, in this case as a way of paying homage to Gypsy spirits.[78] Pop songs that discuss local Afrodiasporic religious practices feature centrally as well: "Yerbero moderno" (Modern Herb Vendor), a song popularized by Celia Cruz and the Sonora Matancera that discusses sacred plants used in religious rites; or "Mata siguaraya" (The Siguaraya Tree), popularized by Benny Moré, which references a plant believed to embody spiritual energy.[79] Musicians intersperse such pieces among others more directly tied to the dead. They transition freely between *plegarias*, commercial pieces, songs with Lucumí texts, and those with Kongo-influenced Spanish.

Plegarias constitute the central musical component of *violines espirituales*, but they are often performed in new ways. As mentioned, instrumental

---

[78] Written by Reveriano Soutullo and Juan Vert, this *zarzuela* debuted in Madrid in 1924. The plot revolves around Amapola, the queen of a group of Gypsies, and various attempts to seduce her on the part of Spanish suitors.

[79] The spiritual and magical forces tied to nature in African-derived religions are documented extensively in Lydia Cabrera's *El monte*; see Cabrera 2023.

3 *Spiritism and* Violines Espirituales

versions are common, something rarely (if ever) heard in a *misa*. Alternately, sung *plegarias* may be included (such as Sindo Garay's "Imagen protectora" [Image of Protection]) that are too complex melodically and harmonically to be easily sung a cappella.[80] These alterations emphasize the frequently presentational nature of *violines*: they include some music that allows audience members to dance or sing along, but other pieces are intended to be watched passively and/or highlight the musical skills of the group.[81] And, of course, ensembles accompany both instrumental music and elaborated *plegarias* with chordal harmonies on the guitar or keyboard and by percussion such as the *claves*, bongo, or *güiro*. These instruments are never used in *misas*; they make the repertoire sound much more commercial. Such harmonizations are especially striking when used to accompany Palo or Ocha devotional songs not traditionally associated with Western instruments.

The relatively elaborate musical arrangements heard in *violines* often include harmonized vocal melodies and choral responses, countermelodies or arpeggios played on the violin, piano, or flute behind vocalists, and instrumental improvisation. The repertoire of the Orquesta Estrellas Cubanas illustrates these tendencies with highly complex arrangements (Oviedo and Pinelli 2011), but they are evident in performances by smaller groups as well. In a *violín* led by María Teresa "Mayté" Rosell in Almendares Park on December 20, 2020, for example, the musicians' interpretation of the folkloric "O María" piece mentioned earlier (Figure 3.5) alternated between instrumental and vocal segments. The ensemble consisted of a guitar, violin, flute, bongo, and two percussionist-singers playing *clave* and *güiro*. Performers began the piece instrumentally, with the violin on the main melody and the flute harmonizing it a third above. Guitar provided

---

[80] Some refer to this piece as "Virgen del Cobre" (Virgin of the Cobre Valley, in eastern Cuba), or "Plegaria a la Caridad" (Prayer to the Virgin of Charity). No exact match for it can be found in the list of Garay's works published by de León (1990), and the song appears to be unregistered with licensing agencies such as Harry Fox. Verónica González, librarian overseeing the Cristóbal Díaz Ayala Music Collection in the Green Library at FIU, has no record of the piece in that collection either. Yet the *Del Caribe* journal published by the Casa del Caribe in Santiago de Cuba (no. 57–8, 2012, p. 126) clearly attributes it to Garay. A version of the song interpreted by *trovador* (singer-songwriter) Eduardo Sosa is available on YouTube: www.YouTube.com/watch?v=0pc_qpW1pUs (accessed June 30, 2021).

[81] Devotion to saints or spirits continues to serve as a source of inspiration for professional musicians. Following the lead of Sindo Garay, for instance, *nueva trova* artist Silvio Rodríguez (b. 1952) and academic composer José María Vitier (b. 1954) collaborated to create their own "Plegaria a la Virgen del Cobre" as part of a larger orchestral and choral work called *Misa cubana* in 1996. Various performances of it are available on YouTube: www.YouTube.com/watch?v=f8VQulxbunQ (accessed June 30, 2021).

FIGURE 3.16 Excerpt of vocal and flute countermelody of "O María" (or "Ave María") as performed in a *violín espiritual*.

harmonic support; the *clave* player tapped on beats two and three of each measure in 3/4 time and the bongo marked beat one and added occasional improvised flourishes. Following completion of the introductory instrumental verse, voices entered; the violin continued doubling the main melody, but the flute switched to an improvised discant line against it (Figure 3.16). At the end of the initial verse section, the ensemble repeated most of the introduction instrumentally, then accompanied the singers in the second "O María, madre mía" section with the flute on new improvised countermelodies. The result was a very polished and highly arranged performance – a far cry from the a cappella songs heard in a traditional *misa*.

In the same way, the Estrellas Cubanas arranged choruses to *plegarias* such as "Sea el Santísimo" (Figure 3.2) and "San Miguel" (Figure 3.6) with three-part vocal settings and elaborate violin lines. Percussive rolls and flourishes on the bongo accompany the "Santísimo" piece, and it is preceded by an improvised cadenza on acoustic guitar.[82] Rhythmic

---

[82] See www.YouTube.com/watch?v=6TH5GbpOp8s (accessed June 30, 2021). The "El santísimo" segment begins this track; "San Miguel" can be heard starting at 4:47.

FIGURE 3.17 Violin double stops behind "Canción a San Lázaro."

double stops on the violin are commonly heard in many *violín* renditions of traditional *plegarias*. A violinist might introduce the melody of a *plegaria* such as "Canción a San Lázaro" (Figure 3.7) instrumentally, accompanied only by guitar and percussion, then switch to double stops as vocalists enter (Figure 3.17, compare with Figure 3.7).

Perhaps the most prominent characteristic associated with the music of *violines* could be described as the *son*-ification of traditional Spiritist repertoire, underscoring the influence of the Cuban *son* or other dance music on many pieces. Most *sones* consist of a strophic verse section in an AB or ABA form, followed by a cyclic, improvisational vamp known as a *montuno*. The *montuno* consists of a repeated harmonic vamp, often four measures long, and specific patterns on the bell, bongo, or other percussion. It serves as the basis of vocal and instrumental improvisation (Moore 2010, 91–100). In *violines*, musicians commonly add such vamp sections to the end of *plegarias*, increasing the tempo of the piece at that point, adopting standard *son* percussion rhythms, and featuring call–response vocals. The shift changes the style of the music, downplaying its introspective or devotional qualities and instead foregrounding rhythmic drive. Climactic musical segments of this nature often inspire participants to dance. Some *montuno*-like sections come from popular music; for instance, the "Canción a San Lázaro" (Figure 3.7) may be followed by the "Babalú Ayé" chorus in Margarita Lecuona's 1939 composition of the same name, later popularized by Miguelito Valdés, Desi Arnaz, and others (Figure 4.4).[83]

Other *montunos* may represent modified versions of existing choruses derived from popular music (most commonly featuring new lyrics), or entirely new *montunos* of the musicians' own invention. Examples of modified choruses include changing the refrain of the *son* "El huerfanito"[84] from its original lyrics – "*Yo no tengo padre, yo no tengo madre, yo no tengo a nadie que me quiere a mí*" (I don't have a father, I don't have a mother, I have no one who loves me) – to "*Yo sí tengo padre, yo sí tengo madre, yo sí tengo a Yalodde que me quiere a mí*" (I do have a mother, I do have a father, I have *Yalodde* [literally, queen or great lady; a Yoruba word associated with Ochún] who loves me). Or musicians may follow a traditional *plegaria* to a *gitana* spirit with the phrase "*Gitana de mis amores, bendíceme*" (My beloved Gypsy, bless me) over a 2mm. i-iv-V-i progression, a newly invented vamp (Figure 3.19). These choruses typically alternate with vocal or instrumental improvisations. Still other musicians may take a traditional antiphonal melody such as "*Yo venzo uno, yo venzo dos*" associated with praise songs to San Miguel (Figure 3.6) and arrange it as dance music with harmonized choruses, driving bell patterns, and violin riffs (*guajeos*) in the background.[85] Similar vamps such as "*Alumbra aquí, alumbra allá, si tú no me alumbras ¿quién me va a alumbrar?*" (Illuminate here, illuminate there, if you don't shed light on me who will?) function as "free-floating" choruses that may appear after almost any Spiritist *plegaria*. As discussed in Chapter 5, final climactic segments in *violines* often include multiple refrains sung in alternation in order to demonstrate the improvisational acumen of performers, their ability to think on their feet and continuously add new embellishments. The use of *son*-like choruses creates a decidedly intertextual element to

---

[83] For a recorded example of this chorus, listen to Miguelito Valdés' version of "Babalú" on YouTube starting at about 1:26: www.YouTube.com/watch?v=20yLoXDE6Ws (accessed July 15, 2021).

[84] "El huerfanito" was written by by Bienvenido Julián Gutiérrez and initially recorded by the Cuarteto Machín in 1931 on the RCA Victor label. It can be heard on YouTube and other online platforms: www.YouTube.com/watch?v=bQ-CmrltoME (accessed July 19, 2021); the chorus begins at about 1:16.

[85] This tag is heard in many live events, but it was also recorded on the Orquesta Estrellas Cubanas *Violín a Ochún* CD, track 2 ("El Santísimo"), starting about 5:30. See www.YouTube.com/watch?v=Oi8U1f4SXEM (accessed July 15, 2021).

3 Spiritism and Violines Espirituales

violines: lyrically and musically they reference Spiritism and broader secular repertoires simultaneously.

While the microdynamics of performances are the subject of Chapter 5, it is worth discussing what song sequences to individual spirits sound like in additional detail here. They vary greatly in length; if a particular deity is of little importance to a given celebration, songs in its honor may be recognized only with one or two brief *plegarias* before the ensemble passes on to other beings, or they may be omitted entirely. On the other hand, song sequences dedicated to spirits central to the event may easily last fifteen minutes or more. Longer sequences usually begin out of time or at a moderate tempo and build toward faster rhythms. A typical *tratado*-like segment focusing on Gypsy spirits might begin with the melody "Ole con ole, gitana" (Figure 3.18), sung out of time against sustained chords on a synthesizer keyboard. Eventually the performers would start playing the same piece in time but at a moderate tempo, supported by antiphonal vocals and improvised discant melodies on a violin in the background. Next, the lead singer might transition to new choruses such as "Gitana de mis amores, bendíceme" (Gypsy, my love, bless me) or "Baila gitana rica hasta amanezca el día" (Dance, lovely Gypsy, till the light of day) over repeated Andalucian cadences (i, bVII, bVI, ii V i) in four-measure phrases, referencing southern Spanish and Middle Eastern heritage lyrically and sonically. The lead vocalist might then increase the tempo and transition the group to a shorter version of the same chorus to add excitement ("Hasta amanezca el día" [Till the light of day]) over a repeated two-measure phrase with extended vocal and instrumental improvisations, until finally coming to an end.

FIGURE 3.18 "Ole con ole, gitana" with chordal accompaniment. This melody is typically sung by a chorus, then improvised on by a lead singer.

FIGURE 3.19 "Gitana de mis amores, bendíceme," alternating phrases between the chorus and lead vocalist.

In the same fashion, song sequences dedicated to Francisca or other Kongo spirits link together multiple *plegarias* and choruses, often emphasizing percussion at moments so as to sonically evoke Palo and *cajón* ceremonies from which many of the melodies derive. Such an *oru* could begin with a spoken Catholic prayer, then the lead singer might lead the group in an a cappella version of "Mamá Francisca" (Figure 3.12), out of time and accompanied only with occasional flourishes on the bongo. On a repeat of the same melody, a guitar or keyboard might begin to fill in chordal accompaniment with the violin playing sustained tremolos or inventing a soft countermelody. After a brief pause at the song's conclusion, the lead singer could lead the group into new *plegarias*, this time harmonized and with a rhythmic pulse from the outset, such as "Francisca" (Figure 3.20). These melodies are often interpreted in a lively fashion, with rumba clave and bongo patterns derived from Cuban popular music, syncopated piano figures, and violin countermelodies. The violinist might play a brief instrumental solo to add variety, or they might play the main melody for a time, giving the singers a chance to rest. The lead singer could eventually bring this

FIGURE 3.20 "Francisca" with chordal accompaniment.

plegaria to an end, then begin again at a slightly accelerated tempo but without guitar or piano, foregrounding percussion and voices only. They could then segue to other melodies accompanied in the same way: "Dice Ma Francisca que no tenga miedo," (Ma Francisca says don't be afraid, mentioned earlier) or "Lumbe lumbe" (Figure 3.14). A religious advisor could then end the praise sequence by offering a series of spoken prayers, giving thanks to prominent spirits in the event organizer's *cuadro*.[86]

Some organizers of *violines espirituales* feel a close affinity with Catholic beliefs and choose to organize *violines* in churches rather than private homes. Violinist Abilio Betancourt Bejerano[87] notes that such performances he has taken part in emphasize *plegarias* devoted to Catholic saints and/or classical concert repertoire. Aside from Schubert's "Ave María," works performed often include instrumental versions of "Estrellita" (Little Star) by Manuel Ponce, modern Catholic hymns such as "Santa María de la esperanza" (St. Mary of Hope) and "Santa María del camino" (St. Mary of the Path) by Juan Espinoza, "Virgen mambisa" (Insurgent Virgin, dedicated to the Virgin of Charity and written by Alma DeRojas), waltzes of various sorts, the *zarzuela* aria Lecuona's "Damisela encantadora" (Enchanting Damsel), and similar works.

Trance or direct communication with spirits takes place more frequently in *violines espirituales* than in *violines santorales*. This may be because some mediums are extremely susceptible to communication with their *cuadro*, or because Spiritist possession requires no exacting ritual

---

[86] The descriptions of devotional song sequences to Gypsies and to Ma Francisca are based on musical performances I have observed. Many thanks to Reynaldo Fernández Pavón for helping to transcribe and interpret the pieces in the Kongo sequence.

[87] Interview, May 12, 2021.

cues. As in the case of *misas* themselves, Spiritist trance most commonly takes place during later *violín* segments devoted to more aggressive beings such as Indios or Kongos. Multiple spirits may even compete with one another to speak through a particular medium in a *violín*. Even if no possession occurs, medium organizers will contact the spirits to whom the *violín* was dedicated in the aftermath and ensure they were satisfied with it. As Diana Espírito Santo describes it,[88] "The dead, your dead, need to tell you that they're happy with what you've done. So somebody needs to do the mediating, either through the body or through [divination] of some kind afterwards."

Conclusion

Violines espirituales (and others) draw heavily on the structure and musical idioms derived from creole séances. This is evident in countless ways, such as the incorporation of spoken Catholic and Kardecist prayers, the use of hymns such as the "Padrenuestro," the creation of altars displaying ritual objects honoring the dead, and recognition of prominent spirit *comisiones*. And yet many differences are evident between *misas* and *violines espirituales* as well. The latter might be considered an aesthetically elaborated analogue of the former for presentational purposes. The overall structure of *misas* and *violines espirituales* is similar, but music becomes the central focus in *violines*, including new kinds of music and creating new forms of spiritual resonance. Musicians replace the collective a cappella singing in *misas* with a combination of instrumental and vocal works. The music played may be technically demanding, derived from European concert traditions. It may incorporate praise songs in Afrodiasporic languages, accompanying them on the bongo and claves rather than on traditional drums. It may include popular songs. And musicians transform the many Spiritist *plegarias* they play by adding Western harmonies, extended arrangements, and instrumental and vocal improvisations in the style of dance repertoire.

In their constant movement between religious spheres and beyond, *violines* reflect a fundamental mutability and interreferentiality that speaks to the fractured realities of postslave society. *Violines* represent part of an amalgamated practice that accepts all influences. One event may emphasize praise of a local patron saint; another may pay homage to African ancestors or Gypsies, or entirely different spirits. In musical terms as well, *violines* move constantly between realms of practice. They

---

[88] Personal email, February 3, 2021.

manifest an unusual degree of fugitivity and draw implicit connections and/or juxtapose forms of music that in other circumstances would have little to do with one another.

The relationship between *misas espirituales* and *violines espirituales* is much closer than that between traditional drumming events for the *orishas* and *violines santorales*, the focus of Chapter 4. Ocha worship involves formalized structures, both musical and ritualistic, to a much greater extent than *misas*. *Orishas* must be venerated in a prescribed order and with specific kinds of music and dance. Offerings to them in the form of a *violín* thus represent a more tangible break with orthodox practice, yet they too can also be viewed as expanding and modernizing the parameters of such worship in certain ways that are increasingly attractive to the religious community.

4

Violines a Ochún and *Orisha* Praise

Violines dedicated primarily to the praise of Ochún or other *orishas* (known as *violines santorales* or *violines de santo*) closely resemble the *violines espirituales* discussed in Chapter 3, with a partially distinct repertoire and devotional focus. In *violines* for the *orishas*, Spiritist repertoire combines with popular songs in Spanish and others employing Lucumí texts; performances typically foreground sequences dedicated to a number of individual *orishas*, much as in the case of a *tambor*. Percussionist and *santero* Octavio Rodríguez[1] speculates that the practice of organizing *misas* for spirit guides and the dead prior to Ocha initiation may have contributed to the emergence of *violines santorales* over time. The close ties between *misas espirituales* and Regla de Ocha, discussed in the next section, seem to have resulted in the gradual "Santería-ization" of *misas* (with spirit guides often viewed as linked to *orisha* counterparts), and, as a result, to the greater prominence of Lucumí-based devotional songs in *violines*. This underscores how the religious community continues to experiment with multiple modalities of worship (Balbuena Gutiérrez 2003, 32; Brown 2019).

Violín musicians perform a variety of repertoire in praise of the *orishas*, and they often transform the sound of chants with Lucumí texts by fusing them with dance music, as discussed. Yet performers playfully cross the boundaries separating traditional percussive accompaniment and danceable repertoire by incorporating segments that foreground solo percussion rather than melody or harmony instruments, and by switching briefly to triple-meter rhythms such as those associated with *bembés* (a form of

---

[1] Rodríguez interview, June 2018.

religious drumming). Percussion-only segments add musical variety and intensity to *violín* performance, but they never last too long as musicians don't intend their music to lead to mounting by an *orisha*.

This chapter begins by summarizing the extent to which Spiritist practices have been adopted into all forms of *orisha* worship and underscoring the appeal of religious expression such as *violines* that reference both forms of religion simultaneously. It then describes the significance of the Caridad del Cobre/Ochún to the Cuban people, an important consideration given that most *violines* are dedicated to her/them. The chapter continues by describing the overall format of the *violín santoral* and the musical repertoire associated with the major *orishas* it recognizes, as well as ritualistic acts such as the *brindis* or toast to Ochún. A final segment considers attitudes toward *violines* within the Ocha community, which continue to be somewhat ambivalent.

SANTERÍA AND SPIRITISM

The *misas espirituales* discussed in Chapter 3 developed as a distinct form of religion but now are integral to Ocha religious rites. Cuban *santeros* regularly venerate their *egun*, both deceased family members and *santeros* associated with their specific religious community (González-Wippler 1995, 106–7). They organize *misas espirituales* prior to some formal drumming events for *orishas* as a means of both honoring and placating the spirit world (Castellanos and Castellanos 1992, 195). They stage elaborate, multiday ceremonies to venerate the spirits of *santeros* who die (Valdés Garriz 1991), both funerary rites and tributes (*honras*) a year or more after their passing.[2] Many Ocha healing and purification ceremonies employ perfume, glasses of water, flowers, and other items found on the Spiritist *bóveda* (Sanchez 2000, 7). As mentioned, veneration of the dead has a long history in West Africa[3], and *orishas* themselves are

---

[2] Johnny Frías (personal email, June 12, 2023) notes that ceremonies in honor of *santeros* who have died are typically called *tambores a egun* and that they are followed the next day by a standard *tambor* honoring the same individual's primary *orisha*. The *tambor a egun* has its own unique drumming rhythms and ritual songs. Drummers often perform standing, with drums strapped to their waists. Services may take place in the home of an individual close to the deceased or in a funeral home next to their casket. David Font-Navarrete (personal email, August 8, 2023) notes that songs for the *egun* can be heard not only accompanied by the *batás* but by *bembé* drummers in historical recordings all made by Lydia Cabrera and Josefina Tarafa from the 1950s.

[3] Veneration of the dead is especially prevalent among Kongos, according to Bastide (1971, 161).

understood to be distant ancestors. Most if not all *santeros* receive advice not only from *orishas* but also from spirit guides. And converts to Santería convene multiple *misas* in advance of initiation, as discussed in the following paragraphs. For all these reasons, the line between *egun* and *muerto* or between *santero* and Spiritist can be difficult to draw.

The first step individuals must take within the Lucumí religion is to be baptized in the Catholic tradition. If they were not baptized as a child, they are required to do so as an adult.[4] Prior to being crowned in Ocha, they must take part in three *misas espirituales*: *a misa de iglesia*, a *misa de investigación*, and a *misa de coronación*.[5] A *misa de iglesia* (Catholic mass) takes place first; during the service, the priest mentions the names of the individual's deceased family members. This pays homage to them and ensures that the Ocha ceremony goes well.[6] Later Spiritist *misas* take place at home. The *misa de investigación* reveals the individual's principal spiritual cadre (González-Wippler 1995, 107). *The misa de coronación* takes place a few days before making one's saint. Its purpose is to ensure that all spirit guides have been properly identified, and that they support *orisha* initiation and will not interfere with it. The coronation itself involves ritual singing while adorning the initiate with lilies or other white flowers (see Chapter 3 and Castellanos and Castellanos 1992, 201–2). It formalizes the relationship between a new initiate (*iyawó*) and their spiritual cadre (Feraudy Espino 1999, 36).

Many members of the religious community emphasized to me the importance of holding rites of purification and offerings to the dead prior to a *toque de violín*, something they referred to as a *servicio al muerto*. This takes place in the home where the *violín* is to be played and is overseen by any initiated elder within the religion.[7] Servicios are as crucial as *misas*; they must be conducted prior to all Ocha ceremonies, including *violines*, *toques de santo* (drumming events dedicated to the *orishas*), and celebrations marking the anniversary of making one's saint. Their intent is to advise spirits of an upcoming religious celebration and to seek their blessing. *Servicios* involve preparing gifts for the dead – often laid out on the floor – including coffee, glasses filled with sugar water, flowers, candles, soft drinks, cigars, and rum or cane alcohol. Organizers draw on the floor as well: a semi-circle with nine segments and an offering

---

[4] Nicolás Martínez Palacios WhatsApp communication May 21, 2024 and Gordillo Miraval interview 2021.
[5] Nicolás Martínez Palacios, interview, Jan. 2021, March 10, 2021.
[6] Melena Francis Valdés, personal email, August 6, 2021.
[7] Martínez Palacios WhatsApp communication May 19, 2024.

placed within each one, the lines symbolically marking divisions between the living and dead.⁸ Ritual herbs serve to cleanse the home and rid it of negative energies following the service, making sure that no unfriendly spirit presence remains.⁹ Often, participants sing nine songs for the ancestors and/or spirit guides as part of a *servicio al muerto*. In some cases, the rites may also include animal sacrifices. Following these activities and the singing of ritual songs, organizers ask whether the dead are satisfied or if they require anything else to be done before they offer their blessing.

Some spirit guides are so closely associated with *orishas* that it can be difficult to tell which one is present in a given ceremony. This relates to the controversial issue of whether *orishas* or some aspect of their "essence" mount worshippers in ceremonies, discussed in Chapter 3. Solimar Otero (2020, 78ff.), for instance, recounts attending creole séances in which most spirits invoked had ties to Elegguá, Babalú, or Palo heritage and thus represented multiple forms of Afrodescendant spiritual power simultaneously.¹⁰ She describes Afro-Cuban religions as "sonically intersectional" (79) in the sense that they evoke beings through songs that align with multiple religions. I would argue that this intersectionality extends even further in the context of a *violín* since it sonically references both the sacred and the secular realms.

Since *violines* represent especially hybridized and ambivalent spaces that reference both Spiritism and Santería in nearly equal measure, spirits of the dead occasionally appear in *violines* dedicated to the *orishas*. Sotto (2012, 14–16) describes one such case in which, during a *violín* for Ochún, the spirit of Juan Moreno – a former slave and one of the individuals believed to have first found the image of the Caridad del Cobre (see the following section) – mounted an older woman. Moreno's spirit eventually started reciting prayers to Olofi (a manifestation of the Supreme Being in Regla de

---

⁸ Melena Francis Valdés, personal email communication 2 August 2022.
⁹ González Siones interview, May 2018.
¹⁰ David Brown, a renowned expert on Regla de Ocha, sent this additional comment on the links between *orishas* and spirit guides in a personal email (April 8, 2023):

> My first informants were [Ocha] priests with tons of "*muertos*." One was a María Antonia, who had Yemayá crowned in life and now advised Adolfo about everything. His "Francisco" was Congo/Palo and was the *muerto* intermediary between Adolfo and his Kongo *prenda*. Ramón and Adolfo had different kinds of *misas*, but the most significant ones were "*misas paleras*" which addressed the whole spirit matter hierarchy from top to bottom, starting with the 'spirits of light' (e.g., *Hermana de la Caridad*), moving through the orishas – but really ... spirits with ties in life to the *orishas* – and then to the material congos ... [When] Francisco possessed Adolfo, he gave verbal advice and cleaning, and wielded the tibia bone that his *prenda* carries. They topped [these events] off with a salsa party.

Ocha) in Lucumí, again underscoring the complex interplay between religious spheres in practitioners' lives.

DEVOTION TO LA CARIDAD AND OCHÚN IN VIOLINES

The refined sound of much *violín* repertoire appeals strongly to the tastes of Santería's Ochún and her Catholic counterpart, La Caridad del Cobre (Virgin of Charity), and the linking of most *violines* to this figure has undoubtedly contributed to their popularity. La Caridad, Cuba's patron saint, evokes both a sense of religious devotion and nationalist fervor. Her image appears constantly in iconography, visual art, film, and literature, and she is the inspiration for both concert repertoire and popular song. Initially understood as a local mixed-race incarnation of the Virgin Mary, she is now viewed as emblematic of the Cuban experience: "Neither Catholic saint nor African *orisha*. She is now Cuba's saint ... the Virgin of Charity officially and clearly Ochún among my friends" (Espinosa Mendoza 2012, 23).[11]

The origins of La Caridad and related saints can be traced back to cults of devotion to the Virgin Mary in the Byzantine Empire beginning in the seventh century, and later in Europe. Fernando Ortiz remains an authority on this subject; his posthumously published book on La Caridad includes extended discussion of representations of the Virgin in Spain (e.g., Nuestra Virgen de la Caridad in Sanlúcar de Barrameda and in Illescas) and their relation to those in Cuba (Ortiz 2012). Iconographic depictions of Cuba's Caridad are very similar to their Spanish antecedents, differing only by virtue of a somewhat darker skin tone in many representations and the fact that the Cuban saint holds a child in her arms. According to early written accounts, two Indigenous boys (Juan and Rodrigo Hoyos) and a ten-year-old Black slave named Juan Moreno (mentioned earlier) first encountered an image of La Caridad floating in the water in the Bay of Nipe, near the town of Mayarí. Following their departure from shore they found themselves caught in a fierce storm and began praying to save themselves. The storm lifted suddenly, and in its wake they came across an image of the Virgin floating in the water. The three first took the relic to Barajagua and later to El Cobre valley in the early 1600s, where a shrine was built in its honor.

---

[11] "Ni santa católica, ni oricha africana. Santa cubana y punto ... Caridad del Cobre oficialmente y Ochún a secas para mis amigos."

Within a century, local residents (including Black and Indigenous groups) began worshipping images of La Caridad, with some attributing miracles to them. Indigenous communities understood La Caridad as a representation of the deity Atabey (also Atabex); Benítez-Rojo (1996) describes her as a goddess of fertility, rivers, and lakes (similar in that sense to Ochún), and as the supreme deity of the Taino pantheon recognized throughout the greater Antilles. The African slave community expanded throughout eastern Cuba in the late eighteenth century, and its members increasingly read La Caridad through a Black lens, with *cabildos* established in her name in Santiago and other nearby towns (Cueto 2014, 34). The overthrow of the Oyó empire in the 1830s resulted in large numbers of captives arriving in Cuba from present-day Nigeria and Dahomey. They understood La Caridad to be Ochún, a goddess of love and fertility who lives in rivers: playful and flirtatious, quick to dance and laugh, a companion of Changó and Yemayá, and an intimate friend of Elegguá (Bolívar 1990, 116). Thus, Europeans, Blacks, and Native groups all viewed La Caridad from unique perspectives.

"Cachita" (as La Caridad is known affectionately in Cuba) did not assume prominence as a national icon until the late nineteenth century. Prior to that time, devotion to her remained the purview of poorer communities on the eastern side of the island. Her renown spread rapidly during the Wars of Independence, however. *Mambises* (insurgents against Spain) invoked her name prior to engagements during the Ten Years War (1868–78) and carried images of her into battle. General Antonio Maceo is said to have worn a medallion bearing her likeness; president of Cuba in Arms Carlos Manuel de Céspedes prayed to her publicly after victorious battles (Ortiz 2012, 251–2); and prominent Black generals of the wars (Agustín, Juan Pablo, and José Candelario Cebrecos) grew up in the valley of El Cobre itself near La Caridad's shrine. Affinity for the saint grew as a means of supporting devotion that did not follow established Spanish paradigms and that spoke to the diverse backgrounds and experiences of the masses:

Juxtaposed to the official body of worship sanctioned and promoted by the Catholic Church, an institution characterized by its class-based, racist, and pro-Spanish positions, the veneration of a *criolla* virgin of color by a group of devotees of like color was rooted among the popular sectors of society ... [It was] part and parcel of the idea of an authentic Cuba found in the country's heartland, a Cuba linked to the image of Martí and the flag, to the full panoply of symbolic representations constituting *cubanía*. Little by little, the Cuban festival of Our Lady of Charity, celebrated on 8 September, gained ground against other Marian celebrations. (Iglesias Utset 2011, 41)

By the early twentieth century, La Caridad achieved widespread recognition even in western regions of the island and in whiter, more affluent areas, supported by the rapidly growing number of private Catholic schools established at that time and a clergy consisting increasingly of Cuban rather than Spanish priests (Cueto 2014, 66–9). In 1916 Pope Benedict XV officially declared her Patron Saint of Cuba, at the request of war veterans.

Clearly, divergent perspectives on (and representations of) race and religion exist in tension within the figure of La Caridad. Most often she is depicted as a *mulata*, a mixed-race woman with much lighter skin than the dark Virgin of Regla aligned with Yemayá. Other artists depict La Caridad as *cobrizo* or copper-colored and thus more associated with Indigenous heritage, or even as white (Ortiz 2012, 262–3). Such varied renderings of *mulatez* symbolically negotiate Cuban national identity in particular ways to distinct audiences. Competing constructs of La Caridad can be understood as existing in uneasy tension with one another, an example of Benítez-Rojo's (1996, 21) syncretic signifier "made of differences." Many today describe La Caridad simultaneously as a Catholic saint, as Ochún, and possibly representative of Spiritist beliefs as well. Notions of *caridad* or charity are a central element of Spiritism, defined as offering help to those in need through acts of purification and blessing, and in the way spirit guides offer advice about how to resolve the problems of the living (Espírito Santo 2015, 35). More broadly, the *comisión María* and related forces also tie spirit guides to Cuba's patron saint:

> Catholicism, Santería, and Spiritism are one in the cult of the Caridad. It is not even necessary to have faith to feel the need to celebrate her. Perhaps patriotic sentiment tells a Cuban deep inside that [she] is the Patron of Cuba. Perhaps a Spiritist initiates a session by focusing on La Caridad, inspired in the meaning of the word. Surely Catholics align their beliefs in the discovery of Nipe Bay ... It is logical that the Lucumí practitioner would repeat legends and songs to Ochún, venerating the goddess of the river and notable companion of Changó. None of that matters, it's all the same thing. The figure is ours: Cuban, mestizo, African, Spanish, white, with or without faith, but it all embodies *cubanía*. (Cuéllar Vizcaino 1950, 97)[12]

---

[12] Catolicismo, espiritismo y santería son uno en el culto de la Caridad. Ya no es preciso tener fe para sentirse ligado a su celebración. Acaso un sentimiento patriótico dice el cubano muy pecho adentro que la Caridad del Cobre es la Patrona de Cuba. Acaso un espiritista desarrolla en una sesión el tema de la Caridad inspirándose en la significación de la propia palabra. De seguro que el católico afinca su creencia en el hallazgo de Nipe ... Es lógico que el creyente lucumí repita las leyendas y los cantos de Ochún venerando a la

Within Regla de Ocha, Ochún's many *caminos* or incarnations further enrich and diversify her meanings to practitioners. She is simultaneously understood to be Ochún Yeyé Moró, sensuous, vain, and full of life, fond of music and dance; Ochún Ololodí, a warrior, diviner, and dutiful wife of Orunmila; Ochún Awé, intimately tied to death and sadness; and Ochún Kolé-Kolé (also known as Ochún Kolé or Ibú Kolé), eldest of all witches and divine messenger of Olofi, living in poverty and eating only what Mayimbe the vulture brings to her (Castellanos 1996, 45, 73);[13] she also appears in additional forms (see Benítez-Rojo 1996, 15; Mason 1992, 294–7). All *orishas* embody the complexities of human life; as such, they represent the gamut of personalities and manifestations linked to broader concepts, metaphors, forces of nature, and principles, rather than a single entity (c.f. Matory 2018, 236ff.).

While the Caridad construct often serves to unify, she is also a Catholic saint aligned with dominant institutions. In that light she can be viewed as a colonialist imposition quite distinct from the African-inspired Ochún that much of the local population understands her to be. Lázara Menéndez Vázquez (2012, 10–11) describes La Caridad and Ochún as representing *opposing* models of viewing and structuring reality: one is a local variant of the Virgin Mary, a symbol of Western beliefs and religious conquest; the other is an African queen from the city of Oshobgo, a central figure in the religion of the oppressed who symbolizes cultural resistance. Menéndez Vázquez notes that many leaders of the Cuban Catholic Church continue to view any association between La Caridad and Ochún as a satanic perversion, and not something to be celebrated. Images of La Caridad and Ochún do not always share the same religious spaces, nor are they revered in the same way, and two deities' relationship with their devotees may differ significantly. Ritual *soperas* (ceramic tureens representing the physical presence of an *orisha*) never appear on Catholic altars, for instance, even if *santeros* are more inclined to include images of La Caridad in their sacred devotional practices. Conflicting readings of Cuba's patron saint thus speak to both division and to shared *cubanía*. The cultural meanings associated with

---

doncella del río que fue la notable compañera de Changó. Nada de esto importa. Todo viene a ser la misma cosa. Es algo nuestro, cubano, mestizo, africano, español, blanco, con fe o sin fe, pero que constituye la cubanía.

[13] See also https://ashepamicuba.com/en/ibu-kole/. David Font-Navarrete (personal email, August 8, 2023) notes that *mayimbe* is the Kongo term for vulture, and that vultures may be viewed as an incarnation or avatar or Ochún.

La Caridad and Ochún allow them to represent many things to individuals in the context of devotion and music making.

VIOLINES DE SANTO

Bárbara Balbuena Gutiérrez (2003, 7) recognizes five different kinds of ritual celebration associated with Regla de Ocha: the *tambor* or *wemilere*, the most sacred form required for formal events such as initiation and that foregrounds performance on consecrated *batá* drums; the *bembé* and *güiro*, often understood as "lighter" and less formal events involving unconsecrated percussion of various sorts; the *cajón de santo*, discussed in Chapter 2; and the *violín*.[14] Formal *tambores* (and especially those performed as part of initiation ceremonies) may involve elaborate preparations over multiple days, including the *misas espirituales* discussed earlier, sung prayers to Olorun (Lord of the Heavens) and Olofi (the Supreme Being), the offering *coco* to the *santos*,[15] animal sacrifices, distinct private and public praise ceremonies,[16] and a ritual meal. Most *violines* condense this sequence of events considerably. Those organizing a *violín* may prepare a *misa* or offer *coco* to their *orisha* prior to the event, and they must offer a *servicio al muerto*.[17] They may or may not feed their *orisha* with a ritual offering ahead of the music making.[18] Immediately preceding musical performance, sung or chanted prayers are typically offered to Olofi and Olodumare requesting their blessings, and to one's *egun* and spiritual advisors, in private.[19] Ritual rum may be poured on the floor as

---

[14] A useful introduction to these distinct styles on video was released by David Font-Navarrete and Kenneth Schweitzer, entitled *Lucumí Music: Singing, Dancing, and Drumming Black Divinity*: www.YouTube.com/watch?v=VdmM1aF10jA (accessed July 20, 2023). *Batá* drumming can be heard starting at 3:55; *güiro* music at 9:10; *bembé* music at 12:10; Iyesá music (yet another style now linked to Lucumí drumming practices) at 13:27; and a *cajón* ensemble performing *orisha* music (in a *cajón de santo*) at 17:11.

[15] This involves literally offering the *orishas* pieces of coconut in combination with ritual prayers and as a form of divination; see Cabrera (2023, 379ff.).

[16] These are known respectively as the *Oru del Igbodú* (literally, a ritual praise sequence in a sacred room) or *oru seco* involving only drums, usually in a private area with an altar; and the public *Oru de Eyá Aranla* ("praise sequence on the patio" or in a more public space that involves drumming, song, and dance; see Ortiz 1981, 296ff.; Balbuena Gutiérrez 2003, 45ff.).

[17] Johnny Frías (personal email, July 24, 2023) mentions that a *servicio al muerto* precedes a *tambor* as well, and that it may simply consist of placing out offerings of food for one's *egun*.

[18] Duquesne Mora interview, April 2022.

[19] Del Pilar interview, November 2020.

an offering to the spirit world, and perfumed water or *cascarilla* may be placed near the door so that guests can ritually cleanse themselves as they arrive, as would be the case in a *misa*.

The altars or *tronos* (thrones) associated with *violines de santo* resemble those dedicated to spirit guides, with subtle differences. Figure 4.1, for instance, depicts the altar of a *violín* dedicated Ochún organized by a *santera* named Yenny. It is typical in that it features representations (from left to right) of the *orishas* Obatalá, Ochún, and Yemayá on top, with cloths in each of their colors covering ritual *soperas* or tureens. Obatalá's *sopera* and corresponding white cloth or *manto* are visible on the left. A statuette of the Caridad sits at the base of the gold-colored cloth representing Ochún (alongside a can of Bucanero beer, as Ochún enjoys beer and wine), while a representation of the Virgin of Regla sits in front of Yemayá's blue cloth. On the floor in front of the altar (an area known as *la plaza*), ritual offerings to the *orishas* can be seen. In this case, yellow sunflowers associated with Ochún figure prominently, as well as bottles of rum, fancy yellow bows, brass bells, yellow candles, and light-colored fruits such as pineapple, coconut, and oranges, all of which Ochún enjoys. At the base of the altar one sees ritual necklaces (*elekes*) displayed, in Changó colors of red and white. To the left of the *trono* stands a doll between two ornamental conga drums, under a nightstand with glasses of water on it; this represents a *gitana*, Yenny's primary spirit guide linked to Ochún.[20] The nightstand with glasses of water (a *bóveda*) represent her *cuadro espiritual* (spirit guides).

Other items commonly found on *tronos de santo* include homemade sweets or cakes, bracelets (*manillas*, especially gold-colored if intended to honor Ochún), fans (*abebé*), ritual whisks or plumes (*iruke*), such as used by Oyá when she dances, and Elegguá's crooked staff (*ogó*). The specific composition of the altar of course depends on the *orishas* being honored.[21] In events for Ochún, elegance is a must: devotees offer her perfume, flowers, and honey, and instrumental music is foregrounded at

---

[20] Personal WhatsApp communication, May 2024.
[21] Balbuena Gutiérrez (2003, 43) provides a list of additional items typically associated with *orishas* that may appear on altars: a small silver or white bell to call to Obatalá, a seed pod from the flamboyant tree to call to Oyá, a maraca painted white and blue to sound for Yemayá, etc. She views the *trono* tradition as influenced by the Altares de cruz used in folkloric Catholic celebrations derived from southern Spain (see also Moore 2006, 203–4). David Brown's book *Santería Enthroned* (2019) remains the most comprehensive source of information on ritual altars in Regla de Ocha devotion.

FIGURE 4.1 Yenny's altar, prepared for her *violín* dedicated to Ochún, Nuevo Vedado, Cuba. April 24, 2022. Photo by Melena Francis Valdés.

times on the violin to strike the correct tone.[22] *Santeros* salute the altar in a formal manner immediately upon entering the home.[23] Guests may also

---

[22] Espinoza Casanova interview, March 2022.
[23] Villas Junco interview, March 2021. Melena Francis Valdés (personal email, April 10, 2023) provides additional insights into appropriate ways to salute the altar:

> An *aleyo* salutes the altar kneeling, because he/she has not made Ocha. A *santero/a* salutes the altar in a specific manner depending on [who their guardian angel is]. If your guardian angel is female (Ochún, Yemayá, Oyá), then you salute laying down to one side first,

leave a little money in a *jícara* (a bowl made of dried gourd) in front of the altar to help the organizers with the expense of the event.

Early celebrants such as Aurelia Crespo dedicated all *violines* to Ochún, but more recently *santeros* organize them in honor of other *orishas*. Most of the events García Lacerra observed as part of her master's thesis research were dedicated to Ochún, for instance, but about 10 percent were performed in honor of Yemayá. Another 20 percent paid homage to figures such as "La Milagrosa," La Virgen de Regla, La Caridad del Cobre, Elegguá, Oyá, and Ogún (García Lacerra 2015, 27, 43). Any *orisha* may request a *violín* of devotees through divination, but some enjoy them more than others.[24] Ochún requests *violines* most frequently, given her love of pretty melodies, romance (hence the prominence of boleros and romantic songs typically performed), dancing, and the sound of the violin itself. Lázaro González Siones describes the violin as a sublime instrument and difficult to play. When used in religious contexts, he says "it is like giving a bunch of flowers to a lady."[25] The prominence of the violin in mariachi ensembles makes their repertoire attractive to Ochún as well. Other *orishas* said to be especially appreciative of *toques de violín* include Obatalá, known for his calmness and

> placing your hand on your hip and then turn to the other side with had on hip. If your guardian angel is male (Changó, Obatalá), then you lay your whole body down straight.
>
> As a further indication of how many houses of worship incorporate ritual salutes and offerings into *violín* worship, consider this description by Ivor Miller of *violín* he attended in Havana in March of 1994:
>
> Before I could enter the house (as *Iyawó*), water in a gourd was brought and libation poured [while intoning the chant] "omi tutu, ana tutu, ile tutu" [meaning cool or peaceful water, cool road, cool home]. Then I entered. A mat was laid in front of Ochún's throne, I was given the silver bell of Obatalá, and prostrated myself to greet Ochún. *Santeras* of the house blessed my prayer and I saluted them. Then a *santero* came to ask Ochún if the ceremony could be opened. While another *santero* kneeled (the man whose Ochún [ceremony] it was) before Ochún, the *santero* prayed and picked bits off of his *cocos*. While the opening [spoken] chant for Ochún was said, the kneeling man rang Ochún's bell. All *santeros* present, including me, put our right hand to the floor to support the prayer. Ochún was satisfied, and the violinists began playing "Ave Maria" ... Before the music started, two candles were placed before Ochún and lit. Thus she has been prayed to, awakened by the bell, given light through the candles, and now is serenaded with sweet music.
>
> Ivor L. Miller Papers, Amherst College Archives and Special Collections, Amherst College Library.

[24] Johnny Frías (personal email, July 24, 2023) makes the important point that *babalawos* or other intermediaries actively pose such questions to the *orishas*, and therefore the extent to which *violines* are requested depends on whether intermediaries approve of such celebrations and ask *orishas* about them.

[25] Lázaro González Siones interview, May 2018.

tenderness;[26] and Yemayá, as mentioned, *orisha* of motherhood and queen of the sea. To *santeros*, the ocean is a site where the dead reside and do work on behalf of the living (Otero 2020, 16); perhaps for that reason *violines* that fuse Ocha and Spiritist practices appeal to her, and to Oyá as guardian of the cemetery. *Santeros* dedicate fewer *violines* to warrior *orishas* (Ogún, Ochosi, Osun), and some in the religious community consider it inappropriate to do so.[27] The popularity of *violines* dedicated to La Caridad del Cobre has grown among *santeros* and non-*santeros*. In fact, more *aleyos* now organize *violines* than initiates themselves, and since they have not yet made their saint they typically dedicate them to La Caridad rather than Ochún.[28]

Ritual musicians organize *orisha* songs into *orus*: formal groupings of pieces that salute major deities in a prescribed order.[29] In drumming events, these sequences are carefully organized, with as many as twenty-four *orishas* recognized every time (Ortiz 1965, 387–408). *Violín* performers adopt the same general model, but with greater flexibility and recognizing only half a dozen of the most prominent deities. Melodies with Lucumí texts represent only about a third of the total repertoire played, with the remainder sung in Spanish or performed instrumentally (García Lacerra 2015, 8, 35). Musicians try to follow a standard order of praise songs, but patrons may have their own ideas about what should be played and they sometimes request significant changes or additions to the repertoire.[30]

Violines de santo begin with a series of slower pieces in front of the altar, essentially identical to those in a *violín espiritual*. The first piece performed is most often an instrumental version of "Ave María" on the violin, significant since La Caridad represents an incarnation of the Virgin Mary. This may be followed by a musicalized version of the "Our Father" prayer (Figure 3.15) or by *plegarias* associated with the Spiritist tradition such as "O venid protectores" (Figure 3.4) or "Misericordia." *Plegarias* in this context offer praises to supreme beings (*espíritus superiores*) of all religions, the Catholic Trinity, and their counterparts such as Regla de Ocha's Olofi and Palo's Nsambi who are perceived as linked.[31] Some consider these slower initial pieces the equivalent of the *oru seco* in *batá* drumming in that they ritually purify and consecrate

---

[26] Gordillo Miraval interview, January 2021.
[27] Gordillo Miraval interview, January 2021.
[28] Anonymous interview, March 2021.
[29] The origins of the term *oru* are unclear; Ortiz (1965, 281) suggests it may derive from *oro*, meaning word or conversation; *orín*, meaning chant; or *orun*, referencing "the invisible world" to which religious songs are directed.
[30] Anonymous interview, December 2020.
[31] Espinosa Casanova interview, March 2022.

the performance space.³² Some also view such *plegarias* as a form of paying homage to the *egun* and spirits prior to praise of *orishas* (García Lacerra 2015, 55).

Following this repertoire, musicians typically salute Elegguá and occasionally warrior *orisha* collectively with a musical song or sequence. Their *oru* often consists of one or more songs performed either instrumentally on the violin or with the full ensemble. They might include a ritual Lucumí *rezo* (nonmetrical hymn), such as "Bara suwayo,"³³ accompanied by the sound of percussive rolls on the bongo, the shaking of a maraca, or violin arpeggios. Other devotional songs to Elegguá are more often performed in upbeat versions, usually in 4/4 time with accompanying violin background figures and retaining the call–response format. Examples include "Aso kere-kere me yé," "Sosa sokere," and "Ochiminí" (Figure 4.2).³⁴

Alternately, musicians might choose to dedicate a song to Elegguá in Spanish, such as "Como soy tan chiquitico" (Because I'm So Small; Figure 4.3) in this context since Elegguá is understood to be small and childlike in certain respects³⁵ and because he is aligned with the Holy Child of Atocha, an incarnation of the child Jesus. The original melody to "Como soy tan chiquitico" appears to derive from Spiritist traditions³⁶ that recognize the Child of Atocha as one of many forces associated with Catholic *comisiones*. Performers in *violines* often extend it with one or more improvisatory vamp sections that foreground a repeated chorus such as the example provided below. This practice serves to reinforce the associations between the song and the *orisha* Elegguá (since his name appears in the chorus); it also makes the musical structure conform more closely to commercial dance repertoire and allows for improvisational spontaneity. Aside from the example transcribed below, other common choruses used in conjunction with the same *plegaria* include lyrics from the Mexican *son jarocho* "La bamba," with an altered melody: "*Para subir al cielo se necesita una escalera larga, y otra chiquita*" (To climb to heaven one needs a long ladder and

---

[32] Anonymous interview.
[33] For a musical transcription of the *rezo*, see Altmann (1998, 11). Mason (1992, 58) provides a possible translation. Typically this piece would be accompanied on the *batá* drums by the *Lalubanché* rhythm in 12/8, but in the context of a *violín* the musical accompaniment is rhythmically simpler.
[34] Transcriptions of these melodies can also be found in Altmann (1998, 30, 32), and possible translations in Mason (1992, 64).
[35] David Font-Navarrete notes (personal email, August 7, 2019) that Elegguá in Yoruba is called "Baba Kekere," or "Small Father/Elder."
[36] See for instance the third song listed on this Spiritist website: https://marina3246.webnode.es/misa-espiritual/musica-misa-espiritual/ (accessed June 27, 2023).

FIGURE 4.2 "Ochiminí," a traditional praise song to Elegguá as interpreted by the Orquesta Estrellas Cubanas. This melody would traditionally be accompanied by the *chachalokafun* rhythm on the *batás* (see Moore and Sayre 2006, 155). Here the *güiro*, bass, and violins perform in the style of a *charanga* band, vamping on the dominant chord, D7.

another short one). Listeners link the meaning of this refrain to Elegguá since it discusses heaven, and because the phrase "*otra chiquita*" brings to mind the word "*chiquitico*" in the song title.

Porque soy tan chiquitico/Because I'm So Small

Porque soy tan chiquito	Because I'm so small
Todos me dan con los pies	Everyone kicks me with their feet
Deja que yo sea grande	Wait till I get bigger
Y me sepa defender	And know how to defend myself

Chorus/Vamp

Como soy tan chiquitico	Since I'm so small
Yo voy a ver	I'm going to go see
A mi padre, Santo Elegguá	My father, the *orisha* Elegguá
Para vencer	Who will lead me to victory

4 Violines a Ochún *and* Orisha *Praise* 113

FIGURE 4.3 "Porque soy tan chiquitico," melody and antiphonal refrain.

Clearly, musicians have multiple options as they perform sequences to *orishas* in the context of a *violín*, which include performing instrumental pieces, vocal popular repertoire, or Lucumí praise songs in standard or modified form at any given moment. They thus control many aspects of the tempo and dynamics of an event to elicit the most favorable response from their audience. In decades past, *violines santorales* tended to be relatively calm and contemplative, and some clients today still ask that musicians foreground Spiritist *plegarias*, instrumental boleros, *danzones*, and related songs that lend themselves to relatively passive or introspective engagement. But increasingly, organizers and audiences enjoy a livelier ambience. The option of playing such music may or may not be discussed with organizers prior to a *violín*, so it is often incumbent on musicians to "read the room" and determine what to play on that basis. Some first perform various songs for Elegguá and/or warrior *orishas* that emphasize percussive, danceable grooves, then switch to a romantic piece such as "Madrecita" by Mexican singer José José (since Cubans associate it with La Caridad as the "mother" of the Cuban nation). Performing very different repertoire in alternation adds variety to the set and helps musicians determine whether the crowd prefers to listen reverentially or to dance and sing, and whether they are more comfortable with Lucumí or Spanish-language lyrics.

Following praise of Eleggúa, *violines santorales* have little fixed structure, though performers usually salute the *orisha* to whom the event is dedicated last and in a more extended fashion. Most commonly, major *orishas* such as Obatalá, Changó, Babalú, Yemayá, and Oyá receive some recognition (though not in any fixed order). Between *orus*, musicians play lyrical boleros or other instrumental music featuring the violin since such music is especially appealing to Ochún, as noted.[37] While this results in abrupt changes between segments and between liturgical and popular music, all aspects of performance are understood as devotion. The overall trend is to save the fastest, longest, and most danceable segments for the final half hour; Chapter 5 includes a close examination of these sequences. String players frequently set down their violin and switch to hand percussion or vocals during "hotter" moments. Climactic repertoire often foregrounds a combination of traditional Lucumí melodies and songs in Spanish.[38] Pieces dedicated to Eleggúa and/or a final performance of "Ave María" frequently end the performance.

Depending on the preferences of the organizer and the audience, songs associated with Kongo religions may be included in *violines santorales*, including those dedicated to Ochún. As discussed in Chapter 3, they are more common in *violines espirituales*, yet they can be appropriate in the context of *orisha* worship. Devotees view Ochún as having resonance across religious systems; since many *santeros* recognize Palo deities as an influence in their lives, failing to sing to them as well could be viewed as a slight, as musician Emir Molina del Valle observes (see following quote). Additionally, *santeros* may have spirit guides including *congos* that they wish to honor as

---

[37] Common instrumental pieces in a *violín* dedicated to Ochún include the Mexican *canción* "Estrellita" by Manuel Ponce, the waltz "Dolores" by Waldteufel (op. 170, 1880), and boleros such as "Aquellos ojos verdes" by Nilo Menéndez and "Madrigal" by Puerto Rican Felipe "Don Felo" Rosario Goyco. Younger performers try to update their romantic pieces by including songs by contemporary artists like Prince Royce (e.g., "Darte un beso"), Marco Antonio Solís, and Gilberto Santa Rosa.

[38] Rafael Espinosa Casanova interview, March 2022.

part of the *violín* who were *paleros* in life or who demonstrate a preference for such repertoire:

[Let's say] you are a child of Ochún, and perhaps you also have a religious foundation in Madre Chola who is the entity representative of Ochún in Palo Monte. What if [Madre Chola] says to you: "What about me? Why haven't they played anything in my honor in this *violín*?" That could result in jealousy among the *santos* ... Well, why don't we sing to her?: *Chola nguengue, nguengue Chola* [she will prefer that traditional] music in 2/4 time.[39]

Songs to Babalú Ayé/San Lázaro feature prominently in many *violines de santo*; this reflects the importance of the *orisha* throughout the country, the many religious festivities held in his honor, and the countless pilgrims that visit his shrine outside of Havana each year (Hagedorn 2002). More broadly, the inclusion of songs to Babalú underscores the fact that motivations for organizing a *violín* often derive from a desire for healing of some sort or resolution of a physical ailment. Perhaps for this reason, Babalú is the *orisha* who most commonly mounts participants in the context of a *violín*.[40] Ochoa (2020, 8–9) offers a useful description of how St. Lazarus is discussed in the New Testament and the ways the construct of the saint in Cuba has been fused with that of the *orisha* of pestilence from present-day Benin, Togo, and Nigeria.

As in the case of Elegguá, songs dedicated to Babalú may be sung in either Spanish or Lucumí, and derive from multiple sources. Traditional devotional chants performed for him include "Baba-e baba soroso"[41] and "Tanakana sokuto,"[42] and may be accompanied either with percussion patterns evocative of a triple-meter *bembé* (often played on bongo and bell) or in harmonized dance form. At least as often, musicians perform pieces in Spanish, such as the pop song "Babalú" by Margarita Lecuona from the 1930s, even though its depictions of *orisha* worship from the perspective of the present could be viewed as objectifying or even racist (Lecuona was a white middle-class

---

[39] Interview, April 2022.

> Ud. Es hija de Ochún. ¿Y si Ud. tuviese un fundamento de palo de Madre Chola que es la entidad que representa a Ochún en el Palo Monte? Y ese fundamento le dice: '¿Y yo? ¿Por qué no me han tocado a mí dentro del violín?' ... Ahí viene un celo santoral ... Bueno, ¿por qué no vamos a tocarle (canta): *Chola nguengue, nguengue Chola*, y eso está en una ritmática de 2 por 4.

> See also Balbuena Gutiérrez 2003, 122–3 for brief discussion of Palo songs incorporated into *violines*.

[40] Betancourt Bejerano interview, March 2021.
[41] See Altmann (1998, 77).
[42] See Altmann (1998, 84).

FIGURE 4.4 Chorus to Margarita Lecuona's "Babalú." In most *violines*, the vocals and violin *guajeo* depicted here are accompanied by bongo and guitar or keyboard.

composer and a noninitiate). Sometimes performers incorporate only the chorus of that song, foregrounding the name "Babalú Ayé" in alternation with improvisatory vocals or instrumental lines (Figure 4.4). They often play the Spiritist *plegaria* for San Lázaro in the same sequence as well (Figure 3.7). The refrain of the song "Me voy pa'l pueblo" (I'm Heading to Town) by Merceditas Valdés may appear in altered form as a similar vehicle for improvisation, with the original lyrics (*Me voy pa'l pueblo, hoy es mi día, voy a alegrar todo el alma mía*)[43] changed to "*Voy al rincón todos los días, a Babalú yo le doy la vida.*"[44] Singers may improvise multiple choruses in Spanish dedicated to Babalú or other *orishas*, one after another, as a means of demonstrating lyrical dexterity and keeping ritual content fresh and exciting. In this sense, performance dynamics approximate the improvised vocals and melodic shifts associated with lead singing in more traditional drumming events.

Song sequences to Obatalá usually appear in *violines de santo*, in part perhaps because this *orisha* is one of the most powerful, a knowledgeable and wise presence, creator of mankind with the power to resolve "all problems that face human beings" or that arise between *orishas* and humans (Pedroso 2013, 71). Given that their sacred color is white, Obatalá is often likened to a white dove or, by extension, the Holy Spirit, and is syncretized with the Virgin of Mercies. *Orus* to Obatalá in the context of a *violín* most often begin with slow, nonmetrical *plegarias* such as the piece transcribed in Figure 4.5. The term *plegaria* in the context of *orisha* worship refers to slower, contemplative sung prayers in Spanish, similar to those offered to spirit guides. The "Plegaria

---

[43] "I'm headed to town, today is my day, I'm going to make my soul happy."
[44] "I'm going to El Rincón [San Lázaro's shrine] every day, I offer Babalú my life."

a Obatalá" exists in many variants but typically transitions to a moderate bolero or *tango congo*[45] accompaniment in the second verse, and eventually to a *son*-like improvisatory vamp with a refrain such as "*Obatalá, tú eres la luz, el fundamento del Lucumí*" (Obatalá, you are the light, the foundation of the Lucumí religion).

Plegaria a Obatalá, Lyric Excerpt [Out of time]

Obatalá, tú creaste la naturaleza	Obatalá, you created the natural world
Tú eres lo más grande, Olofi	You are the greatest, Olofi
Obatalá, tú que todo lo puedes	Obatalá, you can do anything
Llévate lo malo	Take away all evil
Devuélvele al mundo la paz	Return peace to the world

[Bolero/tango congo rhythm]

Sin tí no hay santo, tú eres la luz	Without you there are no saints, you are the light
El fundamento del Lucumí	The foundation of Lucumí practice
Obatalá tú que todo lo puedes	Obatalá, you who can do anything
Llévate lo malo	Take away all evil
Devuélvele al mundo la paz	Return peace to the world

Following one or more *plegarias* in Spanish, many groups perform more traditional devotional songs to Obatalá such as "Obatalá kunawa," "Akete oba," "Yale yale," or "A la koko e."[46] In some cases these melodies are played in traditional form, but more typically their rhythms are "straightened" so that the original melody (which might have been heard over triple-time rhythmic accompaniment) is altered so that it fits over duple-meter accompaniment. Sometimes musicians change the melodies of the chants as well so that they can be played against a particular harmonic vamp or *montuno*. In such cases, only the text remains unaltered to reference the original version. As an example,

---

[45] The *tango congo* rhythm first gained popularity in popular songs (typically by white composers) referencing Black heritage during the 1920s and 1930s as part of the *afrocubanismo* movement (Moore 1997, 73). Richard Huntley (personal email, June 3, 2023) notes that *tango congo* is similar to the *rezo* rhythm for Obatalá and may derive from that source. Grupo Ilu Aña has a recording entitled "Obatalá that features the *rezo* rhythm during the first thirty seconds: https://bit.ly/4b7VsRk.

[46] See Altmann (1998, 106–8) for transcriptions of several of these melodies. According to Nelson Aboy and Ramón Torres Zayas (personal email, June 30, 2023), "Obatalá kunawa" means "Obatalá approaches" and "A la koko e" (also "A la ewe ikoko eee") references the leaves of the malanga plant that are often used to present gifts to the *orisha*. Together they can be translated as "Obatalá approaches the malanga leaf."

FIGURE 4.5 "Plegaria a Obatalá," initial out-of-time melody and chorus.

Figures 4.6 and 4.7 contrast the traditional melody of "Obatalá kunawa" as it would be sung over the *ñongo* rhythm on *batás* and then as it is usually played by *violín* ensembles with an altered rhythm and melody. The chants still alternate with improvised lead vocals, as would be heard in a *tambor* (and/or with instrumental solos), but in the context

FIGURE 4.6 "Obatalá kunawa" as sung traditionally. A recorded version is available on the Abbilona CD release *Obatalá 1*, track 4, 7:33.

FIGURE 4.7 "Obatalá kunawa" sung in duple meter and with its melody altered so that it conforms to a i-iv-V-i minor harmonic vamp in *violín* performance.

of a *violín* lead singers have more freedom to improvise either using traditional Lucumí phrases or Spanish, whichever they feel comfortable with.

The incorporation of music dedicated to Oyá varies greatly in *violines*. In some events, repertoire dedicated to her is omitted entirely. In others, she is referenced obliquely with an instrumental version of "Somewhere Over the Rainbow" ("Detrás del arcoiris"), an allusion to the fact that in some incarnations she wears nine scarves of different colors tied around her waist. Other songs used to praise Oyá include Silvio Rodríguez's "Rabo de nube" (Tail of a Cloud), any piece referencing whirlwinds (one of Oyá's symbols), and songs dedicated to Santa Teresa or the Virgin of Candelaria with whom she is syncretized. In many performances, however, musicians play extended *orus* to Oyá using modified Lucumí songs arranged as dance music. The emphasis worshippers place on Oyá is understandable, given the dual emphasis on Spiritism and Ocha worship in *violines* and the fact that Oyá is an *orisha* who controls spirits of the dead and figures prominently in Ocha funerary rites (Valdés Garriz 1991, 33–4). Songs with Lucumí texts played for her in the context of a *violín* include "Mama loya e," "Oyá Oyá o cheche," and "Ko-ko-ko." All of these pieces are most often heard with duple-meter accompaniment toward the end of *tambores*, and thus they require little alteration in order to be played *son*-style.[47] Perhaps because of their extended use of traditional repertoire, sequences to Oyá often include brief playful transitions to 6/8 time before reverting to a dance beat. Figure 4.8 transcribes one such moment during the chant "Oyansa ma terema."[48]

Songs to Changó often appear in *toques de violín*, not only because the *orisha* is well known and beloved but also because he has a close relationship with Ochún in many religious tales. In some *violines* he is venerated first, together with other male *orisha* (Elegguá, Ogún, Ochosi, Obatalá, Babalú Ayé) and before female *orisha*, as would be the case in a *tambor*; in others, his songs may follow those to Oyá or Yemayá. Repertoire dedicated to Changó may consist of extended *plegarias* in Spanish, short choral refrains in Spanish that alternate with improvised vocals, commercial songs such as "Que viva Changó" (first popularized by Celina González and Reutilio Domínguez), or more traditional chants with Lucumí texts. *Plegarias* or longer songs tend to begin the *orus*, and shorter choral refrains or antiphonal Lucumí pieces end them, often in alternation with one another. The Orquesta Estrellas Cubanas recorded one example

---

[47] See Altmann (1998, 200) for a transcription of two of these praise melodies to Oyá. In *tambores*, they are typically accompanied by the duple-meter *Ichachalekefun* pattern. David Font-Navarrete (personal communication, March 28, 2021) notes that "Ko-ko-ko" imitates the clucking sound made by a chicken.

[48] See Mason (1992, 330), and Altmann (1998, 199) for an alternate transcription of the chant in duple meter. David Font-Navarrete (personal communication, March 28, 2021) translates the phrase "Oyansala terema" as "mother of nine," a reference both to Oyá's multicolored scarves and to her sacred number.

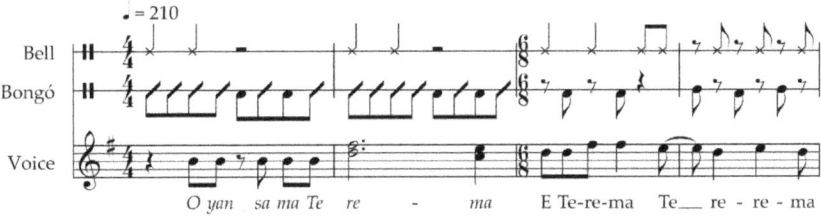

FIGURE 4.8 "Oyansa ma terema," played in duple meter, transitioning briefly to 6/8 time, then back to 4/4. Chorus vocals are in italics.

of a *plegaria* to Changó on their commercial release; the same track later incorporates the other song forms mentioned.[49]

---

[49] See https://open.spotify.com/track/5AJYXaoEFhug7VdAMoxwIo. The *plegaria*, described as anonymous folklore, is interpreted in a slow triple-meter waltz rhythm with this text: "Changó, Changó, Changó. Cuando suenan los tambores siempre le canto a Changó. Cuando suenan los tambores mi cuerpo empieza a temblar. Son los cueros que me llaman

FIGURE 4.9 "El hombre de la guayabera" chorus.

One common choral refrain sung in Spanish to Changó later in musical sequences is *"El hombre de la guayabera"* (The man in the guayabera shirt; Figure 4.9). It references the fact that devotees of Changó are known both as dominant males and as dapper dressers who in the early twentieth century often wore guayaberas or other formal attire.[50] This melody appears to have no antecedent in popular song and may have been spontaneously invented by *violín* performers. Another frequently heard chorus is *"Changó está en el río lavando a los jimaguas"* (Changó is in the river washing the twins), a reference to the Ibeyí (or Ibeyi) or *orisha* twins born to Changó and Ochún who represent duality, unity, and good fortune (Pedroso 2013, 137). The chorus' allusion to the river also ties Changó to Ochún, *orisha* of sweet water, and more broadly underscores the importance of purification rites in rivers as part of Ocha initiation.[51] Lucumí chants to Changó heard in the context of a *violín* include well-known pieces such as "Obalube, obalube oba e," "Kawo e," and "Onileo, onileo, onileo kawo, onileo" (Figure 4.10).[52] Violinists may switch to percussion here in order to add rhythmic intensity and drive. Often, sequences in praise of Changó incorporate ritual songs to the Ibeyí and to Aggayú (an *orisha* of volcanos and other powerful forces of nature who is Changó's father) as well.

Musicians include at least a few praise songs to Yemayá, mother goddess of the sea, in virtually every *violín*. Since most ceremonies celebrate Ochún primarily, devotion to Yemayá signifies in part that the two *orishas* are

y yo tengo que cantar. Y si tú eres creyente, creyente de Changó, yo te invito, ven conmigo a bailar con mi tambor."

[50] Joaquín Fernández Miranda interview, March 2021. David Font-Navarrete (personal communication, July 14, 2023) notes that the phrase *el hombre de la guayabera* has other implicit meanings as well: a man of status, but also one linked to politics and, in Cuba's case, the Communist Party.

[51] My thanks to Ramón Torres Zayas (personal email, July 13, 2023) for this insight.

[52] Altmann (1998, 158) includes a transcription of "Kawo e," and Mason (1992, 192, 201) a possible translation of that chant and "Obalube." David Font-Navarrete (personal email, July 14, 2023) translates *onile* as owner of (a/the) house or (the) world/earth. *Kawo* is a well recognized salute to Changó.

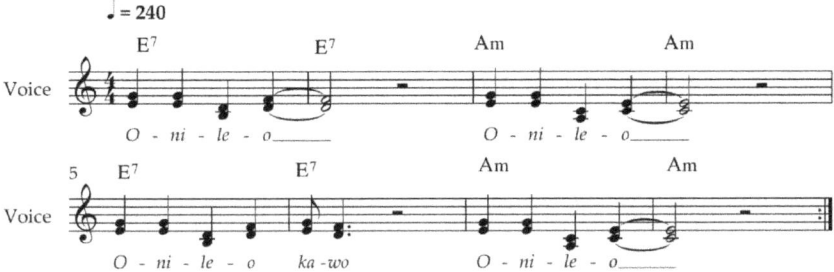

FIGURE 4.10 "Onileo" vamp, alternating between a lead singer and chorus.

viewed as kindred spirits, creatures of water with a special mother–daughter bond (Cabrera 1996), and that many devotees of Ochún describe themselves as *hijas de las dos aguas* (daughters of both salt and fresh water). Tributes to Yemayá may consist of entirely instrumental repertoire such the waltzes "Over the Waves" (Sobre las olas) by Juventino Rosas,[53] "Blue Danube" by Johann Strauss, and the *danzón* "La Virgen de Regla" by Richard Egües and Pablo O'Farrill.[54] All songs with Spanish lyrics that reference the ocean or sailing (e.g., "Marinero"; Figure 3.8), rowing, the Virgin of Regla herself ("A remar," Figure 5.8), flowing water ("Corre el agua,;" Figure 3.9), or related themes are frequently incorporated as well, as are *plegarias* devoted specifically to Yemayá. Songs such as "Corre el agua" or "A remar" (Figure 5.12) make clear the porous boundaries between Spiritist and Ocha repertoire in this sense. The exact origins of Yemayá's *plegarias* are unclear; some may have longstanding ties to Spiritist practice, others are undoubtedly the more recent invention of performers. They are usually in a minor key, and generally include out-of-time segments as well as others interpreted in moderate waltz rhythm or as dance music. Below is a transcription of a *plegaria* in Yemayá's honor performed for me by Roy Vázquez in 2018 (Figure 4.11), one of several heard in devotional events.

---

[53] Martiatu (2008, 58–9) notes that the Mexican composer Juventino Rosas is revered in Cuba, partly because he died there at age twenty-six while on tour and is buried in the coastal town of Batabanó. The author describes Rosas as an ongoing spirit presence in Cuba. In her short story, Rosas is invoked by the playing of "Sobre las olas" and his spirit appears by the altar of a *violín* event watching an elderly Black woman dance to his song.

[54] One version of the *danzón* can be heard here: www.YouTube.com/watch?v=tbfWuQ9L ArU (accessed July 12, 2023).

FIGURE 4.11 "Plegaria a Yemayá."

"Plegaria a Yemayá"

Yemayá, Yemayá, Yemayá	Yemayá, Yemayá, Yemayá
Reina mía, dueña mía, Yemayá	My queen, my owner, Yemayá
Eres la dueña del mar	You are the queen of the sea
Eres grande y poderosa	You are great and powerful
Yemayá, Divina diosa	Yemayá, Divine goddess
Para tí va mi cantar	My song is for you
Protégeme con tu manto	Protect me with your mantle
Y a los presentes también	And all those present
Y si te gusta mi canto	If you like my song
Apártanos del quebranto	Guard us from ruin
De las penas también	And from sorrows as well

Plegarias or extended instrumental pieces for Yemayá typically transition to shorter vocals in a call–response format as a way of gradually building energy and excitement. Musicians may create a tag or vamp at the end of slower pieces to generate audience engagement; such is the case with the Estrellas Cubanas version of the *danzón* "Virgen de Regla," which ends with a chorus such as *"Virgen de Regla, ampárame"* (Virgin of Regla, shelter me) in alternation with flute solos.[55] Musicians may also follow *plegarias* with slower traditional chants such as "Yemayá asesú" or "Soku taniwo."[56] These would traditionally be accompanied by *batá* drums playing the *yakotá* rhythm, but in the context of a *violín* they are arranged as waltzes with prominent violin runs in the accompaniment. Final climactic segments of the *oru* might include faster Lucumí chants, such as "Kai kai kai, Yemayá olodo" (translated by Mason as "Imagine that, Yemayá is owner of the rivers"), "Awoyó aé" (a reference to Yemayá's original incarnation; see Figure 4.12), and "Omio, omio Yemayá" (one of her ceremonial greetings).[57] In order to add further intensity, violinists may switch to bell or maracas at this point. If the band adopts a percussive format, they may use traditional rumba rhythms to accompany choruses in Spanish such as *"Rema, pero rema mi Yemayá"*

---

[55] Listen to their recording of the piece, starting at about 5:00 for the entry of the chorus: https://open.spotify.com/track/okXoVSpYaWfDRfFWheqpso.
[56] See Altmann (1998, 207–8), and for possible translations Hagedorn (2001, 53) and Mason (1992, 306–7). A transcription of *yakotá* can be found in Moore and Sayre (2006, 136).
[57] See Pedroso (2013, 117); Mason (1992, 306).

FIGURE 4.12 The traditional Lucumí chant to Yemayá "Awoyó aé" accompanied by rumba clave on bell, guitar chords, and a percussion solo on the bongo.

(Row, row my Yemayá) or Lucumí songs, or switch to *bembé*-style accompaniment in triple meter.

One of the most important ceremonial events in *violines* dedicated to Ochún is a formal toast or *brindis*, which usually takes place just before musicians play extended song sequences to her. For the toast, organizers may offer alcoholic cider, champagne, or any related beverage; it is not intended to get anyone drunk, only to refresh those in attendance (Martiatu 1998, 44) and to pay homage to Ochún symbolically. The principal organizer invariably takes a glass herself, sometimes together with her spiritual advisor (*padrino/madrina*), and sometimes with a larger serving than those of other guests. Invitees may also participate in the toast, especially initiates (usually women) whose primary *orisha* is Ochún (that is, daughters of Ochún). The *brindis* represents a relatively solemn moment in the ceremony and may include a spoken prayer offered by the principal organizer or their spiritual guide. Accompanying the prayer or just before it, the speaker may softly ring a brass- or gold-colored bell to invoke Ochún's presence, and they may offer honey to Ochún on the altar or put a few drops of honey in their own mouth before they pray.[58] Spoken prayers typically consist of a mix of Spanish and ritual Lucumí terminology. The prayers incorporate ritual names for Ochún (Ori Yeyeo, Yeyé Kare, Ladé Ochún, etc.; see Pedroso 2013, 124) and call on the *orisha* to bless those in attendance and watch over them.[59] They may be accompanied by soft instrumental music on the violin. Following this spoken segment, attendees usually sing a song in honor of Ochún – either a traditional chant such as "Beroní abebe Ochún" or a popular song associated with her, such as "Damisela encantadora," or

---

[58] Espinosa Casanova interview, March 2022.
[59] Pedroso (2013, 125) also includes a common prayer to Ochún with Lucumí text and translation.

FIGURE 4.13 "Beroní abebe Ochún" as sung traditionally in triple meter.

perhaps the birthday song "Cumpleaños feliz" if the ceremony marks the anniversary of the principal organizer's initiation into Ocha. Then participants touch glasses together and often continue by singing another song to Ochún in a moderate tempo.[60] Figures 4.13 and 4.14 illustrate the way that a Lucumí chant like "Beroní abebe Ochún"[61] is frequently transformed in the context of a *brindis* to sound more like commercial dance repertoire.

Following the toast and collective singing, musicians usually perform a more extended series of songs to Ochún since she is the focus of the event. Food and sweets may be offered to guests at this time as well. Ochún's preferred repertoire foregrounds boleros and romantic song, and they may be played at any time throughout the event. Standalone pieces heard toward the end of the *violín* can be relatively sedate and worshipful, such as Sindo Garay's "Imagen protectora" (Protecting Image) or instrumental versions of slower, traditional chants (e.g., "Iyá mi ilé"; see Altmann 1998, 229), or they may be up-tempo pieces – whatever the participants prefer. More danceable repertoire associated with Ochún might include Miguel Matamoros' "Mi veneración" (with its famous chorus "*Si te vas al Cobre, quiero que me traigas una Virgencita de la Caridad*"),[62] Rafael Hernández's "Cachita," or even "Sandunguera" by Los Van Van, an allusion to Ochún's fun-loving nature and skill as a dancer.

---

[60] Some Spiritist events may also include a *brindis* to the principal spirit guide being recognized. In that case, the song performed in their honor will be one that references it in some way.
[61] Again, the term *abebé* references Ochún's fan, and the lyrics of the song discuss the *orisha* fanning herself. *Iyá* means "mother" and *yumu* is one of Ochún's many incarnations or *caminos*. Thanks to Johnny Frías and his *padrino* Alain for these insights.
[62] "If you go to the Cobre valley, I want you to bring me back a little statue of the Virgin of Charity."

FIGURE 4.14 "Beroní abebe Ochún" as performed by a typical *violín* ensemble with string *guajeos* and in duple meter.

Some *violines* wind down at this point with a few praise songs to Elegguá once again, or with "Ave María," or they may continue with longer musical sequences to Ochún before the close. In the latter case, musicians perform sequences of short antiphonal melodies, as in the case of the *orishas* already discussed that represent a sort of musical climax. Pieces featured here may be Lucumí chants performed in a moderate triple-meter time (e.g., "Yeye yeyeo aride u") or in faster duple meter such as "E lade Ochún," "Ore ore," or "A la umba che mache."[63] Yet another option is to switch to a more traditional, percussion-only format; sometimes the guitar is simply turned over in a performer's lap and its body is used as a drum for a time. It may imitate Iyesá rhythms, for

---

[63] See Altmann (1998, 235, 257–8) and Mason (1992, 350, 352, 363) for possible translations, though by no means definitive ones.

instance, which often accompany such chants in a *tambor*.⁶⁴ Depending on the preferences of the host and the musicians, traditional chants such as these may alternate freely with choruses in Spanish from popular songs, or freely invented choruses. The latter might include phrases such as "*Caridad ampárame, ampárame caridad*" (Virgin of Charity, shelter me) repeated in a 4 mm. vamp in alternation with vocal or instrumental improvisation, or the chorus to Rafael Hernández's "Cachita" played on its own ("*Cachita está alborotá, ahora baila el chachachá*" [Cachita is going crazy, now she's dancing the chachachá]).⁶⁵ An emphasis on spontaneity and freely invented choruses characterizes these final song sequences, as explored in Chapter 5.

While many members of the religious community embrace *violines* as an attractive alternate modality of *orisha* worship, the practice does not appeal to everyone. Some interviewees suggest that *violines* tend to be too rowdy, too secular in focus, and that, as a result, they stray from their mission of divine veneration. Some note that *violín* audience members often arrive expecting to be entertained; they believe that such a mindset has led to the expansion of ensemble instrumentation from one or two solo violins to a miniature dance band, and that the repertoire larger groups play does not lend itself to a focus on the spiritual. For his part, *santero* and religious scholar Lázaro Pedroso considers *violines* too much of a departure from tradition. He argues that worshippers have been experimenting too freely with diverse musical content. He feels *santeros* adopt such practices from one day to the next, accepting any new fad: "Unfortunately it's 'monkey see, monkey do.' It only takes one member of the religious community to try something new that occurs to them and share it, then others repeat the same thing."⁶⁶ In this way, Pedroso asserts, established devotional practice is being corrupted by newer trends.

---

⁶⁴ My thanks to Richard Huntley (personal email, July 19, 2023) for this insight. Iyesá rhythms may be performed by *güiro*, *batá*, and *bembé* ensembles and represent adaptations from distinct Iyesá drum ensembles. See Delgado (2001, 2008) for additional info about Iyesá rhythms and their historical presence in Cuba.

⁶⁵ Music scholar Rafael Lam (personal email, September 12, 2023) notes that the chorus first appeared on the LP *Orquesta Aragón* in 1955 (RCA Victor MKL 3070). That group seems to have added it to the original Rafael Hernández composition. Listen to this recording starting at 1:05: www.YouTube.com/watch?v=dfLnNPrZvFE (accessed November 9, 2023).

⁶⁶ Lázaro Pedroso, Facebook Messenger, August 1, 2022. "Desgraciadamente esto es 'mono ve, mono hace'. Basta que un creyente haga algo que se le ocurrió y lo divulgue, va a venir otro atrás y lo va a repetir."

The fusion of Ocha and Spiritist practices strikes some listeners as inappropriate as well, even if they also recognize the importance of spirit guides in the lives of many *santeros*. Luis Manuel Leyro finds *violines* dedicated to Ochún or other *orishas* inappropriate because such deities already have a defined liturgy in the form of drumming, dance, song, and distinct rituals:

> A *violín* from my perspective is an invention created to worship Ochún from a certain perspective, but it has no religious foundation. A *violín* dedicated to the *egun* [or spirit world] is more appropriate … but such an event dedicated to Ochún is not logical. Songs like "El Santísimo," "La Gitana," that is spirit music … if you mix one [repertoire] with another you just get a crazy blend.[67]

To Leyro, celebrations of one's ancestors, spirit guides, and *orishas* should all be conducted separately. He emphasizes that *santeros* have long paid tribute to the *egun* and to *muertos*, but always independently so that spirit energy will not cross with that of the *orishas*. Emilio Gordillo Miraval extends the argument further, asserting that *violín* performance is not even appropriate for all forces of the dead such as Kongos. To him, the spirits of African slaves in Cuba would have no interest in the European-derived violin, and thus worshipping them with that instrument makes no sense.[68] Clearly Ocha and other religious practice continues to experience significant changes on various fronts; those represented by *toques de violín* do not represent established practice by any means.

Of course, large numbers of *santeros* appreciate the boundary-crossing manifest in *violín* worship and are drawn to it precisely for that reason. Rafael Espinosa Casanova sees no confusion in the simultaneous use of Ocha, Spiritist, Catholic, and Palo music, for instance. To him, *violines* accurately reflect the complex spiritual lives of the local community:

> If you organize a *violín* for your *orisha*, it is a beautiful thing to place a *bóveda* to one side [of the *orisha* altar] because that covers everything. If you are singing to Changó in Yoruba, you can sing to him for a time [and] as part of the event you can represent your Spiritist side, so it's a double celebration you're offering … You can start off singing in Yoruba but suddenly switch to "*Siete con siete, siete na' má, siete, tiene siete rayo'*."[69] Now you're singing for the Kongo world and Changó at the same time, you see? That way you can kill two birds with one stone … Or you

---

[67] Manuel Leyro interview, April 2022. "El violín para mí es un invento que se hizo para congratular de cierta manera a Ochún, pero eso no tiene fundamento. Suena mejor un violín a egun, por ejemplo … pero a Ochún no tiene lógica … Si tú mezclas una cosa con la otra, estás hacienda como decimos nosotros un 'sancocho'."

[68] Gordillo Miraval interview, January 2021.

[69] Siete Rayos is the Palo equivalent of Changó.

can sing to Ochún, but you can sing to the Gypsy too so that the Gypsy you have there on your *bóveda* also recognizes the offering. And that way things turn out prettier and better.[70]

CONCLUSION

My approach in this chapter has been to synthesize overall tendencies in *violines de santo* by comparing video recordings of multiple events (Chapter 3 adopts a similar approach). Many *violín* videos are available on YouTube so that readers can view them and draw their own conclusions about how best to describe such devotion. Synthesizing broad tendencies associated with *violines* is challenging for many reasons: because the practice continues to develop; because little established orthodoxy surrounds it; because of the tremendous diversity of music that performers draw from; because they alter content significantly based on the wishes of event organizers; and because the music they perform is often chosen on the spur of the moment. Thus, much *violín* music making is emergent, created in a fluid dialogue between ensembles and audiences. Chapter 5 explores specific gatherings and song sequences in detail to capture the details of such microdynamics.

Musical fugitivity , a constant movement between styles and repertoires, represents a central element of *violines*. Popular songs may be repurposed in praise of an *orisha*, for instance, or a pop song melody may have its lyrics changed slightly for the same purpose or a different purpose. Musicians invent choruses and add them to the end of established repertoire, or they change the rhythm or melody of a song so that it blurs distinctions between the sacred and the profane, the popular and the folkloric. Musicians complicate boundaries between multiple religious systems as part of the same process. Transformations of repertoire in *violines* can be viewed as far-flung signifying on local Caribbean religious

---

[70] Si tú le estás haciendo un violín al Santo, sería bonito poner una bóveda al lado, porque eso te da la cobertura de que si tú le estás cantando a Changó en Yoruba, puedes cantarle en un momento determinado a Changó [y a la vez] dentro de la fiesta metes a la parte tuya espiritual y es una celebración doble que le estás haciendo ... Estás cantando en Yoruba pero ahora ... [Canta:] *Siete con siete, siete na' má', Siete con siete, siete na' má', siete, tiene siete rayo'* ... Estás cantándole a la tierra conga, y le estás cantando también [a Changó] ... ¿Te das cuenta? ... Tú a veces puedes con un disparo matar dos pájaros ... Tú le cantas a Ochún, pero tú puedes cantar a la gitana y cantas la gitana para que la gitana que tú tienes ahí en la bóveda también perciba eso. Y así las cosas salen más bonitas y mejor.

experience, involving not only wordplay but soundplay that creates new linkages and meanings across disparate realms. Any interpretation of such performance must recognize a sense of multidimensionality to music, lyrics, and ritual action (Font-Navarrete 2021). The interpretive act of listening even to traditional *orisha* music, with its oblique lyrical references, is endlessly complex, and further transformations in the context of a *violín* require attention to many new details.

Violines demonstrate the dynamic, emergent nature of all religions and the ways that Afrodiasporic devotion in particular weaves together elements of physical and metaphysical experience. Such practices are "dynamic, ever transforming and ever transformative" (Meadows 2023, 6). *Violines* incorporate new forms of Cuban music into contexts of worship, especially from commercial sources. They combine sounds in a way that collapses distinctions between conceptual categories and creates new spaces of ambivalence and possibility. In the same way that Otero (2020, 85) describes *redobles* or refractions among spirits that simultaneously intensify or multiply relationships between them, the music of the *violín* both elides and blurs sonic and ritual space, concealing and revealing an array of connections and convergences.

5

Performance Dynamics in *Toques de Violín*

INTRODUCTION

The preceding chapters have made apparent the degree to which *violines* represent a space of transformation and intersectionality in which multiple musical and religious influences combine. The boundaries that tend to be crossed or blurred most consistently involve religious devotion and commercial music making of various sorts, resulting in what García Lacerra (2015) and others perceive as a tension between the sacred and the festive. Musical repertoires intersect in various ways as musicians perform: through the adoption of musical elements associated with dance music or folkloric repertoire when singing to spirits or *orishas*; by incorporating lyrical or melodic references to popular songs (for instance, choral refrains); by alternating between Spanish and Lucumí lyrics when singing to *orishas*; and by encouraging hand clapping and dancing in a style reminiscent of Cuban *son* as an accompaniment to religious worship, to cite only a few examples. This process resembles the "cohesive acts" described by Warden (2006) in *cajón* performance to an extent, especially the fusion of distinct musical modalities into new forms of expression. But intertextuality and boundary-crossing are arguably even more striking in the case of *violines* since they involve harmonic as well as rhythmic shifts and the incorporation of diverse commercial repertoire in addition to local Black folklore.

This chapter focuses on the overall structure of *violines*, the performative choices musicians make in such contexts as they assemble and move through repertoire, and the ways many groups now strive to make their music appear as spontaneous and exciting as possible to elicit more audience participation. An ability to engage listeners and to surprise or entertain them with unexpected shifts represents an important skill for *violín* ensembles that compete with one another for work; performers demonstrate this aspect of their skill by transitioning from one genre to another, suggesting new choruses for audience members to sing, taking solos, inventing background figures behind vocals, and so on. Such decisions take place constantly.

This chapter begins by providing an overview of all the music performed in a few distinct *violín* events to underscore the extent to which they frequently differ from one another. It considers the genres group members choose to foreground and the overall sequence of their activities, which often alternate between precomposed works and at least partially spontaneous jam sequences involving call–response singing in alternation with improvisations. The final sections of the chapter explore the dynamics of particular climax sequences in greater detail. Much as in the case of other traditional forms of Black Cuban music – vocal *tratados* with Lucumí texts, Palo songs, rumba, *danzón*, *son*, etcetera – musicians at peak moments are expected to foreground their instrumental and/or vocal skills. Using precomposed *plegarias* as a point of departure (which function roughly like the head of a jazz standard), they often segue into vamps that shift to multiple new melodies. The emphasis on inventiveness and keeping the audience entertained frequently leads to intertextual play and humor.

A COMPARISON OF REPERTOIRE IN THREE VIOLINES

The content of *violines* can be evaluated in many ways, but perhaps most clearly in terms of the repertoire they select. Various styles of music can predominate, be de-emphasized, or be excluded entirely. Several questions came to mind as I looked through recordings of *toques de violín* and began to compare: How would I characterize the overall musical progression in this devotional act? How much of the music derives from Spiritist traditions or the Catholic Church versus popular song, folklore, or other sources? How much of the music has Spanish-language lyrics versus lyrics in other languages, and how much is entirely instrumental? Is all the music accompanied by harmonic and melodic instruments? How much of the music is precomposed or improvised? I also found myself wondering how much of the music had unambiguously religious associations, though that issue often proved difficult to determine, as is discussed in the remainder of the chapter.

Some of these questions, and my focus on the repertoire of discrete performances, were inspired by the publications of Bárbara Balbuena Gutiérrez (2003, 117–20) and Miraima García Lacerra (2015, 78–9), both of whom document the repertoire of ceremonies they observed in detail. Neither analyzes *violines espirituales* specifically, and neither describes the variety of performance styles that I encountered, but they offer many useful insights. Balbuena Gutiérrez divided the *violín* music she witnessed into Spiritist songs versus others dedicated to the *orishas* but performed primarily in Spanish. García Lacerra identified three distinct segments in the music making she analyzed. The first, characterized as religious/ritualistic, included an instrumental "Padrenuestro" and "Ave María," then a series of unspecified songs to Elegguá. The second, labeled an *oru* for spirit guides, included primarily *plegarias* in Spanish. The third, labeled the *oru del eyá aránla* or main public devotional event, included a ritual toast to Ochún, a series of traditional songs and *plegarias* devoted to major *orishas*, and a closing segment foregrounding songs to Elegguá. I extend their analysis by considering multiple distinct performances that deviate to an extent from this paradigm, and by taking a closer look at the microdynamics of *violín* music making.

DANAI'S VIOLÍN

As an initial example of a *violín* performance, consider one that took place in the home of a *santera* named Danai in 2021 (Figure 5.1). This was relatively unique in that the performance featured only a single violinist playing alone, and for that reason the music was relatively subdued and reverential in nature. The organizer chose this format because of the Covid-19 crisis, as larger gatherings were discouraged at the time and hiring a single musician seemed safer.[1] This stripped-down format provides insights into what *violín* devotion may have sounded like prior to the 1970s, when groups tended to be smaller and had not all incorporated percussion. Danai's was the shortest performance I documented, lasting only about forty minutes (see Figure 5.2).

In this performance, more than 75 percent of all the music consisted of instrumental melodies, a higher percentage than in other *violines*. Catholic and Spiritist repertoire made up nearly half of the repertoire, and about a third involved popular music.[2] All songs sung by those in

---

[1] Danai Pérez Domínguez, "WhatsApp communication 7 May 2024."
[2] Admittedly, the categories of analysis used here are not mutually exclusive – i.e., a song can be both a *plegaria* and in Spanish, or instrumental and Spiritist. My calculations are intended only to provide a sense of broad tendencies.

FIGURE 5.1 Danai Pérez Domínguez relaxing with invited guests following her *violín* and *brindis*, Nuevo Vedado, Cuba, November 15 2020. Left to right: Danai Pérez Domínguez, Mirta Maray Salcedo Suárez, and Neisy Fonseca. Photo by Melena Francis Valdés.

attendance (four in total: about ten minutes of music or 25 percent of the event) had Spanish-language lyrics, and most of the instrumental pieces had implicit Spanish lyrics; only two Ocha praise songs were included, and only in instrumental versions. At least a third of the repertoire consisted of popular music. Perhaps most strikingly, nearly all the music was precomposed. The violinist appeared to invent a few introductory melodies and to play with the standard melodies of some songs a little in performance, but otherwise his playing was interpretive rather than improvisatory. This aspect of the musical offering contrasts sharply with most other *violines* heard today.

A *violín* repertoire guidebook that María Teresa Gómez Noguera inherited from her father Tomás, dating from the 1950s, suggests that Danai's event conforms roughly to performance practices of the mid-twentieth century. A great deal of the music played at Danai's house consisted of discrete precomposed songs, for instance, rather than the more improvisational call–response sequences common today; Tomás' guidebook suggests a similar approach. Specifically, Tomás writes that in a *violín de santo* "First

5 Performance Dynamics in Toques de Violín

Duration	Title
6:52	An instrumental rendition of the "Padrenuestro" song (Fig. 3.15) and two versions of "Ave María" in combination, Schubert's and Gounod's
1:26	An instrumental version of "Porque soy tan chiquitico" (Fig. 4.3)
2:25	A sung version of the folk *plegaria* Ave María (Fig. 3.5)
3:17	A sung potpourri of the *plegarias* "Sea el Santísimo" (Fig. 3.2) and "La luz redentora" (Fig. 3.2)
4:02	Instrumental versions of the *plegarias* "San Miguel" (Fig. 3.6) and sung versions of "La luz" and "O venid protectores" (Fig. 3.4)
3:01	"Madrecita del alma querida" by Mexican singer José José, instrumental
3:30	"Damisela encantadora" by Ernesto Lecuona, instrumental
3:32	Danzón "Virgen de Regla" by Richard Egües and Pablo O'Farrill, instrumental
3:27	Tango, "El día que me quieras" by Carlos Gardel, instrumental, segueing to the bolero "Contigo en la distancia" by César Portillo de la luz, instrumental
2:19	*Plegaria* to Obatalá, instrumental
4:04	Preparation for the *brindis*; instrumental version of the chant "Beroni abebé Ochún" accompanied by the ringing of a bell. Then a spoken prayer followed by singing of the "Cumpleaños feliz" birthday song
2:32	A second rendition of the chant "Beroni abebé Ochún" followed by "Imagen protectora" by Sindo Garay
2:27	A final reprise of Schubert's "Ave María," instrumental

FIGURE 5.2 Repertoire in Danai's *violín*.

one plays for the dead," presumably with pieces such as Schubert's "Ave María"; "[s]econd one opens [with a piece for] Elegguá"; and then, after a piece dedicated to Ochún, it suggests continuing with "numerous fine instrumental works" like waltzes or "La bella cubana" by José White.[3] Interestingly, Tomás' guidelines for music making in Spiritist-oriented *violines* (included in the same notebook) is more detailed than those for Ocha-related rites and includes dedicated sequences to Kongos, Gypsies, and Indians in addition to other *comisiones*. This suggests that Spiritist-oriented

---

[3] "1ero se le toca un poco a los muertos. 2ndo se abre con Elegguá el violín al santo. 3ro si es para Ochún como primer número la plegaria a la Caridad del Cobre. Después valses o números finos instrumentales como por ejemplo 'La bella cubana'."

violín performance was at least as common at the time, and possibly predates the broad popularity of *violines de santo*, as discussed in Chapter 2.

YENNY'S VIOLÍN

Many *violín* praise events follow a structure similar to Danai's, with the caveat that these days more performers usually participate, more traditional Ocha songs are included, and, at least during later sequences, musicians have more freedom to riff instrumentally or vocally. Yenny's *violín* from April 2022 (Figure 5.3), involving a violinist, guitarist, and bongo player, represents a good example of these tendencies. Much of the initial ceremony conformed closely to Danai's: it began with instrumental Catholic numbers, proceeded to Spiritist songs, and included a *plegaria* in Spanish to Elegguá early on. Just like Danai's event, songs sung in Spanish predominated and popular/romantic songs constituted much of the overall performance (about 40 percent): "Camino verde" by Spanish vocalist Antonio Molina; "Alma, corazón, y vida," a Peruvian waltz by Adrián Flores; the Cuban bolero "Corazón en cristal" by Enrique Pessino, etcetera. Yet the musicians also chose to include *orus* in Lucumí dedicated to Oyá and additional Lucumí songs for Yemayá, Obatalá, and Elegguá. And, in an extended song sequence to Ochún toward the end, the group also included many spontaneous additions, such as a bongo solo and multiple invented choruses, some taken from popular dance repertoire. The latter included lines such as *"No me voy a disgustar . . . a la hora que tú me llames no me molesto"* (I won't get mad, whatever time you call it won't upset me), derived from a recording by La Orquesta Aragón,[4] and others designed to get audience members dancing such as *"a derecha . . . a izquierda"* (step to the left . . . to the right) or *"abajo, abajo, abajo, abajo"* (down, down, lower, lower).

The primary factors distinguishing Yenny's *violín* from Danai's were its length (ninety-six minutes in total, more than twice as long as Danai's), a significantly greater percentage of Lucumí songs (a little over eleven minutes of such music, roughly 12 percent of the total), and en emphasis on *montuno* jam sections following *plegarias* to San Lázaro/Babalú and La Caridad/Ochún (as noted, slower *plegarias* often serve as a point of departure for improvisation). Precomposed pieces still constituted about two-thirds of the performance, but improvised call–response sections with

---

[4] The song in question is "No me voy a disgustar" by José Beltrán Guzmán, written about 1980; it can be heard on Spotify: https://open.spotify.com/track/005IqSzlUZtMfLrBikdvk1 (accessed May 27, 2024).

5 *Performance Dynamics in* Toques de Violín 139

FIGURE 5.3 Musicians performing in Yenny's *violín*. They include director and bongo player Osvaldo "Mambo" Blanco. Hugo Álvarez performs on guitar, and Hugo Cruz on violin. Photo by Melena Francis Valdés, Nuevo Vedado, Cuba, April 24, 2022.

more overt audience participation predominated in the remaining third. I view Yenny's event as relatively traditional given its heavy emphasis on popular song and on slower romantic pieces, but also as indicating the ways that *violín* devotion has changed in recent decades. A form of praise that began as largely contemplative has increasingly incorporated overt influences from Ocha repertoire and dance music.

Eduar's *Violín*

Eduar's *violín*, also from 2022, provides an example that differs significantly from both celebrations discussed thus far and suggests the flexibility of *violín* devotion as a musical form. Eduar, a violinist in the Orquesta Sublime *charanga* band and a child of Ogún, had been instructed in a spiritual reading (*itá*) to play his violin for Ochún every year and to make other offerings to her. Perhaps this was in part due to his special abilities on an instrument known to appeal to that *orisha*. The altar he prepared featured the colors of Ochún and Yemayá prominently, but the cake he commissioned had Ogún's colors. In the performance, Eduar played with his uncle Abilio (also a violinist, director of the Orquesta Sublime, and of the *violín* ensemble itself), and a guitarist (Cecilio) who doubled on percussion (Figure 5.4). The musical set began in relatively standard fashion with an instrumental "Padrenuestro" melody, Schubert's "Ave María" (also instrumental), a series of five sung *plegarias* in the folk Catholic/Spiritist tradition, another song for *gitanas*, then the Puerto Rican bolero "Madrigal." Shortly thereafter, the sound of the group shifted to praise of the *orishas*. The group performed "Porque soy tan chiquitico" for Elegguá (Figure 4.3), then the guitarist turned his instrument over and used it like a *cajón*, initially beating out a duple-meter rhythm to accompany traditional songs in Lucumí such as "Elegguá, Elegguá asokere" (Figure 6.7), "Sosa Sokere," and "Elegguá ago añá." The two violinists switched to bell and maracas at the same time, as a complement to the sound of the percussive slaps

FIGURE 5.4 Performers in Eduar's *violín*. They include director and lead violinist Abilio Betancourt Bejerano (left), second violinist Eduar Marzán Betancourt (center), and guitarist/lead vocalist and percussionist Cecilio Arozarena (right). The ensemble is called Violines Abilio. Photo by Melena Francis Valdés, April 26, 2022.

5 Performance Dynamics in Toques de Violín 141

FIGURE 5.5 A duple-meter rhythm accompanying *orisha* songs in Eduar's *violín*. Higher notes in the guitar line represent slaps on the edge of the guitar body while lower notes represent lower-pitched hits in the center.

on the body of the guitar. The resulting composite rhythm was reminiscent of the Iyesá rhythm played on the *batás* (c.f. Coburg 2004, 62–3), and also of *danzón* clave (see Madrid and Moore 2013, 72).

I list all music played by Violines Abilio in Figure 5.6 so that readers can evaluate the structure of their performance, the extent to which it aligns with or diverges from the performances for Danai and Yenny, and also the way that the ensemble chose to play particular sequences using only traditional praise songs accompanied by percussion, as in a *tambor*. Consider the relative length of the boleros and instrumental pieces performed, for instance, in comparison with the *oru* in praise of Eleguá, Ogún, and Ochosi; Obatalá, Changó, and Oyá; and, especially, Ochún toward the end. Instrumental pieces in this fifty-six-minute performance collectively lasted only about thirteen minutes – roughly 15 percent of the set. Songs sung in Lucumí lasted about twenty-one minutes in total, representing more than a third all music making. Songs in Spanish, while also numerous, lasted only sixteen minutes in total. Call–response

Duration	Title
3:00	Instrumental versions of the "Padrenuestro" prayer and Schubert's "Ave María"
12:10	*Plegarias*: "Gloria Jesús, Gloria María"; "Ave María/Del cielo ha bajado; "Sea el Santísimo"; "La luz redentora"; "Que luz tan divina"; "Gitana de mis amores"
2:15	"Madrigal," an instrumental bolero
2:05	"Somewhere Over the Rainbow," instrumental
3:00	"Como soy tan chiquitico," *plegaria* for Eleggúa
3:30	Traditional Ocha songs for Eleggúa, Ogún, and Ochosi accompanied by percussion, initially in 4/4 and later 6/8
2:00	"Damisela encantadora," instrumental
2:00	"A mi manera" (My Way), primarily instrumental
1:30	*Plegaria* to Obatalá (Fig. 4.5)
5:30	Traditional Lucumí songs for Obatalá, Changó, and Oyá with percussion-only accompaniment
3:40	An *oru* for Yemayá consisting of an instrumental version of "Sobre las olas" (Over the Waves), then the sung *plegarias* "Marinero, marinero" (Fig. 3.8) and "A remar" (Fig. 5.8)
2:15	Traditional Lucumí songs in praise of Yemayá
3:00	Songs for Ochún: "Imagen protectora," sung, and "Madrecita," instrumental
1:15	*Brindis* for Ochún
10:30	An extended final sequence of primarily traditional Lucumí songs to Ochún, Ogún, and Eleggúa. The lead singer sings final chant in Spanish, however: "*Que vengan los bocaditos*" (Bring Out the Sandwiches), a humorous call for organizers to end the religious offering and start offering food to guests.

FIGURE 5.6 Eduar's *violín* repertoire.

improvisatory sections were more prominent in Eduar's *violín* as well (this mostly corresponds to the Lucumí segments), many of them involving percussion-only accompaniment. While precomposed music and popular songs still constituted about half of the overall performance (roughly thirty-three minutes), this *violín* clearly takes more direct inspiration from traditional drumming.

THE MICRODYNAMICS OF PERFORMANCE

One aspect of *violín* vocals that deserves further discussion is the way lead singers often move back and forth between Spanish and Lucumí in praise of the *orishas* – a practice that would not be considered appropriate in most drumming events. When calling the *orishas* to earth is the priority, singers use ritual African-derived speech (Lucumí) only. Since *violines* do not generally attempt to provoke an *orisha*'s presence, however, singers have more license to approach the event however they choose. In the final sequence of Eduar's *violín*, as one example, the lead singer transitions freely between praise songs to Ogún in Spanish, such as *"Yo subo a la loma y llamo a mi Ogún/ Y Ogún me responde en el nombre de Dios"* (I climb the hill and call to my Ogún/ And Ogún answers me in the name of God), and traditional melodies such as "Aguanileo Ogún mariwó" and "Amalá Ogún arere." Other singers make similar transitions between Spanish and Lucumí, for instance by leading in a chorus to "Elegguá, Elegguá, asokere" and then responding with a lead vocal in Spanish that quotes the lyrics to "Como soy tan chiquitico."[5] Sometimes lead singers respond to choruses in Lucumí with Spanish phrases as well; when improvising lines against a praise song to Oyá such as "Oyansa ma terema" (Figure 4.8), they might sing *"Terema, cosa buena,"* mixing Spanish and Lucumí; or, when singing to Changó, they might say *"Onileo, claro que llegó."* Clearly, the freedom performers have to transition between languages of praise extends to the most sacred repertoire.

The "broken up" musical flow and pacing of *violines* deserve further consideration, given that it deviates from other religious music making among *santeros*. As mentioned, most drumming events build in energy and tempo toward a final climax. By contrast, *violines* tend to intersperse boleros, slow *plegarias*, or pop songs with faster sequences (Balbuena Gutiérrez 2003, 116). Such alternations can be seen in Eduar's *violín*: one moment he and Violines Abilio play a series of driving, traditional praise songs to warrior *orishas*, then they switch to "Damisela encantadora," a slow waltz. Other up-tempo praise songs in the same performance transition to "Over the Waves," another slow waltz. Many other performers consciously alternate between *"temas suaves"* (smooth or calm pieces) and more upbeat or danceable ones. This approach has

---

[5] Abilio Betancourt Bejerano (personal WhatsApp communication, April 1, 2024) underscores the importance of transitioning back to Lucumí texts following segments in Spanish. "This is necessary so that the attendees can participate more in the *violín* by dancing and helping with the choruses ... 'Para que se muevan.'"

various advantages. It provides musical variety and it gives performers (violinists, percussionists, singers) a rest at particular moments since they can switch between multiple modalities rather than play danceable pieces all the time. Even audiences interested in dancing may appreciate such breaks. Perhaps most importantly, the constant tempo and genre shifts keep the event energy from becoming so intense that it would logically lead to mounting by an *orisha*.

Tempo and mood shifts take place not only between distinct sequences, but within them. In Chapter 4 I mentioned that while the basic pulse of most performance in *violines* draws from duple-meter dance repertoire, some performers shift to 6/8 briefly to add rhythmic excitement and variety (see Figure 4.8) and to play between the boundaries of sacred music and dance music. In Eduar's performance, the group not only referenced 6/8 time but sustained a 6/8 pulse under many chants, adding additional drive to those sequences. During the initial *oru* to the warrior *orishas*, for example, the lead singer began to sing the chant "Elegguá ago, Elegguá ago Añá" in duple meter (using the Iyesá-like rhythmic accompaniment transcribed in Figure 5.5), then continued to sing the same piece as he transitioned to a 6/8 rhythmic base (Figure 5.7). The group maintained the new 6/8 pulse as the *akpwon* (ritual lead singer) entoned a shorter version of the same chant ("Alaroye demasankio Elegguá ago Añá") and through various other praise songs to Ogún and Ochosi ("Amalá Ogún arere," "E afereo," "Ochosi ayiloda ala malaode," etc.). As in Figure 5.5, the 6/8 rhythmic base was performed on the body of a guitar with an accompanying bell and maraca. The rhythm played on the guitar does not follow any standard pattern, but instead is loosely

FIGURE 5.7 A triple-meter rhythm accompanying *orisha* songs in Eduar's *violín*, apparently representing an adaptation of the batá's *ñongo* pattern. Thanks to Richard Huntley for help with the transcription. For notated versions of standard *ñongo*, see Coburg (2004, 64) and Moore and Sayre (2006, 140).

evocative of rhythms associated with *ñongo* on the *batás*. Rather than playing the large *iyá* drum's "busy" figure every other measure, as would be traditional, however, the percussionist in Eduar's *violín* plays it every measure, against both sides of clave. This creates a complex polyrhythmic accompaniment to the antiphonal vocals.

Overall tendencies in *violín* performance dedicated primarily to spirit guides are similar to those described earlier to the *orishas*, with a few differences. Spoken prayers in Spanish tend to be incorporated more frequently and to last longer in Spiritist *violines*, especially early on; these appear to mirror spoken prayers heard in *misas* themselves. More of the musical set focuses on *plegarias* dedicated to themes of light and clarity; to San Miguel, San Lázaro, or the Virgin Mary; and to *indios*, *congos*, or *gitanas*. Palo-derived songs are heard more frequently too, as well as songs with *bozal* lyrics instead of extended sequences in Lucumí. During some *orus* to the spirits of former African slaves, musicians may employ fast triple-meter rhythms in percussion-only segments reminiscent of traditional Palo ceremony. Percussion of this sort usually only lasts a few minutes, however. Generic choruses inspired by Spiritist imagery feature prominently as the basis for improvisation – for example, choruses such as "*Alumbra aquí, alumbra allá*," mentioned in Chapter 3, or "*Baila, baila Cachita a la luz de la caridad*" (Dance, dance Cachita in charity's light"). Significant segments of the set involve improvisation of some sort – nearly half, in many cases.

Finally, many of the popular songs employed in *violines espirituales* are distinct from those used in *violines de santo*. In one performance I witnessed, the stylized lullaby "Drume negrita" (Sleep, Little Black Girl) by Bola de Nieve was used to accompany the final *brindis* since the *violín* was dedicated to the spirit of an African slave ("La negra," mentioned in Chapter 3). The same *violín* featured an extended version of the pop song "Danza ñáñiga" by Irakere.[6] Despite its title's reference to Abakuá culture, the lyrics of this song do not discuss Black religions and seem only to recount a story of unrequited love: "*No sé, no sé vivir, no sé, no sé soñar, las puertas se me cierran si tú, si tú no estás.*"[7] Of course, the

---

[6] *Ñáñigo* is a pejorative term used by Spanish colonials to refer to members of the Abakuá secret society. The origins of the word *ñáñigo* has roots in southeastern Nigeria/southwestern Cameroon and refers to *íremes*: masked ancestral spirit dancers; see Miller (2009).

[7] In translation: "I don't know, I don't know how to live, I don't know, don't know how to dream. Doors close before me if you aren't here." Many versions of the piece are available online, including this heavily blues-inflected rendition featuring Omara Portuondo on lead vocals: www.YouTube.com/watch?v=opqyLd9UGyI (accessed August 30, 2023).

yearning for another in the context of a *violín* could be viewed as spiritual in nature rather than physical. The lead singer in the event I observed described "Danza ñáñiga" as a gift to all *egun* so that they would offer their mantle of protection to those present. Other popular songs heard in Spiritist *violines* include "Sun sun babaé," recorded by Celia Cruz. The lyrics of "Sun sun babaé" discuss a small black hummingbird, yet according to Fernando Ortiz they implicitly reference Kongo rituals (Ortiz 1991, 114).[8]

One way that musicians add to the excitement in *violines* of all sorts is to incorporate rhythmic breaks into their sets that imitate the sound of dance bands; musical sequences in a *violín* organized in November of 2020 demonstrate this tendency clearly. The group there consisted of two violinists, a guitarist, and a bongo player who also sang most of the lead vocals. The latter had a unique performance style that involved playing his bongo with his open left hand and a metal tuning wrench held in the right; he used the wrench to hit a bell on beats 1 and 3 of the 4/4 measure and to hit first the smaller *macho* head and then the larger *hembra* on beats 2 and 4 as part of his modified *martillo* ride pattern.[9] This performer made percussive shifts of various kinds central to his improvisations, sometimes by momentarily shifting to 6/8 but more typically by introducing a number of distinct breaks, marking them by hitting the bell and the *hembra* drum head simultaneously and loudly. Sometimes he used the breaks to lead in a new chorus, marking the transition between lead vocals and the entrance of other singers with rhythmic flourishes, as in Figure 5.8.

Alternately, the lead singer in this group sometimes played a break instead of singing a lead vocal line to surprise listeners. For instance, he might let the chorus finish responding to him with "Sosa, sokere" and then play two quarter-note triplets in one measure followed by a full break on the downbeat of the next measure, after which the chorus entered once again. At other moments, the same performer might build intensity by switching from *martillo*-based accompaniment to straight

---

[8] The *sunsún* (or *zunzún*) is a small black hummingbird native to Cuba; see, for instance, www.cubaplusmagazine.com/en/environment/zunzun-cuba-hummingbird.html (accessed September 2, 2023). Cary Peñate's dissertation (2021, 272ff.) includes a more extended discussion of "Sun sun babaé," its meanings as discussed by Ortiz and others, and its use in early Cuban film. According to Manuel López Martínez (n.d.), the song was popularized originally in folkloric ensembles associated with the parrandas de Zulueta, in Remedios.

[9] See Moore (2010, 95) and CD track 11 for further information on the *martillo* pattern and a recording of it.

5 Performance Dynamics in Toques de Violín 147

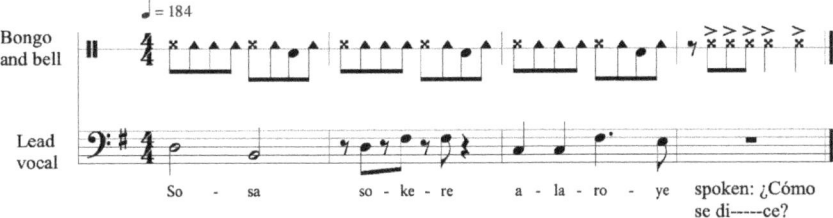

FIGURE 5.8 Sketch of a simple bongo drum break used to call in the chorus of a new praise song for Elegguá, "Sosa sokere." "X" heads indicate bell hits, triangle head represent muted strokes on the bongo's smaller *macho* head, and lower notes represent open tones on the larger *hembra*.

FIGURE 5.9 Straight quarter-notes on the bongo, used instead of a standard *martillo* pattern to generate musical interest during call–response singing. Lyrics in caps indicate the choral response. The break in measure eight leads back to a *martillo*-style accompaniment.

quarter-notes played simultaneously on the bell and *hembra* head of the bongo as he continued to sing (see Figure 5.9). Just like a dance band might do in order to build excitement, he would sustain the quarter-note accompaniment for multiple measures, slowly getting louder, then use a syncopated *cinquillo* rhythm or similar pattern to mark a transition back to the *martillo*. The bell itself often served as an additional source of minor spontaneous improvisations throughout the show; sometimes the bongo player would strike it two or three times, marking eighth notes at the beginning or end of a given measure, before returning to his ride pattern to generate variety. In general, he used breaks and alterations to signal to other musicians in his group that he wished to transition from one refrain to another or to initiate a change to the accompaniment in other ways.

Yet another technique used by musicians in some *violines* to add variety is to insert a *masacote* or *bomba* breakdown section into song sequences. In modern *timba* (or Cuban salsa) music, *bomba* sections involve relatively "empty" moments in which harmonic instruments such as the bass and keyboard drop out along with the brass section, leaving only percussion to sustain the vocals. These moments take the overall energy of the group down to allow for a final climactic build-up thereafter. The bass player in *bomba* segments often slaps the instrument's strings rhythmically on beats 3 and 4 of the 4/4 measure to add to the percussive groove, or plays glissandi or other arhythmic sounds against the percussion (González Bello and Casanella 2002). Guitarists and violinists can adopt this same approach in a *violín*: at certain moments they all stop playing melodic or harmonic accompaniment at the same time, either switching from violin or guitar to hand percussion or continuing to sing but not playing their usual instrument. The guitarist may rhythmically slap the body of his guitar on beats 3 and 4 for a time, imitating the bass. Later, the violinists and guitarist enter again as a group with harmonic strumming and *guajeo* melodies, making the group sound suddenly fuller and more energetic.

The addition of new, invented choruses constitutes perhaps the most important way to add interest to a *violín* during its final climactic segments. This tendency was mentioned briefly in the context of Yenny's celebration but merits further commentary. Just as in the case of a *tambor*, lead singers in any ensemble play a key role in sustaining energy as they transition from one musical idea to the next. They essentially "drive the bus" in the sense that all other musicians and singers follow their lead, and their decisions make or break the overall musical dynamics. Others in the band and in the audience respond to their cues with the appropriate vocal responses; percussionists sometimes are forced to alter their patterns to accompany the new vocal lines appropriately, and of course the whole group's melodic and harmonic patterns must often shift in response as well. Percussionists or instrumentalists may be featured with a solo and become the center of attention during jam segments, but only briefly. Singing lead thus involves constant decision making about the overall direction of performance, with other ensemble members supporting the transitions that singers initiate.

The added chorus phrases that help *"poner la timba"*[10] or add excitement and get audiences involved are most typically in Spanish, though some include well-known phrases in Lucumí also. Most often, the resultant melodies are conceived so that they fit within a simple four-measure harmonic loop or vamp identical or similar to the music played previously; this ensures that the transition to the new segment will be relatively seamless. Some choruses reference particular *orishas* or spirit guides; in extended devotion to Babalú Aye, for instance, singers might introduce choruses such as *"Por ahí pasó, por ahí pasó, Babalú Ayé y nadie lo vió"* (He just went by, just went by, Babalú Ayé, and no one saw him). Alternately, in a Spiritist or other context the singer might reference his Catholic counterpart with the chorus *"San Lázaro bendito, San Lázaro ven tú, ahí están tus hijos pidiéndote salud"* (Blessed St Lazarus, St. Lazarus come, here are your children asking you for good health). Or, when singing to St. Theresa/Oyá, a typical new chorus might be *"Santa Teresa madre, Santa Teresa de Jesús, allí viene el misionero, viene dando luz"* (St. Theresa my mother, Jesus's St. Theresa, there comes the missionary, he brings light).

Even more often, the new choruses introduced by lead singers are generic in the sense that they have no direct association with specific *orishas* or spirits and can be used at any time. Some derive from popular songs and are introduced in their original form, such as the chorus of "Oye como va" by Tito Puente. Others represent adaptations of popular choruses. One example is the refrain of the song "El guarapo y la melcocha" by Eduardo Saborit from the 1940s: *"Toma guarapo por la madruga', lo bueno se queda, lo malo se va"* (Drink cane liquor in middle of the night, the good things stay, the bad things go). In the context of a *violín*, performers alter these lyrics and instead sing phrases such as *"Siá cará, siá cará, lo bueno pa' 'quí, lo malo pa' llá"* (*Siá cará, siá cará*, a phrase used in rituals to purge evil spirits, also means "let good things stay here and bad things go away"). Still other invented choruses seem to be created spontaneously by singers themselves who adapt them as needed to a given performance. In a Spiritist-oriented event one might hear *"Tra la la, media unidad, fe, esperanza y caridad"* (Tra la la, spirit medium, faith, hope, and charity), for instance. Or, *"Voy a hacer un violín, voy a hacer una serenata, esta fiesta no se termina hasta mañana por la mañana"* (I'm going to organize a *violín*, a serenade, this party won't end until tomorrow morning; see Figure 5.10, chorus #1). Of course, after introducing such

---

[10] Percussionist Rafael Espinosa Casanova used this phrase in an interview as he described the importance of adding new choruses in the context of *violín* performance. The term *timba* has an interesting etymology; see Perna (2005, 97ff.) for further information.

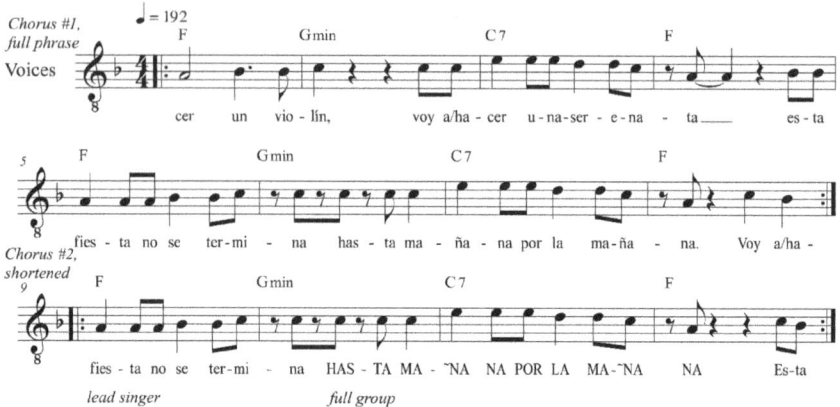

FIGURE 5.10 "Voy a hacer un violín." Two versions of a newly invented chorus as commonly incorporated into performances.

a phrase, the chorus would repeat it and then the lead singer would have the chance to improvise new melodies and/or text in alternation with it. Eventually it could also be shortened to add energy, with the lead singer and chorus singing only the second half in alternation (Figure 5.7, chorus #2).

ANALYSIS OF A MUSICAL SEQUENCE TO YEMAYÁ

The foregoing commentary provides some feel for the spontaneous elements that lead singers and instrumentalists adopt to make events more interesting, but only a closer look at particular sequences can truly underscore the constant improvisatory dynamics that surround present-day *violines*. This is especially true toward the end of a performance. As a first example, consider a celebration organized by Nadia Milad Issa and her *madrina* in May of 2023 in honor of Nadia's primary *orisha*, Yemayá (Figure 5.11). This *violín* began with song sequence to Elegguá, a few *plegarias*, and a birthday song for Yemayá (referencing Nadia's spiritual birthday as an initiate). Next came instrumentals and slower pieces: the Erroll Garner ballad "Misty"; "Leyenda de un beso" (Legend of a Kiss) from the Spanish *zarzuela* mentioned in Chapter 3;[11] and

---

[11] The Spanish rock group Mocedades famously covered the same *zarzuela* melody, adding original lyrics and entitling their modified piece "Amor de hombre." Thus, many listeners associate it with their group rather than with the original production. See www.YouTube.com/watch?v=aEKiTSZzego to hear the Mocedades version (accessed September 6, 2023).

5 Performance Dynamics in Toques de Violín

FIGURE 5.11 Nadia's *violín*. Nadia Milad Issa organized this performance in consultation with her *madrina*, Natividad de la Cruz Chivas "Oñí Odé" in May of 2023. The featured performers include Ubaldo Machado Valdés (percussionist, far right in the white cap), Omar Nilo González Álvarez (violin, bottom left), Judith Caridad Deulofeu Suárez (violin), and Raúl Alejandro Montane Salgado (guitar).

a second bolero, "El ciego" (The Blind Man) by Antonio Machín. "El ciego" eventually segued into a series of spontaneous choruses performed chachachá style; the first chorus derived from the final phrase of the piece's lyrics, "*Por tí, solo por tí*" (For you, only for you), with musicians singing it over a i-i-ii-V, 2-measure vamp in A minor. The lead vocalist in this segment (the guitarist) improvised lyrically and melodically against the group vocals, just as one might in a bar or on a concert stage. Other choruses sung over the same harmonic vamp thereafter included "*A la playa yo quiero ir a bailar, porque el niche me invita a guarachar*" (I want to go dance at the beach, because the Black guy has invited me to have a good time), featured recently in Omara Portuondo's version of "Quizás, quizás, quizás" in her Carnegie Hall show;[12] and "*De cualquier malla sale el ratón, oye, de cualquier malla*" (A mouse slips out of any net, hey, any

---

[12] www.YouTube.com/watch?v=gCt5ghkkIMY (accessed September 6, 2023). The "el niche" chorus dates back many decades and was first incorporated as a tag to the *danzón* "El niche" written by Félix Reina in about 1940. It can be heard in this recording by Antonio Arcaño's group, for instance: www.YouTube.com/watch?v=LK4dHNVQtwo (accessed September 15. 2023). Composers and interpreters constantly modify such lyrics in order to mention their own group or a particular lead singer at a given event.

net), a chorus taken from the 1964 Cheo Feliciano dance hit "El ratón" (The Mouse).

While the sequence described in Nadia's *violín* leans heavily toward commercial repertoire, musicians invoked *orishas* overtly thereafter with an extended song sequence dedicated to Obatalá and later with a climactic sequence dedicated to Yemayá. Yemayá's music began with a precomposed *plegaria* in D minor and a similarly precomposed arrangement of "Yemayá asesú" in D major. From there things began slowly to increase in intensity. First the lead singer introduced the Lucumí praise song "Kai, kai, kai, Yemayá olodo" in G major, making the other musicians follow his lead as he switched keys, harmony, and tempo. His solo vocals repeated essentially the same lyrics as the chorus, improvising new melodies only. The singer (in this case the lead violinist, Omar, who continued to play *guajeos* at the same time) followed more or less the same approach during the next two Lucumí songs he introduced: "Ladi oke, ladi oke"[13] and "Awoyó aé" (Figure 4.12). However, each required a slightly different harmonic structure to support the melody (e.g., I-V-V-I vs. I-I-V-I vs. V-V-V-I), forcing the accompanying guitarist to quickly switch his pattern (the second violinist had switched to bell). At this point the violinist/*akpwon* switched to a series of Spanish-language *plegarias* in the same key but all with slightly different harmonic accompaniment as well: first "A remar" (Figure 5.12), then "*Yo vivo en el agua, con el camarón, y a nadie le importa como vivo yo*" (I live in the water with the shrimp, and no one cares what I do) followed by "*Sirena, sirena,*

FIGURE 5.12 "A remar," one of many *plegarias* devoted to Yemayá, usually performed in alternation between a chorus and lead singer.

---

[13] See Altmann (1998, 224) for a transcription and Mason (1992, 312) for a possible translation.

sirena de la mar, yo saco la suerte del fondo de la mar" (Siren, siren, siren of the ocean, I find my luck at the bottom of the sea). This sequence ended with a faster reprise of "A remar."

Next, the same lead singer took things up a notch in terms of tempo and improvisatory activity. Staying in the same key, he first brought the group to a full stop on the word "*re-ma*" (row), then, using a new solo vocal, he transitioned to a shorter and apparently spontaneous variant of the "A remar" *plegaria*: "*Rema, que si no rema no va a viajar*" (Row, cause if you don't row you won't travel). After he had introduced this line, the full band entered again at a brisk tempo (over a I-I-V-I vamp in the same key, G) as the crowd repeated it. In alternation with the new chorus, the lead singer began to alter his lead lines, introducing new phrases that rhymed with the chorus but changed the focus a bit. Some of his improvised phrases focused on traveling and may have been inspired by the fact that Nadia was a US citizen and had flown to Cuba to visit her spiritual advisor (*madrina*) for a few days. Thus, she herself had recently traveled and would soon do so again. The call–response lyrical sequence is transcribed below, with italics denoting the chorus. Many of the improvised lead lines elicited peals of laughter from the dancing crowd, as well as exclamations such as "*¡pa' la Yuma!*" (Let's head to the US!).

Rema, que si no rema no va a viajar   *Row, cause if you don't you won't travel*
Rema, que si no rema te va' a quedar   Row, cause if you don't you'll be left behind
Rema, que si no rema no va a viajar   *Row, cause if you don't you won't travel*
Rema, que si no rema no va a llegar   Row, cause if you don't you'll never get there

The lead singer then introduced a new chorus over a shorter two-measure phrase, "*Rema pa' ahí, rema pa' 'llá* (Row over here, row over there) with a simpler harmony, V-I, and new melody. For the first time he stopped simultaneously playing violin *guajeos*, instead gesturing with his hands and encouraging the crowd to repeat back the new refrain. The gesturing also helped the guitarist catch the sudden harmonic change. Musical accompaniment at this point consisted of bongo, bell (played by the second violinist), and guitar. The lead vocalist soon switched to spoken rather than sung interjections as he jokingly shifted the focus from Yemayá to travel abroad, and by extension to the better material living conditions in the US and elsewhere which inspire many Cubans to emigrate. Later lines even suggested that Cuba itself is being taken on an unknown journey of economic misery and that the singer himself might prefer to leave.

Rema, pa' ahí, pa' allá	Row over here, row over there
Rema, pa' ahí, pa' allá	*Row over here, row over there*
Remen pa'l mar pa' que vayan pa' allá	Row to the ocean so that you get [to the US]
Rema, pa' ahí, pa' allá	*Row over here, row over there*
Mira que la cosa está mala por acá	[spoken] Look, things are bad over here
Rema, pa' ahí, pa' allá	*Row over here, row over there*
Lleven pollo, no vaya a ser que venga a fallar la luz	[spoken] Bring chicken, just in case the power goes out
Rema, pa' ahí, pa' allá	*Row over here, row over there*
¡El azúcar también se perdió, caballero!	[spoken] There's no more sugar either, friend!
Rema pa' ahí, rema pa' allá	*Row over here, row over there*
¿Hasta dónde, dónde nos van a llevar?	[spoken] Where, where is this all taking us?
Rema pa' ahí, rema pa' allá	*Row over here, row over there*
Rema, pa' ahí, pa' allá	[sung] Row over here, row over there
Rema pa' ahí, rema pa' allá	*Row over here, row over there*
Te aconsejo que en avión te vayas pa' allá	I advise you to take a plane over there
Rema pa' ahí, rema pa' allá	*Row over here, row over there*
Oye, que en el día hay mal tiempo allá	[spoken] Hey, in the day there's bad weather there
Rema pa' ahí, rema pa' allá	*Row over here, row over there*
Tremenda tormenta, tormenta en el mar	[spoken] Horrible storm, storm on the ocean
Rema pa' ahí, rema pa' allá	*Row over here, row over there*
Rema, pa' ahí, pa' allá	[sung] Row over here, row over there
Fui a buscar mi pasaporte y todavía no está	[spoken] Went for my passport, it's still not ready
Rema pa' ahí, rema pa' allá	*Row over here, row over there*
Rema, pa' ahí, pa' allá	[sung] Row over here, row over there
Yo que quería viajar en la semana que viene	[spoken] I wanted to travel there next week
Rema pa' ahí, rema pa' allá	*Row over here, row over there*
Me parece que me voy a quedar	[spoken] I think I'll stay [over there]
Rema pa' ahí, rema pa' allá	*Row over here, row over there*
Rema pa' ahí, rema pa' allá	[sung] Row over here, row over there

The "rema" sequence ended shortly thereafter with another full stop by the band at the beginning of the chorus and an improvised vocal line on the syllables "*a-lei-lo-lei-lo lai*" and a drawn-out "Yemayá...," similar in style to a rumba singer's initial *diana* vocal line or the vocals associated with *música jíbara* in Puerto Rico.

Without taking a break, the group's bongo player (Ubaldo) then took over the role of lead vocalist and transitioned the group into a fast groove in 6/8 employing bongo, bell (on clave), the body of the guitar as a third percussion instrument, and Omar playing double stops on open A and D strings (Figure 5.13). First the new lead singer shouted out the line "*Todo lo malo*" (Everything bad) and the crowd immediately replied "*Pa' 'llá*" (Away from us). The lead singer continued with a long list of things that he wished participants to be rid of – including ugliness, sadness, evil, pain, and war – to which the chorus responded with repetitions of "*Pa' 'llá.*" The lead singer eventually made the crowd laugh by yelling out "claustrophobia," implying that participants might be getting tired of being in such close quarters with one another. Next, he switched to discussing good things instead of bad. This required everyone singing the chorus to be listening closely to him and to switch their response to "*Pa' 'cá*" (Over here) instead of "*Pa' 'llá*" from one moment to the next. Some didn't make the transition in a timely way, leading to considerable laughter once more. The "good things" mentioned in lead vocal lines included some that might be expected, such as health, money, and a home to live in, but others were tied to the previous theme of travel (including passports and visas) which got the group laughing yet again. Nadia's *violín* concluded with a performance of "Damisela encantadora," a prayer and *brindis* to Ochún and Yemayá, and a few final songs dedicated to those two *orishas* as well as Changó, los Ibeyí, and Elegguá.

FIGURE 5.13 A segment of music accompanying the "Todo lo malo" antiphonal segment in 6/8 following the *oru* to Yemayá. The vocals, *claves*, and violin depicted here are accompanied by bongo hits and slaps on the body of a guitar.

A SEQUENCE OF CHORUSES TO THE SPIRIT WORLD AND BABALÚ

While Nadia's *violín* helps underscore the centrality of spontaneous, improvised performance dynamics as a central element of *violines*, segments of Ileana's celebration from 2018 demonstrate the ways that intertextuality and aggressive musical borrowing from popular repertoire can serve the same purpose. The *violín* ensemble in her event consisted of electric keyboard, violin, bongo, and a lead singer playing hand percussion (Figure 2.3). The group began their devotion with the Chucho Valdés composition "Danza ñáñiga," described earlier, a spoken Padrenuestro prayer, and later praise songs dedicated primarily to African spirits. As the performance progressed, musicians included songs to figures such as San Miguel and the occasional instrumental bolero such as "Te quedarás" (You'll Stay With Me) by Alberto Barreto. Next came an extended sequence to *gitana* spirits organized largely around call–response singing that ended with the song "Sun sun babaé," then a return to praise of African spirit guides such as Ma Francisca. Movement between short religious songs and popular refrains began at this time as the lead singer first introduced Spiritist repertoire such as "Congo de Guinea soy" (Figure 3.13), then the chorus of a Daniel Santos recording with the Sonora Matancera from 1950, "¿Dónde va José?"[14] The singer apparently chose the Santos piece because the name "José" appears prominently in the song's refrain and segued nicely to the next traditional chant to an African spirit guide they performed, "Aguaragua José." The full lyrics of the Sonora Matancera piece discuss an individual named José walking to the foot of a mountain to pray about various things troubling his mind (including losing his faith!) and thus they relate in a general sense to the topic of devotion.

The climax of Ileana's *violín* consisted of a series of songs first for Babalú, then for Ochún and other *orishas*, the latter consisting primarily of borrowings from popular music. In paying homage to Babalú, the lead singer began with a slow, out-of-time version of Margarita Lecuona's composition of the same name, then a long improvised segment based on the chorus of the same piece (Figure 4.4). Most of the improvised lead lines focused on issues of spiritual cleansing and health ("*limpiamos la casa/limpiamos todo lo malo, Babalú Ayé*" [cleanse the house/clean away everything bad, Babalú Ayé]), perhaps chosen because one of the

---

[14] The Santos song can be heard on YouTube: www.YouTube.com/watch?v=e_9y5tb5l64 (accessed August 11, 2023); the chorus starts at 0:35.

individuals in attendance had mentioned struggling with an illness. Next, the violinist took an open solo over the same ii-V-I-I changes and ended it by leading in the alternate *"Voy al Rincón"* chorus for Babalú mentioned in Chapter 4. This continued for about a minute, then the group reprised the main verse of "Babalú" at a slower tempo to conclude. After a pause, the lead singer spoke about the importance of praising Babalú, describing him as a strong presence in African religions, but also in the land of the dead. She sang a series of traditional Lucumí pieces dedicated to him ("Baba e, baba soroso," "Towe towe," "Tanakana soku tó," etc.),[15] accompanied only by percussion, before segueing to popular repertoire.

Prefacing the final *oru* (interestingly, she described it as a *cuadro*, likening the music to a spiritual quadrant), the lead singer noted that she would dedicate it primarily to Cachita/Ochún, *"para que terminen de ripiar"* (so that those in attendance would end the celebration dancing like crazy), and that it would conclude the ceremony. She called for spiritual unity and peace. Musicians in the group clearly viewed the song sequence they then initiated as a climax. They began with a rendition of Rafael Hernández's "Cachita," and after about seventy-five seconds switched to the frequently heard chorus *"Cachita está alborotá, ahora baila el chachachá"* (discussed in Chapter 4) over a ii-V-I-vi progression in C. About thirty-five seconds later, the ensemble switched to the chorus of "Vuela la paloma" by Félix Reyna.[16] Its lyrics consist of this phrase: *"Vuela la paloma a su palomar y vuela que vuela para no tornar"* (The dove flies to its nest, it flies and flies, never to return; see Figure 5.14). The *"vuela"* chorus was twice as long but used essentially the same progression as the earlier Cachita vamp, so transitioning to it was simple in a musical sense. Most listeners associate white doves with Obatalá rather than La Caridad, however (see, for instance, the lyrics of the Plegaria a Obatalá discussed in Chapter 4), so introducing this refrain suggested that many *orishas* and spirits would be referenced in the segment, not only Cachita. Listeners may also have understood the song more literally, given that in its original version a male singer called for a woman he cared about (represented by a dove) to return to him.[17]

---

[15] See Altmann (1998, 77, 80, and 84) for transcriptions. In her verbal preamble, the singer stated she would be singing in Arará, a language derived from the Dahomey region of Africa, yet most of these chants were clearly in Lucumí.

[16] "Vuela la paloma" was popularized in the United States by Tito Rodríguez; his version can be listened to here: www.YouTube.com/watch?v=5RFPLOZCxro (accessed September 11, 2023).

[17] The lyrics of "Vuela la paloma" are available here: www.musixmatch.com/es/letras/Tito-Rodriguez/Vuela-la-paloma (accessed September 12, 2023).

FIGURE 5.14 Sample chorus and lead line of "Vuela la paloma," a song by Félix Reyna. Italics indicate the chorus.

Typically, members of the ensemble improvised on each chorus in this final segment for a minute or less before introducing a new musical idea.

After about forty-five more seconds, the lead singer transitioned to a phrase taken from the song "Quimbombó con salsa" by Narciso Valdés Iglesias.[18] The lyrics of the refrain are "*Salsa, salsita, como me gusta el quimbombó con salsa*" (Sauce, sauce, how I love okra in [red] sauce). Musically, this transition also worked smoothly because the accompanying chords were nearly identical to those in the previous chorus. Lyrically, however, the "Salsa, salsita" chorus created new questions about religious interpretation. It could be read as simply celebrating salsa dance music, since countless songs use food as a metaphor for tasty music making and sensuality. Alternately, the chorus could be read as a reference to Changó, given that okra is one of that *orisha*'s sacred foods. However the audience members understood "Salsa, salsita," my impression overall was that the choruses chosen by this *violín* ensemble moved farther and farther from direct associations with religious themes as the potpourri progressed. The bongo player (Rafael), who also sang, played a key role in supporting the lead singer by cueing audience members at

---

[18] The earliest known recording of "Quimbombó con salsa" is by Francisco Fellove and *tresero*-arranger Niño Rivera, who released it in 1979 on the LP *Fellove*, (Areito LP-3803). Many thanks to Verónica González at Florida International University's Green Library for help tracking down this information. Alfredo Rodríguez, Patato, and Totico recorded a popular version of the piece in the United States on their *Sonido Sólido* LP a few years later (1983).

appropriate moments as the next chorus began, helping them respond appropriately to each new antiphonal melody.

Next, the musicians (lead by the bongo player) segued to the refrain *"Estaba la langosta en su salsa y no me la comí porque estaba muy salá"* (The lobster was sitting in its sauce, but I didn't eat it because it was too salty), also in a major key but with a slightly different harmony (I-ii-V-I). Initially, band members played the full chorus, then cut it in half to add excitement (see Figure 5.15). The refrain has many possible readings. If one wanted to link the phrase to *orisha* worship, the mention of lobsters could associate it with the ocean and, by extension, with Yemayá.[19] However, the meanings of the chorus in everyday parlance are varied; perhaps this very ambivalence made it attractive to listeners. Sánchez-Boudy's *Diccionario mayor de cubanismos* (1999, 391), for instance, defines *"langosta"* as slang for "ass": this includes examples such as *"Esa mujer tiene una langosta muy bonita … Esa mujer está como la langosta"* (That woman has a great 'lobster' … That woman is [tasty] like a lobster), among others.[20] And *estar salao* typically means to have bad

FIGURE 5.15 "Estaba la langosta" chorus as performed in Ileana's *violín*, in full and shorter versions.

---

[19] Diana Espírito Santo, personal email, March 2, 2021.
[20] My thanks to Cristóbal Díaz Ayala for this insight (personal email, March 4, 2021), and to Agustín González García (personal email, March 3, 2021) for weighing in on the interpretation of the chorus.

luck or to experience something unpleasant. Thus, the phrase could be interpreted as meaning that someone (presumably a man) was tempted by a woman's lovely body but decided not to pursue her because of her disagreeable temperament or a similar factor. Rafael Lam has written about the history of this chorus, tracing its origins to carnival celebrations in the 1940s associated with *charanga* bands from the town of Bejucal who process through the street during the Christmas season. Since then, many artists have incorporated the chorus into commercial music making, beginning with the vocal ensembles Las D'Aida and Los Zafiros in the 1960s. The dance band NG La Banda continued the same trend, for instance in their 1994 song "Échale limón."[21] In that recording it appears toward the end as part of a sequence of new choral and instrumental interludes, much like the improvised music making described in this *violín*, and the meanings of the lyrics in that context are just as open to interpretation.

Following a few repetitions of full and shorter versions of the "lobster" chorus, the lead singer guided the group to additional refrains: First she sang "*María Luisa, no seas mala, llévame contigo pa' la playa*" (Maria Luisa, don't be cruel, take me with you to the beach). The transition to this melody took the keyboardist and violinist by surprise for a moment, since the harmony required for the new eight-measure vamp was slightly different, but they soon caught on. The chorus has been used by various performers for years and may derive from carnival music, as was the case with the *langosta* melody; in 2016 it also featured in a pop song entitled "Mi María Luisa" by the Puerto Rican band La Tribu de Abrante.[22] "María Luisa" thus represented a piece that listeners might have heard on the radio or in other contexts. It could be read as extending discussion of ocean themes and thus aligning with the overall focus on Yemayá in the service, the principal *orisha* of the organizer's spirit guide in life (see Chapter 3). Or, it could simply be understood as a fun-loving dance piece.

With the next chorus, the singer stood up, raised her arms, and sang "*Manos pa' arriba los que están, manos pa' arriba las pepillas/ Quien no baila con Okán Oñí, por lo menos se aflojan las rodillas*" (Hands up everyone here, hands up young fashionable folks. Anyone who won't dance with Okán Oñí [and here she gestured toward the band members]

---

[21] The song can be heard here: www.YouTube.com/watch?v=CMj7WIHa2VQ (accessed September 12, 2023); the "langosta" chorus begins at about 5:52.

[22] The Tribu version of the song and its music video can be seen here: www.YouTube.com/watch?v=27IKARwJGfE (accessed September 12, 2023).

will at least loosen up their knees). The "*Manos pa' 'rriba*" chorus represents an adaptation of one first sung by the rumba ensemble Yoruba Andabo; it can be heard on their 2016 release "Rumba con amor,"[23] again demonstrating how *violín* musicians often incorporate very recent works into their repertoire, as well as traditional songs. The singer here merely substituted the name of her own ensemble (Okán Oñí, meaning "heart of honey" in Lucumí) for the original name Yoruba Andabo. Slightly over a minute later, she paused the group and then led in a new chorus at a slower tempo and with a distinct four-measure harmonic accompaniment (I-IV-V-V): "*Mira como te maté*" (Literally, "look at how I killed you," but in this context meaning "see how I knocked you out/outdid you/bested you," which might be understood as making reference to the strength of the spirit forces being honored in the performance, or to the strength of the music making). This chorus too comes from Yoruba Andabo; it appeared on at least two of their releases: "Ponte pa lo tuyo" (Do Your Thing) on the 2014 album *Rumba cubana dale cuero*, and "La gozadera" (The Good Time) from the 2015 release *El espíritu de la rumba*.[24] Just like *violín* performers, the members of Yoruba Andabo incorporate multiple choruses into their compositions, and in performance sometimes freely integrate choruses originally associated with one piece into another. This same aesthetic of spontaneity clearly permeates *violines*.

The Okán Oñí ensemble ended their musical montage with a final chorus: "*O o o, cantaré una rumba para egun, oñí abbé*" (Oh, oh, oh, I will sing a rumba for spirit guides, honey fan) over a I-IV-V-I vamp. After a short time, the singer cut the chorus in half, singing only "*Una rumba para egun*," to which the chorus responded "*Oñí abbé*." It was a typical ending piece for the ensemble; on another occasion when performing in a *violín de santo*, the group changed the final phrase to "*una rumba Yemayá, oñí abbé*" and/or "*una rumba pa' Yalodde, oñí abbé*" in

---

[23] Thanks to Yunior Terry (personal email, Februry 23, 2022) and Maya Berry (personal emails, September 12–13, 2023) for help tracking down the origins of the chorus. The lyrics of the original version are as follows: "*Manos pa' arriba los que están, manos pa' arriba las pepillas/ Quien no baila con Yoruba Andabo, por lo menos se le aflojan las rodillas.*" The "Rumba con amor" track can be heard here: www.YouTube.com/watch?v=JZaqsSaQemw (accessed September 13, 2023); the chorus first enters about 2:55.

[24] The "*Mira como te maté*" chorus can be heard on YouTube beginning at 5:30 in the song "Pónte pa' lo tuyo"; see www.youtube.com/watch?v=9d8GptLXML4&list=RD9d8Gpt LXML4&start_radio=1 (accessed February 27, 2025) ; in "La gozadera" the same chorus enters at 5:25: www.YouTube.com/watch?v=jr9ysreMvqo (accessed September 13, 2023).

alternation. As the group ended, the lead singer commented on the final lyrics by saying "*Oñí* is honey. *Abbé* is a shortened version of *abebé*, or fan. [It suggests] that with the honey that sweetens our lives and a fan we must always fan and sweeten ourselves in the presence of the *egun*."[25] Next came a toast to Ileana's spirit guide, a few spoken prayers, the singing of "Se van los seres" (The Spirit Beings are Leaving) and the spreading of perfume on the back of the neck of those present before they departed.

CONCLUSION

The preceding chapters discuss common structures and standard repertoires in *violín* devotion, but this chapter emphasizes the importance of spontaneity and musical/verbal play to a successful devotional event. Performers' choices made on the spur of the moment add a great deal to the dynamics of the show and the degree of engagement of those attending. Singers make unexpected lyrical substitutions, switch to entirely new choruses, and cue changes to the harmonies musicians must play, the tempo and meter of a piece, or the instrumentation of the ensemble; they suggest breaks or transitions between sung segments, cue instrumental solos or background fills, segue quickly between musical repertoires, etcetera. This emphasis on spontaneity parallels the dynamics found in many other ritual events – for instance, decisions made by an *akpwon* at a *tambor* about which ritual melody to sing next, how to improvise vocal lines in response to the chorus, how and when drummers choose to make rhythmic shifts to accompany new ritual chants, or how they vary their individual parts in dialogue with other percussionists and with singers. But in certain respects the range of options available to *violín* musicians is even greater than that of percussion-only groups: because the types of music considered appropriate in a *violín* are significantly expanded, because the use (or temporary suspension) of harmony provides additional sonic possibilities, and because singers freely switch between Spanish, Lucumí, and other languages as well as incorporating instrumental repertoire. All of this takes place in a context that draws more or less equally from elements of religious music and popular dance music, with some influences from folkloric genres as well.

[25] "Oñí es miel. Abbé es un diminutivo de abebé que quiere decir abanico. Lo que quiere decir, que con la miel que nos endulza y el abanico, siempre tenemos que abanicarnos y endulzarnos juntos a egun."

The case studies examined here demonstrate the extreme elasticity of *violines* relative to many other performative modalities and the role of the lead singer in navigating its musical changes and transitions. One moment a *violín* can sound essentially like a *cajón*, employing percussion patterns reminiscent of *rumba guaguancó* or related genres to accompany vocals. The performance might then switch to a dance music groove with violin fills, or to a 6/8 rhythmic base reminiscent of the *batá*'s *ñongo* rhythm, or foreground a bolero or concert repertoire. *Violines* can be shaped to satisfy the expectations of those with profound knowledge of traditional Lucumí, Spiritist, or other religions, or it can cater to those with virtually no ritual knowledge. The lead singer guides every aspect of the set, evaluating audience reactions and, largely on that basis, deciding when to introduce new material, when to lead transitions, when to be jokey, when to extend or end a sequence, and so on. Much like US blues artists, lead singers in a *violín* develop a unique repertoire of stock choruses and lead vocal phrases in various idioms that they adapt to any given sequence.

The bewildering musical and lyrical intertextuality of *violines* never ceases to amaze me, and I hope I have been able to convey some sense of that aesthetic here. The constant movement between popular music and religious music in performance exemplifies this, as do frequent musical citations of songs in folkloric idioms by Yoruba Andabo or the *charangas* of Bejucal. While based largely in Spanish-language texts and rhythms derived from the *son*, *violines* gesture outwards to encompass virtually every other musical style Cubans listen to. It is noteworthy that many recordings of recent years demonstrate similar intertextual tendencies; dance band tunes by NG La Banda, Los Van Van, and Havana D'Primera often fuse *son*, Ocha melodies, jazz influences, carnival melodies, and rumba in their compositions.[26] Perhaps all of this speaks to a desire to fuse multiple aspects of lived experience in new ways, to no longer separate the religious and the secular, or the traditional and the contemporary.

The lyrics employed in *violín* songs/choruses have meanings that lend themselves to diverse interpretation, whether in Spanish or in other languages. Such choruses may discuss over-salted lobster tails, hearts of honey, okra in red sauce, trips with María Luisa to the beach, or any number of

---

[26] Havana D'Primera's "El paso de la bailarina," for instance, quotes the carnival piece "Uno, dos, y tres" and the famous rumba chorus "*El yambú no se vacuna*," as well as the *langosta* chorus discussed earlier in this chapter. See www.YouTube.com/watch?v=9R r1zgn9NRE (accessed September 13, 20203). *Timba* repertoire has long been described as a sort of "inter-genre" that moves between stylistic boundaries by critics; see Moore (2006, 125ff.).

other topics. These coded phrases mirror the similarly oblique meanings associated with more traditional praise songs. Even if the literal meaning of Lucumí chants for the *orishas* are understood by devotees (which is frequently not the case), for instance, translating them fully requires substantial knowledge of the deities' various incarnations on earth, the stories of their lives, and their individual characteristics. Akiwowo and Font-Navarrete (2015, 45) have discussed the issue, writing that:

> The texts of Yorùbá and Lucumí sacred music are often obscure in meaning, and knowledge of the textual and esoteric content of ritual music is highly regarded among devotees. Drummers and singers, like other ritual specialists, are reservoirs and mediators of Yorùbá *ijinlè*, or "deep Yorùbá." While individual devotees may have very limited knowledge of specialized, ritual language, it is understood that òrìsà respond to the "mystical potency" of words and music ... especially if they flow from musicians' command of literal and symbolic meanings. (Akiwowo and Font-Navarrete 2015, 45)

It appears that the appeal of "deep meanings" within African-derived ritual language of this sort has permeated *violín* performance as well, even if the lyrics employed are in Spanish and taken from popular culture. Other forms of Cuban popular music adopt coded texts of this sort that require insider knowledge to be understood, most often of Black religious heritage (e.g. Moore 1997, 76–7; Miller 2009, 150–69). The meanings of some *violín* lyrics are not intended to be overtly religious, but most sit at the boundary of religious expression or allude to it obliquely in some way.

I continue to reflect on the fact that long sequences of choruses in Spanish, often taken from popular music, feature prominently in many final climactic musical moments within *violines*, and I wonder what this means. Is popular music foregrounded at such times because it is considered the most enjoyable for participants, the pieces they can identify with most easily or that will likely get them up and dancing? Do musicians emphasize less overtly religious music when concluding *violines* because they want to emphasize the lighter, "festive" aspect of their performance at that time rather than contemplative devotion? Is collective singing and movement so important that the specific lyrics of a show don't matter? Do musicians downplay ritualistic elements in order to distinguish *violines* from other events that intend to summon the presence of an *orisha*? Whatever the case, the final musical sequences which one would expect to be the most overtly sacred tend to be at least as secular as earlier repertoire, if not more so. These moments challenge orthodox conceptions of devotion and lead participants into a space of ambivalence, metaphor, and experimentation.

6

Violines Abroad

INTRODUCTION

Violines as a relatively unorthodox form of devotion have been performed abroad in many ways, underscoring the extent to which they frequently serve as a space of experimentation and innovation. Some practitioners faithfully replicate approaches to worship that developed in Cuba; this is especially true of ex-pat performers raised and trained on the island. Others emphasize the sacred nature of *violín* performance more than in Cuba, preferring rites that incorporate primarily sacred Lucumí melodies and in which the audience sits in silence and observes the musical offering. Their approach might be viewed as linking *violines* with older forms of praise (such as *batá* drumming) in that they use instrumental repertoire to salute all major *orisha* in a prescribed order. Many musicians abroad advocating for the exclusive use of Lucumí melodies are *santeros* or *babalawos* with deep ritual knowledge that they foreground through performance, even as they perform for diverse audiences who may not be familiar with all the musical or ritual elements they incorporate. Still others accentuate the secular aspects of such *violines* further, for instance by incorporating new forms of popular music and/or prerecorded backtracks that emulate the sound of Caribbean dance genres including merengue and soca. Using case studies primarily from the United States, Venezuela, and Mexico, this chapter documents the spread of *violín* performance far beyond Cuba and the ways it continues to develop in new contexts.

CUBAN MIGRATION

One of the primary ways Cuban religions have spread throughout the Americas and beyond is through emigration from the island, a trend that has peaked at moments of political and economic upheaval. Migration to Mexico and the United States began in the 1860s during Cuba's Wars of Independence against Spain, for instance. The revolution of 1959 represented another even more intense period of departures: about 1.4 million Cubans left the island in the wake of Fidel Castro's victory (Duany 2017), settling primarily on the east coast of the United States but also in Los Angeles, Chicago, and other urban centers, in addition to Puerto Rico and elsewhere. The Mariel boatlifts of the early 1980s represented a significant migratory wave, as did the *balsero* or rafter crisis of the 1990s. Between the mid-1990s and 2015, an additional 650,000 Cubans left the island, largely for economic reasons. They continued to relocate to the United States (especially Florida), but nearly half now choose to live in Spain, Venezuela, Mexico and other countries (Duany 2017).

Closer Cuban political ties to Venezuela during the years of Hugo Chávez's presidency (1999–2013) led to cultural and economic exchanges there, and to an expanded Cuban presence in the country overall. These years coincided with ongoing economic difficulties in Cuba that made extended stays in Venezuela an attractive option. Thousands of Cuban doctors, nurses, and paramedics relocated there as part of agreements involving payments of foreign currency to the Cuban government and regular shipments of petroleum to the island at reduced prices. An unknown number of military personnel and advisors from Cuba also visited Venezuela for extended periods (as many as 25,000 by some estimates; see Fonseca et al. 2020, 11), and frequent artistic exchanges. The latter began in the 1970s and 1980s with visits to Havana by musicians such as Ali Primera and Oscar D'León, but continued even more frequently under Chávez.[1] For their part, Venezuelans also traveled to Cuba, including Afro-Venezuelan activists associated with the Frente Francisco de Miranda, an organization created jointly by Castro and Chávez in 2003 to further leftist political efforts internationally.[2]

---

[1] See www.cubaheadlines.com/2008/12/15/14879/cuban_artists_return_venezuela.html and https://venezuelanalysis.com/news/6466/ (accessed October 10, 2023) as example from 2008 and 2011; such exchanges have continued under Nicolás Maduro.

[2] See, for instance, www.minec.gob.ve/frente-francisco-de-miranda-fue-creado-hace-20-anos/ (accessed October 10, 2023).

The Cuban migrant presence in Mexico has not seen the same dramatic surges evident in Venezuela and the United States, but Mexico's longstanding friendly ties with Cuba have led to both the frequent exchange of artists and the steady migration of Cubans to Mexico through the years. Areas of Mexico with a significant Cuban presence now include Mexico City, Puebla, the Yucatan, and the state and city of Veracruz. Cuban musical genres including the *habanera*, *danzón*, mambo, chachachá and *nueva trova* all acquired large audiences in Mexico over a span of many decades, leading Cuban musicians to visit or relocate there. Little detailed information exists on early Cuban migration to Mexico, but officials began to study the phenomenon in the 1990s as numbers increased. García Pérez (2012, 144–5) determined that the official number of Cuban immigrants arriving in Mexico increased from about 3,000 annually in the early 1990s to about 6,600 a year by 2000; the total number of official Cuban residents is now estimated to be about 22,000,[3] and many more have been granted Mexican citizenship. This of course excludes the countless undocumented migrants who cross into the country or who come on short-term visas and decide to stay. Illegal immigration has surged over the past two decades as Cubans use Mexico as the principal route by which they arrive at the US border.

VIOLINES IN NORTH AMERICA

A recent interview with violinist, bassist, and educator Yunior Terry Cabrera[4] (Figure 6.1) provides some insight into *violín* performance in the New York City area that perpetuates many traditions established in Cuba. Terry emphasizes that Ocha devotion there is dominated by Newyoricans (people of Puerto Rican descent living in New York) who constitute his primary clientele. Some travel to Cuba to become initiated, others do so locally. Terry often performs by himself rather than in a group, largely for economic reasons. Each performer contracted must be paid between $200 and $300, thus requesting a trio or quartet can exceed the budget of many organizers. On occasion Terry performs alongside percussionists (either two *cajones* or *cajón* and *tumbadora*, thus fusing the *violín* and *cajón de muerto* formats), in which case he

---

[3] www.eluniversal.com.mx/articulo/periodismo-de-investigacion/2017/05/15/cubanos-en-mexico-los-que-no-llegan-eu/ (accessed October 10, 2023).
[4] Yunior Terry is a professional musician but also teaches at NYU: https://as.nyu.edu/faculty/yunior-terry.html (accessed February 24, 2025).

FIGURE 6.1 Yunior Terry (left), performing in 2014 in an event organized by Octavio "El Papa" Sotolongo (top right) and his cousin (lower right). Photo by Juan Caballero.

will do more singing; when performing alone he plays only instrumental music. Interestingly, Terry notes that Puerto Rico itself does not have much of a *violín* performance scene,[5] but that Puerto Rican immigrants in New York have embraced the practice, influenced by their Cuban neighbors.

Terry learned to play *violín* repertoire in the Camagüey area from his father (Eladio Terry, himself a prominent performer in the *charanga* Maravillas de Florida) and other relatives. He participated in devotional events in Camagüey in the late 1980s and early 1990s before moving to Havana to pursue advanced studies of music at the National School of the Arts (ENA). He continued playing *violines* in the capital, including one prominent performance with the Orquesta Estrellas Cubanas, and later after moving to New York in 2002.

---

[5] Johnny Frías (personal email, October 24, 2023) agrees, though he did witness one *violín* in Puerto Rico while living there in about 2005. The event consisted of 8–12 classically trained performers who played primarily concert repertoire and Puerto Rican *danzas*.

Terry performs primarily *violines de santo* (overwhelmingly dedicated to Ochún) in a format roughly similar to the events described in Chapter 4. However, he tends to play for more extended periods, usually two to two-and-a-half hours in total, including a few short breaks, and he divides his performances into independent sections of sacred and secular repertoire. He begins with pieces like "Ave María" and the "Padrenuestro," followed by "Sea el Santísimo" and other Spiritist songs. The latter to him underscore the importance of spirit guides and *egun* to all Ocha devotion. Terry continues with music dedicated to several of the most widely recognized *orishas*: Elegguá, Ogún, Ochosi, Changó, Obatalá, Oyá, Yemayá, and Ochún. He usually begins sequences to each of them by playing instrumental *plegarias*, or more often slower, nonmetrical praise *rezos* such as "Barasuayo" for Elegguá or "Iyá mi ilé odo" for Ochún. Then he continues with instrumental versions of traditional ritual melodies to each, or other songs associated with them. The overall structure of Terry's devotional music thus mirrors current practice in Cuba. The primary difference in his set as opposed to those discussed in Chapter 4 is its solo violin format, its emphasis on sacred Lucumí melodies as the basis of devotion rather than popular songs or Spanish-language pieces, and the fact that he does not transform or stylize sacred songs in the way that many musicians in Havana do. He feels that the violin creates a contemplative and worshipful ambience that lends itself well to the interpretation of sacred chants in their traditional form. Terry's approach is similar to that of Lisbet Soto (discussed later in the chapter), yet he incorporates more instrumental *plegarias* and plays longer sequences to each *orisha*.

Following musical salutes to the aforementioned deities that last well over an hour, Terry transitions to what he describes as an open section featuring popular music, and (as opposed to the initial devotional section) he takes requests from the audience for songs they'd like to hear. This part of the *violín* includes internationally recognized boleros, tangos, *danzones*, and concert repertoire by Bach and others if desired. It inevitably incorporates Puerto Rican melodies as well: everything from "Cachita" and "Madrigal" (discussed previously) to "Obsesión" by Pedro Flores, "En mi viejo San Juan" by Noel Estrada, and "Verde luz" by Antonio Cabán Vale. Terry initially wasn't familiar with such music and had to learn to play it as part of his adaptation to the New York scene. Following this freer segment, Terry closes his *violines* with a final sequence dedicated to Elegguá. All melodies are performed acoustically on solo violin; he never uses recorded backtracks.

Virtually anywhere one finds enclaves of Cuban ex-pats, they will post excerpts of *violines* on social media, including Canada. Canadian immigration policies have long been tolerant of Cubans; artists frequently visit Canada for that reason, and many have chosen to relocate there. The population of Cuban exiles in the country now is estimated at roughly 30,000.[6] One *santera* using the name "Okán de Niye" (which she translates as "Heart of a Mother"), for instance, has a YouTube channel featuring various forms of *orisha* devotion, including *violines*.[7] In some videos she recites prayers to Ochún in Spanish accompanied by instrumental renditions of "Love Story" by Francis Lai and Carl Sigman. Her most extended post is of a forty-minute *violín* in which the musicians include a Cuban violinist and an Ecuadorian guitarist and singer. They lead off with "El mariachi loco," a cumbia by Román Palomar Arreola, followed by the *cueca* "Cuando pa' Chile me voy" by Carlos Ocampo and Osvaldo Rocha, an adaptation of Venezuelan Simón Díaz's "Caballo viejo," the Mexican bolero "Flor sin retoño" (Flower with No Sprout) by Alberto Cervantes, the Italian hit "Volare," and others. All pieces featured in this performance are popular rather than devotional, though the performers do play in front of a ritual altar.

The Cuban-American enclave in Miami is by far the largest in the United States, as mentioned, and demographically the whitest, yet Afro-Cuban religions have flourished there. Approximately 1.7 million residents of Cuban descent live in Florida now (primarily in Miami-Dade county), with an additional 600,000 spread among other states. Of those who settled in Miami immediately after 1959, only 7 percent identified as Black (Cano Miranda 2016, 168; Duany 2017). Local census data indicates that even as of 2019 more than 75 percent of the Miami-Dade population still identifies as white; the non-white population includes African-Americans, Haitians, and other immigrant enclaves, suggesting that the number of Black Cubans is still small.[8] Palmié (1986, 186) describes the Miami religious scene as involving a "massive diffusion of Afro-Cuban religion" among primarily white Cuban immigrants, and increasingly among (Black and white) non-Cubans as well. This assessment is largely borne out by video footage of *violines* from the area and

---

[6] https://bit.ly/3ELjVjs (accessed February 24, 2025).
[7] www.YouTube.com/channel/UCm8XBLzr4JKrj849LNGMgSw (accessed October 11, 2023).
[8] Dr. Veronica Díaz, sociologist at FIU, personal email, October 3, 2023. https://case.fiu.edu/about/directory/profiles/diaz-veronica.html.

performers who advertise online. Still, migration to Miami has involved multiple waves of Cubans who arrived at different moments; the racial composition of each group is distinct, and each has a unique relationship to present-day religious practices on the island.

Despite having many Cuban friends and academic contacts in Miami, I found it difficult to interview *violín* performers there at length. Some suggested they were willing to talk but kept deferring interviews. Others returned a few phone messages or texts and then stopped, perhaps because of their busy performance schedules and personal lives. As a result, my overview in this chapter is based in part on a brief interview with Abraham Rivero; conversations with local residents such as percussionist and ethnomusicologist Johnny Frías, who has witnessed and filmed *violines* there; and on the many posts of such music making that are available on social media. Thankfully, Miami performers have an ample online presence, so a great deal of that material is available. Cultural anthropologist Corinna J. Moebius describes the Santería community in Miami as "very private" as a rule.[9] *Santeros* there may be wary of the intentions of outsiders due to previous experiences with betrayed trust, or because of the ways the religion has been depicted negatively in the local media.[10]

In general, Miami *violinistas* lean into technology and showy displays. Their video posts include performers in eye-catching outfits, in idyllic venues, sporting custom-made violins with embedded neon lights whose color can be changed in accordance with the *orisha* being honored, and so on. They engage with technology in other ways as well; performers often accompany themselves with prerecorded backtracks that feature elaborate percussive and harmonic orchestration. They use cordless mics to amplify their violins and headpieces with mics attached to project their voices. They have created dedicated YouTube channels, personal Instagram accounts, and Spotify playlists. Most of the videos they upload are sophisticated products that integrate footage from multiple cameras, artsy angles, fades between cuts, and still photos. Their musical recordings online may incorporate reverb and related sound manipulation. In all these ways, devotional performance in Miami is quite distinct from Havana's largely acoustic *violín* celebrations.[11] Aesthetically, the Miami

---

[9] Personal email, October 4, 2023. She is an expert on Little Havana and Miami history; see www.corinnajmoebius.com/.

[10] As one example, see www.nytimes.com/1987/06/29/us/religion-from-cuba-stirs-row-in-miami.html (accessed October 13, 2023).

[11] As an aside, it appears that a limited amount of online advertising of *violín* performance now takes place in Cuba as well; see for instance www.facebook.com/profile.php?

FIGURE 6.2 Tania and Abraham Rivero. Photo courtesy of the performers.

scene strikes the listener as sonically distanced from its origins – perhaps consciously so.

Tania and Abraham Rivero (Figure 6.2) are among the more prominent *violín* performers in Miami, with their own website (www.violinparaoshunmiami.com) and many examples of their music posted online.[12] Both of

---

id=100063684562474&sk=about. Melena Francis Valdés recounted to me that she was recently handed a promotional flyer advertising the services of *violín* performers while traveling in Havana in a *bici-taxi*. Abilio Betancourt Bejerano (WhatsApp communication, April 24, 2024) confirms that many *violín* performers now print business cards and hand them out during performances to potential clients.

[12] #violinestaniayabraham, #miamiviolinist, #violinparaoshun, #laviolinistadeoshun, www.instagram.com/p/CeCk0YhtOTv/. Their YouTube channel: www.YouTube.com/channel/UC983Hf76oWrfrgCH-_JjLiA (accessed October 12, 2023).

them sing and play, Tania on violin and Abraham on both violin and electric keyboard; their services are in high demand. The couple grew up in Havana and studied music formally; their families had strong ties to Spiritist traditions, but not to Santería; neither are *santeros*. They emigrated to Mexico City in the 1990s and played *violines* there, then continued doing so after relocating to Miami in 2003. Tania had more experience with *violines de santo* and initially taught Abraham to perform for such occasions. Since neither has deep knowledge of Lucumí terminology, they do not necessarily know the translation of all repertoire they perform or even the correct pronunciation of various terms, and consult specialists as appropriate, and/or recordings by renowned *akpwon* vocalists such as Lázaro Ros.

While *violines* dedicated to Ochún constitute a majority of the Riveros' professional music making now, they also play *violines* dedicated to Obatalá, Yemayá, and Changó, take part in Spiritist devotion, and perform in other contexts. Their YouTube channel features pieces with religious associations ("Damisela encantadora," the Bach-Gounod "Ave María"), for instance, but also mainstream US pop tunes such as "Hello" by Lionel Ritchie[13] or "Dust in the Wind" by Kansas, with electronically generated accompaniment on bass and drum set. A caption embedded in the "Dust in the Wind" video states that it was filmed at the Biltmore Hotel Miami Coral Gables, and adds "We bring a touch of elegance to your wedding, event or private party."[14]

Abraham Rivero uses Logic Pro software on his computer to create electronic backtracks. Usually he takes samples of *batá* drum recordings and loops them to create a constant ostinato pattern, then adds other instrumental sounds to the mix (such as marimba or electronically generated back-up vocals) to add variety. Abraham knows that sometimes the rhythms he chooses are not what a knowledgeable *batalero* would play against a particular chant, but he tries to choose samples that sound appropriate and that are also upbeat and danceable. Sometimes Abraham also alters traditional melodies so that they fit his arrangement, as discussed later in the chapter. Tania and Abraham endeavor to create a fun and festive atmosphere with their music making, in part to ensure that the performance makes the *orishas* happy rather than sad, as some local clients seem to feel that the sound of the violin is inherently somber. Both performers have great respect

---

[13] https://www.youtube.com/watch?v=p4voCvkNc2M (accessed October 12, 2023).
[14] www.YouTube.com/watch?v=L5hjnfJA-Mc (accessed October 12, 2023).

for the religious aspect of what they do and give thanks to their own spirit guides and to the *orishas* for their professional success.

A short video posted to TikTok and Instagram by Tania and Abraham, entitled "Oshun yeyé moro," provides a good introduction to their sound and style.[15] The piece is interpreted in a fast triple meter with an elaborate backtrack consisting of three-part chorus vocals, a drum set, auxiliary percussion including a *chekeré* or similar instrument, and melodic fills on harp (Figure 6.3). Against this backdrop, Abraham plays synthesizer keyboard and improvises lead vocal phrases while Tania plays simultaneous improvised violin melodies. The result sounds like a large Afropop dance band or a polished studio-produced album rather than a duo, and brings to mind CDs from Cuba of the late 1980s and 1990s such as *Ancestros* by Síntesis (which Abraham mentions as one of his musical influences) and *Cantos* by Mezcla, both similarly featuring Lucumí songs in elaborate arrangements. Abraham's lead vocals mix Spanish and Lucumí phrases. The TikTok post actually includes two chants: the first is an adaptation of the traditional praise song for Ochún "Yeye moro iki";[16] the second appears to be newly composed, perhaps inspired by the traditional melody "Cheke cheke" (Figure 6.8).[17] Tania and Abraham use a shorter, nontraditional version of the "Cheke cheke" chorus as its own responsorial song, with Abraham interjecting lead lines in Lucumí and Spanish such as "*cheke Yalodde*" and "*con su violín.*"[18] The "*cheke cheke*" lyrics reference the jingling of Ochún's bracelets (see Pedroso 2013, 64–5).

Video footage taken of a Miami *violín* by Johnny Frías makes clear that Spiritist repertoire has a prominent place in many Rivero performances too, often interpreted as dance music and played at a brisk tempo. In the performance he documented, prerecorded backtracks have apparently been preprogrammed into a sequence that segues seamlessly from one song to the next. Tania assumes the role of lead vocalist on many numbers and stands next to a sound system so that she can control the entrance and silencing of the backtrack. The duo's repertoire includes a version of "Mamá Francisca" (Figure 3.12) played in brisk 6/8 time, with Abraham

---

[15] www.instagram.com/p/CxG8L5auy1P/ (accessed October 12, 2023).

[16] A traditional version of the "Yeye moro iki" song has been recorded by Abbilona and can be heard on this track, beginning about 2:30, for purposes of comparison: www.YouTube.com/watch?v=vZnkyc57w7I (accessed October 20, 2023).

[17] Listen to this Abbilona recording starting at 1:05 for a traditional version of the song: www.YouTube.com/watch?v=6WlQcGlpGcA (accessed October 20, 2023).

[18] Thanks to Johnny Frías for these insights (personal email, November 30, 2023).

6 Violines *Abroad* 175

FIGURE 6.3 A vocal and harmonic transcription of Tania and Abraham's video "Oshun yeyé moro." Additional elements adding to the elaborate texture including multiple percussion instruments, sustained synthesizer chords, and violin and harp fills.

on keyboard, laying down a syncopated, *montuno*-like pattern in a minor key (with a timbre reminiscent of orchestral bells) to support the vocals and supported by electronic percussion. Thereafter, Tania cues "Corre el agua" (Figure 3.9), perhaps referencing both Yemayá and Palo's Madre de Agua as Abraham changes the chordal accompaniment to a major key over the same rhythm. The two sing vocals in harmony in parallel sixths; occasionally Abraham interjects improvised spoken comments or phrases related to Yemayá (i.e., "Asesú" or "O mio Yemayá") between choral responses to add interest. This dynamic continues during the final piece in the potpourri, "Rema, pero rema mi Yemayá" (Row, row my Yemayá).

A separate video segment from the same event features a song beginning with the phrase "*Todo lo malo, echa pa' llá*" (Everything bad, cast it away), similar to the "*Todo lo malo pa' 'llá*" chorus discussed in Chapter 5 (Figure 5.9). This song alludes to spiritual cleansing, but the musical accompaniment is reminiscent of a Juan Luis Guerra dance tune with its brisk I-IV-V-IV harmonic vamp that imitates rhythmic elements from merengue and soca (especially as Abraham has set the synthesizer to imitate the sound of steel pans). Later song lyrics encourage audience members raise their hands, then lower them, then wave them from side to side.

Tania and Abraham's "Oshun iyesá" video deserves brief mention as well because in addition to instrumental and vocal music it features a hired dancer dressed as Ochún who helps animate the crowd, adding significantly to the event's visual impact.[19] The dancer interacts for a time with the sponsor of the *violín* (a daughter of Ochún), then takes center stage and becomes the focus of attention. My only prior experience with this kind of stylized *orisha* dancing for onlookers is in shows by Cuba's Conjunto Folklórico Nacional and related troupes, but such presentations are not intended to be devotional. The first half of the Tania and Abraham video features a stylized adaptation of the Iyesá chant "Ko ko ko iroko omo iyesá,"[20] performed in a moderate 4/4 tempo and set to harmonies and synthesizer timbres evocative of the 1980s hit "Africa" by Toto. An acoustic version of this same melody can be heard online in recordings by Emilio Barreto.[21] Iyesá repertoire in the context of *orisha* worship represents an adaptation of what were once distinct drumming, song, and worship traditions associated with the Iyesá (or Ìjèsà) people of present-day Nigeria (Delgado 2008); they still persist in a few independent houses of worship. Johnny Frías[22] notes that in Ocha devotion Iyesá segments are typically heard toward the end of the ceremony; the rhythm is considered "lighter" and easily danceable, both because of its 4/4 pulse and because Iyesá rhythms and songs are not intended to bring down the *orishas*. Yet they can be used to accompany sung praises to various deities in addition to Ochún such as Changó, Obatalá, and Yemayá.

Figure 6.4 provides a representative segment of "Ko ko ko iroko omo iyesá" vocals as harmonized and arranged by Tania and Abraham, which can be compared with the traditional Barreto recording referenced earlier. Figure 6.5 transcribes the *batá* rhythm called Borotitilawa (also known as the fourth *vuelta* or rhythmic variant of the *oru seco* for Osain); a computer-generated rhythm inspired by this pattern supports the "Ko ko ko iroko omo iyesá" chant in Tania and Abraham's video. Thus, the rhythm does not imitate Iyesá percussion at all, but instead a distinct duple-meter rhythm for Osain that is similar to it in certain respects.[23] Tania and Abraham's "Oshun Iyesá" video segment ends with Lucumí songs of praise to Ochún from standard Ocha repertoire, also not part of the Iyesá tradition.[24]

[19] www.YouTube.com/watch?v=pOs6he9jKOk (accessed October 12, 2023).
[20] Johnny Frías (personal email, October 19, 2023) notes that "Iroko" refers to the *orisha* that lives in the sacred ceiba tree. "Omo iyesá" refers to Iyesá descendants. The chant in its totality discusses the Iyesá people putting offerings of plantains at the foot of the ceiba tree.
[21] www.YouTube.com/watch?v=Jrms4_nr1RQ (accessed October 12, 2023).
[22] Personal email, October 19, 2023.
[23] Frías, personal email, October 19, 2023.
[24] Frías notes that the various Lucumí songs to Ochún heard later in the video ("Ide were were," "Elade Ochún," "Yan yan Iroko," etc.) derive from distinct parts of the traditional

6 Violines *Abroad*

FIGURE 6.4 The "Ko ko ko iroko omo iyesá" melody, as arranged by Tania and Abraham in their "Oshun iyesá" video.

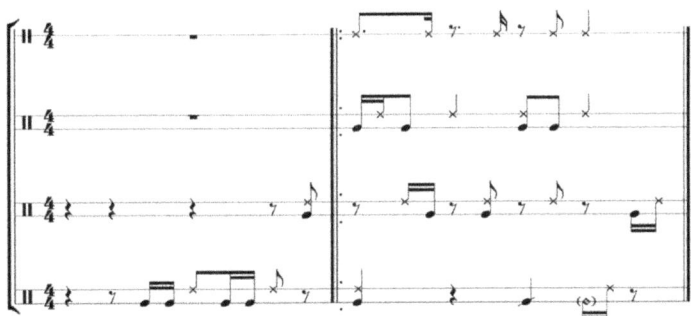

FIGURE 6.5 The praise rhythm to Osain known as Borotitilawa, used as percussive accompaniment to the traditional "Ko ko ko iroko omo iyesá" chant arranged by Tania and Abraham in their "Oshun iyesá" video. The first bar of the transcription represents the initial call and the second the repeating pattern. The top line indicates the implicit clave and lines 2–4 individual drum parts (*okónkolo, itótele, iyá*). "X" notehead indicates slaps on the smaller *chachá* head, and the slashed notehead a muffled note on the *iyá*. Transcription courtesy of Richard Huntley.

oru cantado; most would be accompanied by multiple rhythmic patterns such as *dadá, ibaloke*, and *chachalokafun*, rather than by a single pattern.

Yilian Orama (Figure 6.6) is another prominent performer of *violines* in Miami who has created a YouTube channel,[25] maintains a Spotify playlist,[26] and posts frequently to Instagram.[27] She left Cuba in 2006, where she had already established herself as a *violín* performer, taking up the practice again in Miami as of 2014. Like Tania and Abraham, Orama is both a singer and an instrumentalist, and like them she now creates relatively high-end video uploads, often filmed with multiple cameras. As she is young, she clearly feels at home with digital media, and she openly mentions in posts that she is an initiate and child of Obatalá. Her music incorporates much standard repertoire – instrumental versions of the "Iyá mi ilé odo" chant to Ochún, of "Madrecita del alma querida," famous Cuban boleros such as "La gloria eres tú," etcetera – but also more adventurous material. In a post to YouTube, for instance, she sings two songs to Orula in Lucumí –"Orunmila lade" and "A la iború a la iboya" – alternating vocals with instrumental versions of the same melody on the violin instead of a choral response and accompanying herself with an electronic backtrack that imitates Iyesá percussion.[28] The video is reminiscent of *cajón de muerto* performances discussed in Chapter 2 in the sense that it foregrounds duple-meter rhythms as an accompaniment to sacred vocals. Orama also sings and plays Spiritist repertoire on the violin against *guaguancó* rhythms in other videos.[29] Generally, she alternates in those recordings between instrumental and vocal

---

[25] www.YouTube.com/channel/UCfyN28MTM00rQXtJgZC-mAg. Among her posts are YouTube entire albums of boleros for Ochún: www.YouTube.com/watch?v=YvhGzEhxtSU (accessed October 13, 2023).

[26] https://open.spotify.com/artist/oGVW66MceqDwiNodyzbPrH (accessed October 13, 2023).

[27] www.instagram.com/oshunviolin/ (accessed October 13, 2023).

[28] www.YouTube.com/shorts/ShrS6Sd9yPg (accessed October 13, 2023). The melody is similar to one transcribed in Altmann (1998, 271). A recording of a more traditional version of the piece as performed by Abbilona and accompanied by *batás* is available online for purposes of comparison: https://open.spotify.com/track/1atLWdyy8MGLRjhm295LXj?si=af46654b82be4ded&nd=1 (accessed November 16, 2023). About the lyrics, Johnny Frías (personal email, October 19, 2023) writes:

> The song lyrics allude to Ochún (i.e. called Yeyé moró or Yalodde here) being the *apetebí* (i.e. attendee) of Orula, and by extension [all other] daughters of Ochún ... The final line (A la iború a la iboya, a la iboya ibocheché) [references] how a *santero* greets a *babalawo*; I've heard that Iború, Iboya, and Ibocheché were Orula's three wives (i.e. also *apetebís*).

In all, Frías describes these songs as a general salute or greeting for Orula and all *babalawos*.

[29] www.YouTube.com/watch?v=lriKoFtl2CU (accessed October 13, 2023).

FIGURE 6.6 Yilian Orama, photographed during a *violín* in Miami, 2022. Photo courtesy of the artist.

segments as a means of imitating call–response vocals while performing as a solo artist. The links between *cajón* and *violín* repertoire are perhaps most evident in her video from 2022 entitled "Violín espiritual," in which she collaborates with a percussionist (on *cajón* and congas) and a clave player/singer in an interpretation of two *plegarias* ("Marinero, marinero," Figure 3.8; "A remar," Figure 3.12).[30] In still

---

[30] www.YouTube.com/watch?v=o7ktl6WWmLI (accessed October 13, 2023).

other posts she generates backtracks that recreate the sound of *batá* drums playing the "Borotitilawa" rhythm (Figures 6.5 and 6.11) as accompaniment for instrumental renditions of praise songs to Obatalá such as "Akete oba oba."[31] This combination of violin and *batás* resonates with the acoustic work of Luis Peña and Miguel Amín, discussed later in the chapter. Orama's vocal timbre (like that of Tania and Abraham Rivero) is open and relaxed, a far cry from the nasal and slightly strident sound of a traditional lead vocalist (*akpwon*) singing to the *orishas*.

Perhaps the most interesting recent post by Yilian was of herself and a group of friends singing and dancing along to a remake of Adalberto Álvarez's classic song "Y qué tú quieres que te den?" (And What Do You Want Them to Give You?) The original recording from 1992 generated controversy within Cuba because of its foregrounding of Lucumí chants and other Black religious references.[32] Prior to that time, officials largely prohibited religious themes in dance music, but the Álvarez release became wildly popular and helped usher in more inclusive cultural policies (Moore 2006, 221). The song's success led to countless recordings of music with Afro-Cuban religious themes in later years. In 2015, BIS Music released a new and extended version of the same song, more than eleven minutes long; its accompanying official video features dancers dressed as *orishas*, multiple lead singers, *batá* drummers, a full dance band orchestra, and footage of crowd response to the performance in a large concert setting.[33] The 2015 version incorporates numerous new Lucumí chants to the *orishas*; it functions as a sort of mini-*oru* itself because it salutes so many of them in order. Segments dedicated to Obatalá, for instance, include praise songs such as "Obatalá ta wini wini," as well as phrases in Spanish including "El que tenga algo blanco, ¡que lo saque!" (Those who have something white [Obatalá's sacred color], *pull it out!*) and "Paloma libre me lleva pa' la loma" (The free dove [one of Obatalá's symbols] takes me to the hills). Other *orishas* saluted include Elegguá, Ogún, Changó, Orula, Babalú Ayé, Oyá, and Yemayá, and the recording also references Palo

---

[31] https://YouTube.com/shorts/YeT2i2xuB64?feature=share (accessed October 13, 2023). Thanks to Richard Huntley (personal email, September 25, 2023) for identifying the Borotitilawa/Obanla rhythm in this example, also known as the fourth *vuelta* of Obba in the *oru seco*.

[32] The 1992 recording can be heard here: www.YouTube.com/watch?v=owmwtw43f8s (accessed October 13, 2023).

[33] The song's remake with accompanying video can be viewed here: www.YouTube.com/watch?v=24lHSU35Aqs (accessed October 13, 2023).

religions.[34] The accompanying video is fascinating, with footage of now-deceased Adalberto Álvarez at various stages of life, other iconic Cuban performers such as singer Omara Portuondo and pianist Frank Fernández, virtuosic dancing and drumming, etcetera. The footage creates a fast-paced mash-up of the sacred and the secular, mirroring the varied content of *violines*.

Orama's Instagram post[35] from September 2022 depicts her playing on the violin while the 2015 version of "Y qué tú quieres que te den?" plays through a sound system in the background. She filmed herself for the post during a religious celebration for Obatalá that she had organized. The audience members (approximately twenty in all) consist mostly of women dressed in white who sing along to each new chorus as it is introduced. Yilian clearly knows the recording well; her violin solos enter during recorded verbal interjections by band members, over lead vocal segments, or imitate the melodies of instrumental interludes. She stops playing when she and the audience members sing choruses. At one point she introduces her *padrino* or spiritual godfather and proudly displays footage of an altar constructed in honor of Obatalá. The audience combine salsa-style dance steps with ritual choreographic elements such as pretending to twirl Oyá's ritual *iruke* (whisk) over their heads as her name is mentioned, or brandishing an imagined machete as they sing to Ogún. Yilian's event loses much of the spontaneity associated *violines* in Havana since it involves playing, singing, and dancing along to prerecorded music. In fact, the entire event might be conceived as a form of collective karaoke! But what participants lose in spontaneity they gain in participatory energy, both because everyone can enjoy dancing to a large ensemble and since they are familiar with the recording and can engage with it as a group.

VIOLINES IN VENEZUELA

Violines are now performed in various parts of South America where *orisha* devotion has taken root. This includes Guayaquil, Ecuador, where recent YouTube posts depict a lone performer in front of an altar to Ochún first playing Pachelbel's "Canon" to the accompaniment of a prerecorded orchestral track, and later an instrumental version of

---

[34] The complete lyrics of the new version are also online: www.musixmatch.com/es/letras/Adalberto-Alvarez/Que-Tu-Quieres-Que-Te-Den.
[35] www.instagram.com/p/Ci6A9jTp63m/ (accessed October 13, 2023).

Abba's "Chiquitita."[36] But *violín* performance in Venezuela deserves special mention given how widespread it has become there. This results from various factors, but primarily the relocation of Cuban *santeros* to Venezuela beginning in the 1970s, the gradual spread of Regla de Ocha devotion among the local population, and support for Afro-Latin American religions under the presidency of Hugo Chávez. On early Cuban immigration to Venezuela, Ayoh'Omidire (2014) documents the arrival of many prominent *santeros*, including Domingo Gómez, Evelio Iglesias, Ambiro, Abelardo, and Chiqui Valdez. The religion expanded in the 1990s due to factors including the arrival of yet more Cuban migrants fleeing the economic deprivations of the Special Period,[37] the relative freedom Cubans had to travel to Venezuela at the time, and changes in local government policy. While earlier Venezuelan officials had derided Santería and Spiritism, the Chávez administration described them favorably as creole religions "of the people" (Morán Soto 2015, 199). This legitimized such devotion and brought it into the open for the first time. Local religions fusing belief in Black and Indigenous spirits are widespread in Venezuela and created fertile ground for the adoption of Santería. But local practices do not seem to have fused with Regla de Ocha to date, even if practitioners view Venezuelan and Cuban religions as related to and compatible with one another.

Yanet Trejo and Adolfo León León exemplify the many Venezuelan *violinistas* who advertise their services online (both in Miami and Caracas) and who have adapted the practice significantly, developing a unique performance style. They proudly state that they both worked as members of Oscar D'León's dance band before dedicating themselves to religious music. Trejo, the violinist, performs Lucumí melodies instrumentally – both lead lines and choral responses to them, as appropriate; León León accompanies her using South American goat-toe rattles or the West African djembe drum, as well as ringing brass bells during slower *rezos*. The duo's promotional videos feature *oru* sequences to both Elegguá and Ochún in duple and triple meter;[38] examples include the "Elegguá, Elegguá asokere" chant to Elegguá in 4/4 and (Figure 6.7) and the "Cheke cheke" chant to Ochún in 6/8 (Figure 6.8).

---

[36] See www.YouTube.com/watch?v=iNgrUUXov10 and www.YouTube.com/watch?v=oRAHTJH10pA (accessed October 16, 2023).

[37] Lisbet Soto, in an interview (August 9, 2023), emphasized how much the Ocha religious community has grown in Caracas since the 1990s. She stated "There was a time that for every two rafts [of Cubans] that left for the United States, three planes left for Venezuela. It was incredible."

[38] www.YouTube.com/watch?v=U4adtoryjoM (accessed October 16, 2023).

FIGURE 6.7 "Elegguá, Elegguá asokere kere-kere meyé" chant to Elegguá, performed instrumentally on violin and djembe. Lower noteheads on the djembe line represent open tones; x-heads indicate lighter rim tones, and triangle heads indicate a slap. Transcription courtesy of Richard Huntley.

FIGURE 6.8 Instrumental "Cheke cheke" chant to Ochún on violin and djembe in 6/8 time. Lower quarter-notes on the djembe represent tones played in the center, and slash heads represent lighter hits on the edge.

Another Venezuelan duo with the online names "Awonakosileodo" and "Soy el capitán de arepas" perform instrumental Lucumí melodies on violin with the accompaniment of a single hand-held egg shaker. The resulting sound during pieces in 6/8 time is reminiscent of *joropo* (the best-known folkloric genre in Venezuela), and in fact the shaker egg technique employed (involving largely vertical rather than horizontal motion) does appear to derive from the *joropo* maraca style. In one fifteen-minute recorded sequence[39] the duo performs what might be described as a full *oru seco* using melodies rather than rhythms, a ritual instrumental salute to all major *orishas* in prescribed order. They begin with slow *rezos* to Elegguá accompanied by a straight eighth-note pulse. Gradually they accelerate, first performing chants in 4/4 to Elegguá (which sound a bit like cumbias because the percussionist accents downbeat) and continuing with others dedicated to Ochosi, Obatalá, Babalú Ayé, etcetera, most in 6/8 time. The shaker pattern used to accompany triple-meter chants represents an elaboration of the standard bell pattern that accompanies *bembé* and *güiro* music in Cuba and derives ultimately from West African repertoire. This sequence ends with a series of songs for Ochún, and then to Elegguá once again. Tellingly, this violinist reads all the melodies off sheet music, suggesting relatively recent engagement with Ocha practice.

One of the Venezuelan violinists with the longest-established performance career in involving ritual repertoire is Lisbet Soto (Figure 6.9); she claims to have been the first to learn *orisha* melodies there.[40] Soto was exposed to Santería by her mother (a child of Yemayá) but did not become an initiate herself until the mid-1990s. She studied violin from an early age, eventually enrolling in the National Conservatory. In about 1990 she developed a lesion on her left hand that led to an operation and forced her to stop playing music. A few years later she attended an Ocha ceremony in which Obatalá appeared; the *orisha* told her mother that he wanted Soto to play for him. The *padrino* of the religious house (the *casa de santo* of Alberto la Cruz in Caracas) often hired mariachis to play for gatherings, including religious ones. But Obatalá made clear he didn't want to hear that repertoire. Soto felt unable to comply with his request, given the pain in her wrist. But the *orisha* said that if she played for him she would regain her performance abilities. Slowly she began learning sacred chants for Obatalá, transcribing melodies sung by the *padrino*. Her resulting performances were well received by *santeros*, and over time she found that she could indeed play without pain. Soto eventually expanded her repertoire to include all major *orishas* by attending *tambores* and transcribing additional melodies. She became an initiate in 1995, and requests for her to perform *violines* grew to such an extent that in the early 2000s she left her office job and devoted herself exclusively to music.

[39] www.YouTube.com/watch?v=VLCUOFDZ1F8 (accessed October 16, 2023). See especially the performers' transition to 6/8 time at about 3:00.
[40] These and the details below were provided by Soto in an interview (August 9, 2023).

6 Violines *Abroad*   185

FIGURE 6.9 Lisbet Soto, performing for *santero* Robert Sánchez on his birthday *en santo* in the Venezuelan littoral near the town of Todasana, 2018. Photo courtesy of Lisbet Soto.

Soto now plays for many types of religious celebration: to accompany funerary rites, in honor of "spiritual pantheons" of various sorts including local Venezuelan saints/deities, for secular parties, to celebrate the spiritual birthdays of Ocha initiates, for initiation ceremonies, etcetera. Invitations to perform come all the time from throughout the country: Maracay, Maracaibo, and Valencia, amongst others, and frequently from abroad as well. Soto notes that, as in Cuba, Venezuelan *violines de santo* are typically offered to female *orishas* such as Yemayá, Ochún, and Oyá, or to *orishas* with male and female aspects such as Obatalá. Some of her clients request a *violín* because they live in apartment blocks or other densely populated areas without a sizable Afro-Caribbean religious community and where drumming events are considered too disruptive. When a devotee organizes a *violín* instead of a *tambor*, no one complains about the noise or calls the police. On the other hand, some patrons simply prefer the sound of the violin, considering it most appropriate for the deity they wish to honor. Soto recognizes that with her instrument the religious community can generate

a different energy and make a different kind of supplication ... It isn't the same for me to sit in front of my saint with a drum or to sit there with something more delicate. It isn't the same for you to arrive home and to bring your partner some chocolates or flowers or to bring them beef barbeque, or a sushi combo, the effect won't be the same.[41]

Soto claims to have been the first Venezuelan (and perhaps the first performer anywhere) to develop a complete series of instrumental praise songs to all major *orishas* on the violin.[42] Her approach to devotion is something one would not typically hear in Cuba itself. And, in fact, Cubans visiting Venezuela (including the late singer Lázaro Ros) asked to meet her since her *violines* struck them as so unique. Soto first recognizes all the warrior *orisha* in her *oru*, as one would expect, then continues with others. Usually her audiences just sit and listen to the music in silence, though sometimes they sing along if they know the melodies being played. In order to generate more musical interest, Soto chooses not to play all the songs in the same key but instead modulates between tonal centers. This of course requires decisions about which melody to play in which key and how to transition from one to the next. She tries to imitate what she hears from singers, since they too interpret sacred repertoire in distinct keys. "I connect them one to the other, like a musical potpourri. I can tie a piece in F major to another in the relative minor, moving from F to D minor. Or from F major I create a transition and resolve into A major. And I incorporate rhythmic shifts, breaks, pauses."[43]

Like Yunior Terry, Lisbet Soto never mixes sacred and secular music in performance, but she has started offering sets of popular music to her clientele after the sacred set if asked for it. This is especially common among older Cuban immigrants living in Venezuela who want her to incorporate popular music from their youth. She began learning the repertoire they requested and now can provide sets of older boleros, *danzones*, *danzas*, *trova*, and other genres. She also incorporates some

---

[41] De alguna manera la gente con otro tipo de instrumentos [genera] otro tipo de energía y [hace] otro tipo de ruego. No es lo mismo yo, sentarme frente al santo con un tambor o sentarme con una cosa delicada, no es lo mismo que tú llegues a casa y le lleves a tu pareja unos chocolates o unas flores, o le lleves una parrilla de lomito, un combo de sushi, o sea el efecto no va a ser el mismo.

[42] One example of her *oru* can be viewed here: www.YouTube.com/watch?v=VS_tkwmbV SM (accessed October 16, 2023). The sequence takes twenty-two minutes, roughly the same amount of time as the traditional *oru seco* performed on *batá* drums.

[43] Si yo escucho los cantos de Elegguá, está el rezo y los cantos van nadando en distintas tonalidades. Y se conectan tal cual como un popurrí de música, yo puedo conectar una pieza que está en Fa mayor con una pieza que de pronto modula a la relativa menor, me voy de Fa mayor me voy a Re menor, o de Fa mayor hago un puente y me voy a La mayor. Incluso los cambios rítmicos, los descansos, las respiraciones.

Mexican popular music into her secular sets when the public requests it. Sometimes patrons ask her to play in honor of a specific spirit entity or deceased relative and to recreate the music they enjoyed in life. This of course involves additional research and transcription. Recently, Soto taught her son to accompany her on the piano during popular music sets so that she can offer performance as a duo and create a fuller sound: "I started offering clients the Yoruba music format and the potpourri of popular music on solo violin, and then the duo with added piano which of course provides a completely distinct sonority." In general her performance experiences have been very positive, but sometimes she plays for noninitiates who do not listen in silence during the sacred set. In those cases she may ask them to leave. Despite her strong focus on Lucumí repertoire, Soto says that mountings by an *orisha* during performances are rare.

On occasion, devotees of Venezuelan Spiritism rather than Ocha ask Soto to perform. Prominent spirit groups (known there as *cortes*) she has been asked to play for in that context include the *corte* Calé (devoted to the spirits of delinquents, but also Che Guevara!), la *corte* Libertadora (spirits associated with Bolívar and revolutionary struggle), and la *corte* Chamarrera (associated with the explorer Toribio Alonso de Salazar "El Montañez" and the local religious healer Lino de las Mercedes Valles, among others). Spiritist altars in Venezuela are like those described in Chapter 3 and feature lit candles, glasses of water, flowers, and also images of prominent spirit beings. Patrons may ask Soto to play songs that their spirit guide in life was known to have enjoyed, such as *música llanera* (harp-based plains music), Andean repertoire, or folk music from the Montaña de Sorte region. Well-known Spiritist songs such as "Sea el Santísimo" (Figure 3.2) have circulated throughout the Americas and are part of Soto's *violines*, but most songs requested in that context are Venezuelan and have ties to a particular local entity. The audiences at Spiritist *violines* usually sit and listen, with many smoking cigars and some members communicating with spirits (*transportándose*). Normally after she finishes playing, devotion continues with drumming (in the form of a *cajón* or *tambor espiritual*); it is in that context that spirit beings manifest most often. "What draws the spirits to appear isn't the violin but rather the beating of the drum." Soto describes the Venezuelan Spiritist ambience as quite distinct from *orisha* worship; the two modes of devotion aren't as integrated as in the Cuban ceremonies described previously.

VIOLINES IN MEXICO CITY

Practitioners of Santería established themselves in Mexico following the revolution of 1959 and the immigration of Cuban nationals, first in Veracruz and shortly thereafter in the capital. The scene remained small through the 1970s, then expanded in the 1980s, but became negatively associated with narcotraffickers (Cano Miranda 2016, 165, 170).[44] As in the case of Venezuela, it was the 1990s that gave rise to marked growth in Afro-Cuban religions with the arrival of additional migrants. *Botánica* shops have appeared across Mexico City, for instance, and the Mercado de Sonora near the city center also sells all manner of herbs, ritual statuettes, *soperas*, *collares*, and books on Black religions. Juárez Huet (2013) views Santería as compatible with local forms of mestizo spiritual practice, including *curandismo*, spirit mediumship, divination, and cleansing/healing; for that reason, both Santería and Spiritism have gained acceptance among segments the population. She now describes Mexico as a significant locus of Santería activity, with faith communities in most major cities.

Kunduru is the name of a Mexico City–based *violín* ensemble with a decidedly Cuba-centric style that formed in 2019 and whose personnel consists of two Cubans, two Mexicans, and an Argentine; the group's instrumentation includes keyboard, bass, violin, percussion, and flute.[45] Kunduru's Cuban members (Liñan and Geysinova) typically sing lead as well and are intimately familiar with *violines* as performed in Havana today. Their repertoire foregrounds instrumental popular music, Spiritist repertoire, Spanish-language *plegarias*, and stylized Lucumí chants. The group's founder, Gabriel "Titi" Liñan, is a *santero*, *palero*, and consecrated *batá* drummer; he mentioned to me[46] that creating the *violín* ensemble allowed him both to offer new services to the local religious

---

[44] Links persist between drug trafficking and both Santería/Palo and cults of the Santa Muerte. In 2023, a pop song by Peso Pluma and Junior H (their recent *corrido tumbao* hit "El azul") perpetuated this trend by referencing both the drug trade and including the line "*Dios siempre me cuida y mi gorrita de Elegguá*" (God always protects me, and my ritual Elegguá cap). This journal article discusses the song: https://bit.ly/4bcfMku. See also the article by Roberto Garcés Marrero on references to la Santa Muerte in Mexican music: www.redalyc.org/journal/146/14664836006/html/ (both accessed October 17, 2023).

[45] Specifically, the group members include director Gabriel "Titi" Liñan on bass and vocals, David Silvestre Villarruel Rodríguez on violin, Fabián Flores Muñoz on percussion, Alexis "Jefito" Hechavarría on keyboard, and Geysinova on lead vocals and flute. See their webpage: www.facebook.com/kunduruMX (accessed October 18, 2023).

[46] Personal WhatsApp message, October 17, 2023.

community and to play popular music again, something he had not done for many years. The name "Kunduru" comes from Liñan's interpretation of a story associated with the Ifá sign Otrupon Bekonwa referencing an African string instrument, possibly an antecedent of the modern violin.

Most of Kunduru's music making begins at a slow, contemplative tempo but soon segues into *son*-style dance music with multiple choruses, vocal *soneos*, and instrumental solos. One example of this can be heard in their rendition of Sindo Garay's "Imagen Protectora," eight minutes long and foregrounding improvisation on flute, keyboard, and voice in later sections.[47] Despite the focus on dance music grooves, the crowd depicted in the video consists largely of *iyawós* (recent initiates) dressed in white. Other video postings by Kunduru include the *danzón* "Virgen de Regla" (undoubtedly well received in Mexico, given the strong interest in *danzón* there) which segues into a chachachá and includes choruses such as "*Dáme la calma que alegra mi alma y no sufriré*" (Give me the tranquility that gladdens my soul and I will not suffer) and "*Virgen de Regla, ampárame*" (Virgen of Regla, shelter me).[48] The ensemble also has postings on the "Sonidos del Mar Yoruba" YouTube channel[49] that feature *plegarias* and Spiritist pieces, but that often include dance arrangements as well.[50] Clearly, Kunduru appeals to the local religious community, but it also takes advantage of a broader Mexican interest in *música tropical*.

Venezuelan percussionist Luis Peña and Mexican violinist Miguel Amín have created a very different sort of *violín* ensemble based in Mexico City called "Fantasía Yoruba," one that foregrounds traditional melodies with *batá* drumming (Figure 6.10). They recognize the distinctive nature of their project, noting that most *violín* groups in Mexico have an instrumentation like Kunduru featuring the violin alongside piano, bass, and percussion or that accompanies the violin with electronic backtracks. Both Amín and Peña, by contrast, are initiates in Regla de Ocha (Peña is a *babalawo* and a consecrated *batá* drummer in addition to a *santero*) and have deep knowledge of the religion and its praise songs. Amín makes the point that for *batá* players to perform in ceremonies they require substantial training as well as ritual preparation. He feels that violinists should receive similar training and be able to play extensive

[47] www.YouTube.com/watch?v=ST5lrARh6eo (accessed October 17, 2023).
[48] www.YouTube.com/watch?v=6oZyqwDhjUM (accessed October 17, 2023).
[49] Liñan notes that the Sonidos del Mar Yoruba YouTube Channel is hosted by José Luis Lemus, who invited them to perform.
[50] www.YouTube.com/watch?v=_ibxgYtci-Y or www.YouTube.com/watch?v=wRxwgD5gzw4 (both accessed October 17, 2023).

FIGURE 6.10 "Fantasía Yoruba" featuring Luis Peña, percussion, and Miguel Amín, violin. Note the ritual *gorrita de Eleggúa* worn by Amín. Photo by the author, Mexico City, 2022.

amounts of sacred repertoire as well as popular music. While others offer classical music or mariachi pieces for Ochún, Amín and Peña prefer to foreground only instrumental Lucumí chants and rhythms.

Percussionist Luis Peña is the musical director of the ensemble; he formed it in 2018, shortly after leaving Venezuela because of the difficult political and economic situation there.[51] Peña was born in Maracay and studied Latin percussion as an adolescent. His interest in the *batá* drums gradually led to direct involvement in Santería as a means of learning about them. Peña eventually contacted Amín to play *violines* because he knew of his experience with *música tropical* and other Caribbean dance repertoire as the result of performing in a dance band called La Charanga del Barrio for several years. Initially the duo played mostly popular music together, with Peña accompanying Amín on bongo. But, given his training as a consecrated drummer, Peña felt that the focus of his *violines* should foreground that knowledge.

[51] Most information in this section comes with an interview conducted with the group in June 2022.

Eventually, Peña and Amín decided to include a traditional ritual melody in their set, accompanied by an adaptation of traditional drumming patterns that could be played by a single drummer (accomplished using three unconsecrated or *aberikula batás* mounted on a stand). Since they were unsure how audiences would react, they first performed only the *rezo* "Iyá mi ilé odo" (which had been widely popularized in the Adalberto Álvarez song "¿Y qué tú quieres que te den?" mentioned earlier). The response was enthusiastic; soon they began adding more ritual repertoire, developing their own style, and saluting most major *orishas*. No one in Mexico – or anywhere else – performs quite like this, to their knowledge. The inclusion of *batás* generates considerable interest in the duo and they receive many requests to perform. Peña and Amín believe there is a special quality to the violin and *batá* combination that captures the imagination of listeners, even if a minority find the repertoire less appealing than popular music. They describe the initial segment of their performances in this way: "We are playing a *violín* that is 100 percent Yoruba ... perhaps some people now may think it is strange, but this will make history, it is unique."[52] All of their clients are *santeros* and are directly involved in the religion.

As in the case of other artists discussed, Peña and Amín employ a two-part structure in performance. The first segment, lasting about fifty minutes, consists exclusively of ritual Lucumí melodies played instrumentally on solo violin and accompanied by *batás*. The second section lasts about twenty minutes and consists of popular music. It features Miguel Amín's violin on lead lines, Luis Peña accompanying him on the bongo, and a prerecorded backtrack consisting of piano, bass, and additional percussion. Most patrons choose not to negotiate the specific songs played during the first set and simply accept the performance as offered. This may be because fewer Mexican audience members are familiar with the gamut of ritual melodies to choose from or because they are uncertain what the standard format of *violines* should be. Unlike Cuban ceremonies, the duo's events do not include a *brindis*.

Sometimes Amín and Peña preface their performances by discussing the history of *violines* so as to explain what they are performing and why. Their initial repertoire in events dedicated to Ochún begins with "Ave María" accompanied by *batás*, then proceeds to ritual melodies for Elegguá, Obatalá, and Changó. These are followed by pieces dedicated to Yemayá,

---

[52] "Estamos haciendo un violín cien por ciento Yoruba ... esta forma de violín a lo mejor ahorita hay gente que lo ve así raro y tal pero esto va a hacer historia, porque esto es único."

Oyá, Oduduwa, and finally Ochún. Initially clients only asked them to play *violines* for Ochún, but these days they play for other *orishas* as well. The popular music thereafter consists of international hits like "La rebelión" (The Rebellion, by Joe Arroyo), "La guantanamera" (Woman from Guantanamo, by Joseito Fernández), Willie Colón's "Idilio" (Idyll), Miguel Matamoros' "Son de la loma" (They're From the Hills), etcetera. This segment too is entirely instrumental. While the duo sometimes receive requests to add vocals to their performances, they feel that a *toque de violín* should foreground the violin itself and thus prefer to have it take the melodic lead throughout. They encourage audiences to dance, either by adopting ritual movements associated with particular *orishas* during the first segment or salsa/cumbia steps to accompany the popular music.

The continued use of "Ave María" in Fantasía Yoruba's performances may strike readers as contradictory given their strong interest in Yoruba-derived heritage, but to Luis Peña the song speaks to established practice and to cross-religious influences. He notes that early *violines* began with "Ave María" and he enjoys perpetuating that tradition. He underscores the song's strong religious associations generally; he feels that offering homage to and receiving the blessing of the Virgin Mary remains important since she is a female deity linked to Cuba's Virgin of Charity, and, by extension, to Ochún as well. The only concession to Afrocentric preferences they make is to accompany the piece with drumming, most typically Borotitilawa, which Peña describes as "the third rhythmic variant played to the *orisha* Osain" (*orisha* of herbal knowledge and healing) in the *oru seco*. Figure 6.5 provides a transcription of the traditional Borotitilawa rhythm played on three *batás* by three different drummers; compare it to Figure 6.11, which depicts Peña's modified Borotitilawa rhythm played solo using the stand-mounted *batás*. Peña uses the Borotitilawa rhythm (which he refers to as Obanla) to accompany other melodies, as well including chants to Obatalá such as "Baba fururu" and selected praise songs for Elegguá, Ogún, and, of course, Osain himself.

Luis Peña does not use nearly as many rhythms to accompany ritual melodies as a drummer would play in a traditional *oru cantado* (the publicly sung and danced portion of traditional *orisha* worship in which the melodies Amín plays on the violin would be sung), but he does incorporate about seven distinct rhythms in total (as opposed to the thirty or so distinct rhythms in an actual *tambor*). Rhythms played by Peña include adaptations of *lalubanché* (also spelled *alumbanche*), used in conjunction with *rezos* to Elegguá such as "Bara suwayo"; "*cheché kururú*," used during Ochún's "Iyá mi ilé odo" *rezo*; the Iyesá rhythm used in conjunction with duple-meter chants such as

FIGURE 6.11 Luis Peña's modified Borotitilawa/Obanla rhythm performed solo on all three *batá* drums. Transcription courtesy of Richard Huntley.

"Imbe, imbe ma yeye" for Ochún; *yakotá*, a slower triple-meter rhythm that accompanies melodies such as "Yeye bio bio suo," also for Ochún; and others such as *kan kan* (associated in certain variations with salutes to the *egun*, but also used in sequences to Osun, Obá, Oko, Oyá, and Yemayá) and one of *kan kan's* variants, *cheché kururú* (primarily performed for Ochún and derived from the *oru seco*).[53] Peña's approach to accompaniment, while certainly unconventional in many respects, demonstrates a deep knowledge of heritage. His ensemble's foregrounding of both Lucumí sacred melodies and rhythms inspired in sacred *orisha* practice alter the sound of *violín* performance, bringing it into a closer dialogue with the traditions it emerged from in the early twentieth century.

CONCLUSION

With the exception of repertoire performed by musicians raised in Cuba, such as Yosvany Terry and Titi Liñan of Kunduru, few of the varied styles of *violín* documented in this chapter can be found in Cuba today. Some might not even be well received there, given how different they sound. All of the *violín* musicians discussed here dialogue with Afro-Cuban heritage and incorporate elements of it, yet they have also developed unique fusions,

---

[53] Thanks to Richard Huntley, Johnny Frías, and Luis Peña for insights into these rhythms and their use in traditional ceremonies. The terminology regarding rhythms used in ceremonies seems to differ at times by religious house and by country. Johnny Frías (personal email, October 19, 2023) mentions that the *cheche kururú* variant is not only heard in the *oru seco* but also accompanies *rezos* to Ochún and chants for her such as "Yeye oro yeyeo, yeyé" and "Cheche kururú." The rhythm's name apparently derives from the latter chant.

instrumental combinations, and repertoire. Some lean heavily into technology with sophisticated electronic backtracks and promotional videos, or by performing live on Instagram against pre-existing pop songs. Some emphasize presentational showmanship with hired dancers. Some foreground instruments not typically used in Cuba, such as goat-toe rattles, djembes, or egg-shaped hand shakers, or fuse *violín* and *cajón* formats. Others incorporate new popular songs, including Puerto Rican boleros, Andean *cuecas*, and Venezuelan *música llanera*. Most foreground the sound of the violin itself to a greater extent than is common practice in Cuba today, either as a solo instrument or as the primary focus of instrumental music making. And many of the performers also place a heavier focus on exclusively Lucumí chants, separating sacred and secular musical material into distinct sets and devoting more attention to sacred sequences. Whereas within Cuban *violines* the sacred and secular intersect constantly, in repertoire abroad they often represent distinct musical offerings.

Another prominent trend in *violín* repertoire abroad is what might be described as a conscious blackening of the practice, its engagement with drumming and song sequences that did not constitute a central part (or any part, in some cases) of such performance within Cuba. *Violines* began as a form of worship heavily influenced by Catholicism, Spiritism, and Spanish-language popular song, and the practice developed at a time when close association with African-derived rituals could result in persecution. Performances downplayed Black cultural elements for many years as a result, and the current Cuban public continues to enjoy blurring the boundaries between Black sacred music and other repertoires. But in the twenty-first century, as African-derived religious beliefs are better understood, more widely accepted, and even celebrated, musicians abroad have begun to rethink their relationship to earlier devotion. This is the reason that Lisbet Soto has created a version of the *oru seco* for solo violin that foregrounds ritual melodies, and why Luis Peña has integrated *batás*, the most sacred and complex form of Afro-Cuban drumming, into *violín* presentations by Fantasía Yoruba. In many cases, a mode of worship that once obscured overtly diasporic heritage now embraces it and integrates its influences more centrally in devotional acts.

Conclusion

Sociologist Roger Bastide was one of the first academics to study Afro-Latin American religions in the mid-twentieth century, and in an influential publication (*African Civilizations in the New World*) he emphasized their "fiercely conservative nature" (1971, 128ff.). Bastide noted that many leaders of Santería and Candomblé houses resisted changes in devotional practice; he interpreted their desire to preserve certain forms of Afrocentric heritage as a defense mechanism, the necessary response of a marginal group to a socially and culturally repressive environment. This view of Afro-Latin American religions may have failed to consider sufficiently the constant cultural adaptations religious groups have made since the earliest years of colonization. And yet Bastide's interpretation is insightful. Especially in past decades, Black devotion has centered around the perpetuation of elements perceived as traditional and memories of an African past; many *santeros* continue to resist blending such traditions with external influences. *Violín* worship, by contrast, adopts a very different attitude toward the Spanish language and European-influenced culture that implicitly rejects earlier attitudes.

Afro-Latin American groups, surrounded by a dominant society disinterested in (and frequently antagonistic to) Black understandings of the world, have long faced the possibility of cultural erasure; this tense context required a strategic response. Various options presented themselves, including an oppositionality that rejected all dominant cultural forms (the position described by Bastide); a reinterpretation or translation of dominant cultures through the lens of Afrocentric understandings; an adaptive position that accepted dominant cultures as valid, even desirable; and an integrative stance that attempted to reconcile African and European cultures through the creation of something new. Gerhard Kubik (1994) has explored some of these tactics, and elements of all of them can be found in forms of Black religion and music. Reinterpretation/translation can be seen in the reading of Catholic saints as African *orishas*, for instance, or the use of European Spiritism as a form of honoring African ancestors. Adaptation and integration are especially evident in *violines* and their use of Western instruments, harmonies, and songs derived from Catholicism in devotional contexts. *Violín* performers experiment with the creation of new creolized forms of music making as well.

I view *violines* as a loosely defined space of possibility that developed in a context of oppression and resulted from responses to it. *Violines* of course foreground liminal and fugitive music making that dialogues with many distinct realms, and they emerged in a period of strong bias against Black culture. As David Font-Navarrete (2021, 13) notes, the ways in which practitioners of *orisha* worship have responded to political control through the years "suggest a flexible, adaptable relationship to the notion of religion, arguably as a protective measure against colonial, Jim Crow style, and communist iterations of state authority." Through at least the early 1980s, practitioners had to hide their beliefs and camouflage their interest in African deities and spirit guides, and in the process they developed forms of performance that would not attract unwanted attention or affect their lives adversely. *Violines* thus foreground new forms of strategically transformed ritual on top of countless earlier fusions, representing a reconciliation of Eurocentric and Afrocentric beliefs. Of course, the emergence of *violines* derives from other factors too, including the further integration of Black Cubans into the nation as well as their intimate familiarity with Western music and a desire to include it in all aspects of their daily lives. The prominence of secular elements in *violines* may also result in part from the strongly antireligious orientation of Cuban society since 1959 and the weak influence of the Catholic Church there.

Violines are open to multiple readings: they can be viewed as a concession to Eurocentric and secular tastes, or as a blackening/creolizing of those same practices, or perhaps both tendencies simultaneously. Individuals critical of or uninterested in *violín* practice tend to deride it as a whitened, "diluted," or commercialized version of earlier repertoires. While this attitude is understandable, to me *violines* represent more: they simultaneously suggest the mainstreaming of Black worship, its integration with music making understood as secular, and a reconciliation of multiple modalities of religion. As will be discussed, I also suspect that the popularity of *violines* suggests many in the religious community today lack the same knowledge of Lucumí practices held by earlier generations.[1] It is precisely these aspects of *violín* practice that merit further attention: that they suggest new "ontologies and epistemologies of the acoustic" (Ochoa Gautier 2014, 3) surrounding Afrodiasporic experience and new ways of understanding it.

Scholars of Afro-Cuban religions emphasize the ways in which its musical practices have diversified over time. As regards Regla de Ocha, Bolívar and González (2007, 115) mention that in the mid-nineteenth century the *orishas* only responded to music making on consecrated *batá* drums, but later they came to accept unconsecrated percussion of various sorts, including *bembé* drums, conga drums, and *chekerés* (Balbuena Gutiérrez 2003, 32). From this perspective, the emergence of *cajón* and *violín* ensembles represent newer manifestations of a longstanding tendency. *Violines* especially involve devotion not only on secular instruments but the incorporation of new repertoires as well. Fernando Ortiz's writings from the 1940s and 1950s about the exclusively secular nature of the bongo drum emphasize how much Black religious music continues to change; his pronouncements clearly no longer apply, yet they seem vaguely prophetic in light of the repertoire discussed in previous chapters:

> The bongo drum still hasn't entered the sacred Black spaces of Santería temples. African gods don't understand this instrument with its twin skin heads, even if it looks like a capricious toy of the Ibeyí. It is totally secular, of creole inspiration and derived from the Kongos. It holds itself apart from the solemn, ancient liturgy of Yoruba and Arará gods. Neither Changó, nor Ebioso, nor Abasí, not even Nsambi Mpungo will allow their devotees to dance [in sacred contexts] to the sound of the bongo. Perhaps they will allow it in the new millennium, or when bongo players start imitating *batá* rhythms on six different drumheads. (Ortiz 1955 III, 157)[2]

The diverse elements manifest in *violines* mirror the countless influences contributing to creole Caribbean religions themselves, and perspectives differ over which devotional practices should be perpetuated and which should be purged or reformed in some way. Since Santería has no centralized leadership, religious houses adopt varied positions on these

---

[1] Some of the lack of knowledge about traditional Lucumí chants and rituals outside of Cuba may be the result of the increasing numbers of *santeros* who did not learn the religion at home or as part of community events.

[2] Pero el bongo no entra todavía en los templos de las santerías afroides. Los dioses de África no entienden ese instrumento de cueros jimaguas, que parece un caprichoso juguete de los dioses Ibedyí, pero que es totalmente profano y de espíritu mulato, hijo de congo; ajeno a la solemnidad litúrgica y milenaria de los dioses yorubas y araráes. Ni Changó, ni Ebioso, ni Abasí, ni siquiera Nsambi Mpungo son capaces de permitir que sus hijos bailen al son de un bongo. Acaso lo hagan cuando pronto llegue el milenio o cuando los bongoseros den en seis parches los mismos ritmos de los batá.

matters; some reflect discourses associated with international centers of religious authority (in Nigeria, for instance) while others resist them. Given the conflicting views of practitioners, Rossbach de Olmos (2014) provocatively characterizes *orisha* worship today as a "tradition in conflict." However striking the aesthetic changes or debates associated with *violines*, they need to be understood as part of ongoing, often tumultuous controversies over Afro-Caribbean religious norms more generally. Most controversies center around issues of purity and what is known of precolonial and current *orisha* worship in West Africa, as discussed in Chapter 2.[3] But Caribbean practices diverged long ago from those in Nigeria and have followed their own heterogeneous paths; any attempt at "purification" at this point seems impossible.

Víctor Betancourt Estrada is one of many *santeros* whose writings critique current devotional norms in Cuba even as they underscore the extent of religious fusion. He argues for a return to West African orthodoxy; rather than celebrating New World creole expression in all its complexity, he sees only confusion. In the following quote the author likens the many items found on altars associated with Santería and spirit worship to those in a second-hand antique store:

[W]hen we stand in front of an altar or a glassed cabinet belonging to some practitioners [of Regla de Ocha], it appears that we are in a curiosity shop. There we can see various Catholic images, photos of deceased relatives, vases with flowers, a crucifix, a chalice of the holy sacrament, tureens containing the objects of a certain *orisha*, a Buddha, incense sticks, a Bantu *prenda* for summoning the dead, a Spiritist *prenda*, the image of an *Íreme* (a spirit in the Abakuá religion), the plaster image of an Appalachian Indian, a doll dressed as a Gypsy, multicolored porcelain plates, a cane decorated with colored ribbons and bells, ornaments of porcelain and plaster, a doll dressed as a domestic slave, a doll dressed as a field slave, glasses of water, a cup of water with a rosary hanging from it, an Oriental vase, rattles of different types, a deck of cards, and a doll dressed as a nun, among other objects. The altar's patron gets up early and in front of this display recites an Our Father, an invocation in an incomprehensible language, or a Hail Mary and in his own manner begins to pray to who knows how many gods. (Betancourt Estrada 2007, 11)[4]

---

[3] The Afrocentrist movement gained prominence in Cuba in the 1990s with sustained contact between leaders in the Ocha community and their counterparts in Nigeria (see Chapter 2). The same tendency is evident elsewhere in Latin America; Matory (2005, 23) discusses similar views held by a prominent *mãe de santo* in Salvador, Bahia, who sees no place for Catholic saints or Indigenous spirits in Candomblé worship.

[4] [C]uándo nos paramos frente a un altar o un canastillero de algunos de los practicantes de la [Regla de Ocha] podemos apreciar algo parecido a un [bazar] de antigüedades: Allí podemos ver varias imágenes católicas, fotos de familiares difuntos, búcaros con flores, un

Betancourt Estrada notes other trends he finds disturbing in Cuba's current Ocha practice, including a lack of attention to traditional ritual norms, the commercialization of initiation ceremonies, and a related lack of morality among some spiritual leaders. The provocative title of his book, *La santería: Una tradición en decadencia* (Santería: A Tradition in Decline), aptly summarizes his views on these issues and on the extent of external religious influences on African-derived devotion. One can assume that his views of *toques de violín* would be similarly damning. Betancourt Estrada fails to recognize the attraction of spaces of religious worship that connect and move through multiple realms of experience.

It is interesting to consider *violines* in relation to the substantial literature on liminality and to consider whether they productively dialogue with the concept, especially in terms of the ways the performances described previously blur boundaries between the sacred and the secular and between distinct religions. Sean Williams, in a forthcoming publication,[5] defines liminality as a permeable boundary, "a place of transgression and transformation" and emphasizes that music making often accompanies human states of in-betweenness. The concept of liminality first surfaced in the writings of folklorist Arnold Van Gennep in the early twentieth century; anthropologists, performance studies scholars, and others have expanded his idea ever since. Liminality is foregrounded in many acts of Black Caribbean religious devotion: when *orishas* appear, when initiates are united with their guardian angel, when the dead are venerated after their passing, etcetera. But the kinds of liminality associated with *violines* are of a slightly different nature: they sit at the boundary of multiple religions but also embrace nonreligious influences. *Violines* bear a certain resemblance to the "secular devotion" perceived by Timothy Brennan (2008, 2), in which religious elements infuse certain kinds of African American popular song. The transgressions experienced in a *violín* have nothing to do with rites of

---

crucifijo, un Cáliz, soperas que contienen los objetos de un determinado Orisa, un Buda, palillos de inciensos, una prenda bantú, una prenda espiritual, la imagen de un Íreme (espíritu de la religión abakuá), la imagen en yeso de un indio de los Apalaches, una muñeca vestida de gitana, platos multicolores de porcelana, un bastón adornado con cintas de colores y cascabeles, adornos de porcelana y yeso, una muñeca vestida de esclava doméstica, un muñeco vestido de esclavo, vasos con agua, una copa con agua y un rosario colgando de ella, potiches de porcelanas, sonajeros de diferentes tipos, un juego de cartas, una muñeca vestida de monja, entre otros objetos. El patrono del altar se levanta temprano y ante su altar, reza un Padre Nuestro, una invocación en una lengua incomprensible o un Ave María, que en su propio lenguaje comienza a pedir no se sabe a cuantos dioses.

[5] *Music at the Threshold from the Sacred to the Dangerous*, forthcoming, Oxford University Press.

passage, but instead with making the sacred more mundane and the popular more spiritual. As in the views expressed in some Hassidic texts, *violines* suggest that any sort of music making and the pleasure it produces can play a central role in spiritual uplift and communication with God (Shiloah 1992, 76–7; Fishbane 1998, 160).

The fugitive nature of *violines*, their movement across conceptual and aesthetic terrain, can be understood through the lens of domain collapsing, as discussed by Louise Meintjes and others based on the writings of linguist Charles Pierce. This is especially true of the ways in which performers (perhaps unconsciously) manipulate iconic signs; the way they incorporate recognizable elements of sacred performance – melodies, lyrics, ritual dance steps, rhythms – and weave them together with others linked to commercial music – a bongo drum, a chachachá beat, a violin *guajeo* – collapses distinct performative realms. Musicians enact cultural transformation in this way through the reconfiguration of iconic referents. Meintjes (1990) describes established musical genres as consisting of distinct features that have become familiar to listeners over time and naturalized, crafted into an apparently cohesive unit. She defines domain collapsing as a process by which icons simultaneously represent, connect, and mediate once-distinct experiences (48, 53), and she argues that the symbolic power of music increases to the extent that it links them together. All of music's various components (timbre, pitch, scale, texture, etc.) can serve as independent referents, lending themselves to decidedly complex and multifaceted readings (Turino 1999, 236). I would argue that much of the attraction of *violines* involves the way that they elide realms of social experience, generating new "structures of feeling" (Williams 1977) that recenter Black religious expression relative to popular and concert music, and to present-day sonic experiences more generally.

SACRED–SECULAR MUSICS OF THE AFRICAN DIASPORA

Other scholars of Black music in the Americas have studied religious repertoire that incorporates secular sounds to convey sacred messages in a manner similar to Cuban *violines*; I discuss their publications in order to situation *violines* within broader diasporic processes and consider their relation to such repertoires. Timothy Rommen's work (2007, 2016) in Trinidad, for instance, describes the ways that various forms of Black music from the US and Trinidad – hip hop, Black gospel, R&B, soca/jamoo, dancehall, even salsa/Latin genres – serve as the medium through which evangelical Christians express their faith in God. Rommen details the emergence of fusion musics such as gospelypso in the 1960s, jamoo in the 1980s, gospel dancehall in the 1990s, hardcore gospel soca around 2000, and so on. Obviously these trends have counterparts in the US itself with the spread of Christian rock and rap. The variety of commercial styles incorporated into religious expression in Trinidad is diverse and foregrounds sounds associated with dance music. An important difference between such expression and *violines* is that the lyrics of Trinidadian sacred–secular music are entirely centered on Christianity. Perhaps more tellingly, worshippers in Trinidad's Black Pentecostal community often denounce Afrocentric religions on the island like Shango worship, characterizing them as false or misguided, if not outright satanic. While they embrace many different musical sounds in church services, this community's conception of religion itself tends to be much more restrictive than in Cuba.

John Burdick's (2013) writings in *The Color of Sound* parallel those of Rommen but focus on Brazilian case studies. Like Rommen, the lyrics of the music Burdick examines (such as gospel samba) remain centered on Christian praise, and, as in Trinidad, Brazilian Christians denounce Afro-Brazilian religions: they "reject as the devil's playground all mediumship religions such as Afro-Brazilian candomblé" (10). Burdick describes the use of evangelical Christian devotion as a form of antiracist struggle, noting that distinct subcommunities espouse opposing racial ideologies in pursuit of social equality. Being a gospel sambista, for instance, implies to him the internalization of narratives of national hybridity and the adoption of a vocal and musical style accessible to all races (175–6). Other scenes, such as gospel rap, tend to focus more exclusively on spiritual messages for and about the Black community. This work provides many useful insights into how racial ideologies can manifest themselves in religious music making, but it does not analyze the implications of using commercial music in devotional contexts.

Michael Iyanga's writing engages more directly with the use of secular Brazilian music in religious contexts, particularly in communities that embrace African-derived religions. This author works in the Recôncavo region of Bahia, in northeastern Brazil. His article "Why Saints Love Samba" (2015) notes that samba music and dance (typically in circle-style *samba de roda* format) is performed in numerous contexts, such as during pilgrimages, as an accompaniment to rites of spiritual cleansing (*lavagens*), and most typically in feasts for Catholic saints themselves, who are understood to represent both Christian and African divinities, as in Cuba. Iyanga writes:

[S]amba caps off rollicking patron saint house parties known as *rezas*, each moment of which is marked by ritual music. Standing in front of the home altar, attendees first intone a series of Catholic hymns before gathering in a ring to dance and responsorially sing their saint-saluting sambas. On occasion, this samba can even prompt Catholic saints (and other entities) to possess the host and other guests for a divine dancing and singing distinct from the types of possession rituals characteristic of Afro-Brazilian religions such as Candomblé and Umbanda. (Iyanga 2015, 119)

The use of popular music in these contexts bears considerable resemblance to a *violín*, especially since both can sometimes lead to possession. It appears that popular music not only "caps off" religious ceremonies in Bahia but represents an integral part of them. Iyanga argues that popular music is central to these contexts "because Africans and their descendants effectively reinvented and transformed their Catholic saints, 'converting,' so to speak, the Christian martyrs into samba-loving gods" (2015, 120–1). Is something similar suggested in *violines* through their ritual use of dance music? Is Cuban dance repertoire infused with a new religious sensibility, and is the community "blackening" the aesthetic preferences of Catholic saints in the process? Iyanga's assertion (121) that devotional samba represents an in-betweenness characteristic of Black life in the New World resonates closely with my experiences in Cuba, in terms of its fusions of Catholicism and *orisha* worship.

The same author's recent book *Alegria é Devoção* (2023) takes his earlier arguments further, suggesting that *all* samba dance music in northeast Brazil has ties to religiosity and that conventional Western distinctions between sacred and secular repertoire fail to capture their many commonalities. After documenting the longstanding ties between *samba de roda* and Black religious houses, Iyanga asserts that "samba (and its antecedent forms) were never disconnected from religious contexts" (Iyanga 2023, 257). He continues by insisting that "samba isn't an addendum to a religious celebration, nor is it the 'secular part' ... samba doesn't accompany devotion; it is itself devotion" (258–9).[6] He stresses that musical studies too often characterize samba as unrelated to religion, despite centuries of documentation to the contrary. He makes the important point that writings distinguishing between sacred and profane

---

[6] "insisto que o samba não é um anexo à festa religiosa, tampouco sua 'parte profana' ... o samba não acompanha a devoção; é a própria devoção."

expression fail to capture their fundamentally interpenetrated nature in Afro-Latin American communities (272).

Another study that offers unique insights into similar phenomena is Angelina Tallaj's (2018) article on performances of Dominican Vodú in New York–area nightclubs. She notes that entire Vodú ceremonies can now be viewed in commercial venues rather than in private homes; they often feature live *palo* drumming, the creation of ritual altars, the lighting of fires in the shape of a cross as a form of ritual purification, the blowing of cigar smoke, even the public baptism of new initiates and acts of possession. In the events described by Tallaj, audience members pay to watch religious activity as a form of entertainment, in combination with dance music performances and the consumption of alcohol. Musicians foreground elements of Afro-Dominican rituals while at the same time dressing in flashy attire as part of staged events. Much as in *violines*, Dominican artists perform versions of traditional repertoire, and their actions constantly tack between the religious and the theatrical:

> In a 2012 ceremony in La Nueva Fortuna Restaurant, the drummer added vocal effects to a *palo* song [dedicated] to the deity Damballah Wedo, onomatopoeically depicting the deity's snake character by moving his tongue [like] a snake and improvising vocalizations. At a 2014 ceremony at El Aguila restaurant in the Bronx, the singer, La Piki, shouted out numerous times from the stage: "Who are the single women? Where are the *brujos* [sorcerers]? Raise your handkerchiefs! Hurray for San Miguel!" (Tallaj 2018, 103)

Musicians freely blend elements of many musical styles in such contexts, developing new rhythms and choreographies that dialogue with dance music and Afro-Caribbean religions. Musical examples of such fusion include the Kinito Méndez merengue/*salve*/*palo* hit "Suero de amor" (Love Serum).[7]

Spirit possession, whether actual or contrived, has become central to many Dominican–American club performances, as mentioned. Tallaj describes some shows in which members of the dance orchestra appeared to become possessed by spirits; bandleaders may encourage this since it adds to the impact of their set (104). For their part, young clubgoers too incorporate dance gestures or other movements associated with spirit possession as they socialize. Tallaj interprets this not as a corruption or

---

[7] The lyrics of the Méndez composition conflate love of the deity Ogún Balenyó with romantic love, and the musical accompaniment combines merengue rhythms with traditional *salve* and *palo* percussion and song: www.YouTube.com/watch?v=WcT1riZok8s (accessed October 30, 2023).

mockery of tradition, but as a form of cultural reinvention "through acts of communal dancing, singing, drinking, and trancing together" (99). She characterizes the emergence of religious pop as a valorization of Black diasporic heritage among younger urban Dominicans, perhaps a result of living in the United States where African-derived cultures are more widely accepted.

The dynamics surrounding public religious music making as described by Tallaj differ from and align with *violines* in important ways. *Violines* did not develop in urban immigrant enclaves as a form of collective quasi-nationalist expression, for instance, nor do they represent an attempt to valorize Black heritage (Black traditions dominate Cuban religious life, so such efforts are unnecessary). *Violines* and Dominican club shows both transform religious expression in fundamental ways, however, primarily by secularizing ritual. Both scenes demonstrate a playfulness (even irreverence) in the ways that religious themes are manipulated through performance (the Kinito Méndez song, mentioned earlier, that transforms a sacred chant into a risqué dance tune recalls the choruses sometimes incorporated into *violines* with similarly bawdy content). And, clearly, the musicians in both Tallaj's study and in mine move seamlessly between once-distinct realms of performance, freely modifying older traditions and embracing multiple forms of blackness as they redefine religions in a twenty-first-century context. Perhaps these repertoires should be understood in the way Johnson (2014, 21) describes new forms of spirit possession in the Americas: as open-ended, creative, and "unburdened of any foundational past."

Violines AND RITUAL CHANGE

Of central concern in evaluating *violines* is their significance as a form of devotion relative to more established modes of worship, whether of *orishas*, spirit beings, or other forces. In *violines*, not only does a great variety of repertoire combine, but many styles – such as dancified renditions of religious repertoire, popular songs, or concert music – have no precedent as a central component of Afro-Cuban religious expression. The frequently open-ended musical appropriation found in *violines* can be viewed positively as an expansion of ritual vocabulary, a blackening of the violin's sound in everyday music making, and an extension of the sacred into realms typically thought of as secular. Such changes can also be framed negatively as an impoverishment of past orthodoxies, however; this view of *violines* is especially common among specialists who study and/or practice the extremely complex religious, musical, and textual forms that have long surrounded *orisha* worship. Ethnomusicologist and *santero* David Font-Navarrete, for instance, views the *oru* segments dedicated to spirit entities in *violines* with some concern because he feels that traditional music making is treated too casually or superficially. As a consecrated drummer and a scholar of Afro-Cuban ritual speech, *violín* practice strikes him as excluding many elements of worship that were common in the past. Rather than offering musical salutes to about two dozen *orishas*, for instance (as would be heard in the standard *oru seco* and *oru cantado*), *violines* recognize only about half a dozen of the most well-known deities. The number of traditional Lucumí songs found in most *violines* is significantly reduced in comparison with *tambores* as well; and, of course, musicians intersperse praise sequences dedicated to the *orishas* with others dedicated to many other spirits and Catholic saints. Font-Navarrete views this sort of performance, based on snippets of earlier devotional rites from multiple sources, as "meme-like" in the sense that individual Lucumí *orus* are drastically shortened; they strike him as incomplete, an amalgamation or pastiche created from distinct religious systems. The inclusivity of *violines* makes them inherently disjunct from this perspective: they present a significantly abbreviated version of older rituals as they strive for new levels of cultural integration.

The prominence of Spanish-language songs in the *cajón de muerto* and the *violín* suggests the gradual loss of Lucumí ritual knowledge (or at least the vocabulary associated with it) among some practitioners. This is perhaps inevitable, given the passing of generations and the more distanced relationship younger worshippers have with African-derived influences. Well into the mid-twentieth century, many Cubans still lived in homes with family members who spoke African languages and had parents or grandparents with direct ties to specific regions or linguistic groups there. Today, by contrast, the number of individuals conversant in Lucumí or able to translate the metaphor-laden lyrics of ritual songs continues to decline (Warden 2006, 56). Betancourt Estrada (2007, 9) laments the change, writing that many worshippers now offer praise to divinities "without knowing what they are invoking; they sing *Iyere* (liturgical songs) without understanding their meaning."[8] Consecrated *batalero* Richard Huntley has spoken to me of similar situations he observed in which, during or after ritual performances, musicians

---

[8] "le invocan a las divinidades sin saber que le están invocando; cantan 'Iyere' (cantos litúrgicos) sin conocer el significado de los mismos."

complain among themselves about worshippers' lack of familiarity with the repertoire; he notes that this is especially common when rituals take place in wealthier neighborhoods, suggesting that Ocha knowledge remains strongest in relatively marginal or insular Black enclaves.[9] In general, the relationship of the Cuban religious community to Lucumí praise songs might be likened to that of Catholics to the Latin mass; they have a loose idea of the meaning of the words being sung, but many lack a full understanding of them and increasingly prefer to express themselves in their primary language instead. *Cajón*, Spiritist, and *violín* devotion all represent new "in-between" religious spaces that allow for either the use of Spanish exclusively or the mixing of Spanish and Lucumí with chants such as "*Yo me llamo abukenke.*"[10] Balbuena Gutiérrez (2003, 36–8) notes such tendencies affecting *orisha* dances, as ever fewer participants know the appropriate movements to accompany particular songs. She describes the process as one of gradual "deritualization." I do not agree with this assertion, as current practices remain spiritual and ritualistic, yet their specific form and content are clearly changing.

Violín performers recognize their audiences' new ritual understandings and make alterations to their repertoire accordingly. One performer recalled asking a patron to include chants to Oba (an *orisha* who typically doesn't mount practitioners) in a sequence, only to find that audience members didn't know how to sing the corresponding choral responses. Experiences of that sort have led him to include only the simplest and most well-known chants to major deities and to avoid those with extended lyrics. "Sosa sokere" (for Elegguá), for instance, is a song that virtually everyone knows and that functions well in the context of a *violín*. It is possible that the gradual loss of Lucumí competence has led to greater interest in *violines*, precisely because they require less esoteric knowledge. Along with a lack of familiarity with some older ritual songs, musicians note a tendency for audience members to mispronounce some choral responses to them, often by translating Lucumí phrases into Spanish. In Eduar's *violín* discussed in Chapter 5, for example, participants interpreted the traditional chant "O fenikiya" (a praise song for Ochún) as "*O felicidad*" (Oh happiness)! Johnny Frías

---

[9] Richard Huntley, personal email, April 5, 2021.
[10] This is clearly a phrase that mixes Spanish and Lucumí; it is mentioned by Warden (2006, 56). "Abukenke" might be translated as "one who is abusive and small," a reference to Elegguá's childlike and mischievous nature.

recalls similar cases in which worshippers have transformed the song "Wa lo ñio, wa lo yeo" for Yemayá as *"Pa' los niños, pa' los viejos."*[11]

While the loose, ambiguous format associated with *violines* can be unsettling to traditionalists, I view it as representative of a contemporary moment characterized by relatively free, unselfconscious experimentation with Black heritage. In the context of a *violín*, practitioners now offer more of their musical selves to their gods and spirit guides, and they seem to recognize divine resonance in even the most secular expression. Of course, the popular music often foregrounded in such contexts (boleros and dance music) includes countless Black diasporic features as well (whether one considers instruments, rhythms, the centrality of improvisation, or call–response singing), so perhaps it should not be surprising that such repertoire has now become part of ritual offerings to African deities. As Stuart Hall and others observe, no "pure" cultures exist, and specific forms of Black music have always been emergent and responsive to broader cultural and social influences. Black musical development must be understood "not simply as the recovery of a lost dialogue bearing clues for the production of new musics" – a process that might be understood as reformulations of a shared body of Afrodiasporic musical elements – but instead as "adaptations, molded to the mixed, contradictory, hybrid spaces of popular [and religious] culture" (Hall, 1993, 110).

Afro-Cuban *violines* and religious music continue to develop in innovative ways. The Grammy-winning release *La rumba soy yo* contains a fascinating track called "Un violín pa' Chano" by Lázaro González featuring virtuosic violin solos played against *rumba guaguancó* percussion. It begins with an extended, quasi-classical improvisatory segment and later combines violin and drumming in a big-band Latin jazz arrangement.[12] The chorus of the song, *"Un violín para Chano, ¡qué violín!,"* has a certain religious quality as it evokes the memory and spirit of an inspirational artist from years past. Another interesting phenomenon in the realm of popular music is the emergence of Ocha-reggaetón. Performer Wilson Ogbe-She is a proponent of this new style who, in works such as "Mi prosperidad" (My Prosperity), complicates notions of the sacred and the secular in his own way.[13] Ogbe-She dances and

---

[11] Personal email, November 3, 2023.
[12] www.YouTube.com/watch?v=l2Kiq9X4aWI (accessed November 1, 2023).
[13] www.YouTube.com/watch?v=cpgRZJ_1FAY. Thanks to Johnny Frías for bringing this artist to my attention. See also Wilson Ogbe-She's Spotify playlist: https://open.spotify.com/artist/3j8Gw9SAClwaOmQlZIr3D8 (accessed November 1, 2023).

performs against prerecorded beats as his lyrics discuss the spiritual opportunities provided by Black Caribbean religions. His stage name derives from an Ifá sign exhorting believers not to succumb to adversity. Images in the video accompanying "Mi prosperidad" include Spiritist and Ocha altars, animals being prepared for ritual sacrifice, acts of devotion individually and in groups, and even brief footage of a *violín*. Other videos by Ogbe-She describe the characteristics of the *orisha* Ochún in detail and experiment with musical accompaniment derived from rumba, son/salsa, and other genres.[14]

Wilson Ogbe-She directly promotes innovative experiments with *violines*, including collaborations between violinists and *cajón* groups in a manner reminiscent of Yilian Orama's videos (see Chapter 6). In a June 2023 video filmed in the Sociedad San Juan Bautista of Villa Clara, Cuba, the artist organized a memorial for his deceased relative, Doña Obdulia.[15] It included three violinists, two *cajón* players, a clave player, and a fourth percussionist playing pair of sticks on a wood block. This combination of instruments is highly unusual, but it makes sense given that both *cajón* and violin ensembles can be used to honor the dead. Initially, string players and percussionists performed separately at Ogbe-She's event, but about four minutes in they collectively played a rendition of "La luz redentora" (Figure 3.3), with the *cajón* players imitating *rumba guaguancó*. Later (about 5:45) they segued to a collective version of "Cachita," with the higher *cajón* player shifting to a conga drum pattern reminiscent of Cuban *son* against a straight bell typical of what might be heard in a *charanga* band. These and other postings suggest we should expect many changes in *violín* performance in the future.

Financially, life in present-day Cuba remains very difficult, and yet this has not deterred the religious community from organizing devotional acts. Salary adjustments and other fiscal policies enacted by the Cuban government since 2021 have resulted in substantially increased living costs for the population, to the point of desperation.[16] Economic need has been exacerbated by harsh US embargo policies intended to isolate Cuba, initiated by the first Trump administration and perpetuated under President Biden and Trump's second term, as well as steep declines in tourism and related revenue due to the Covid-19 crisis. Considering these

---

[14] See for instance "La Yalorde," www.YouTube.com/watch?v=cdyfH2BY060 (accessed November 1, 2023).

[15] www.YouTube.com/watch?v=cOeXEOIO0_Y (accessed November 2, 2023).

[16] See https://bit.ly/3QuDW07 or https://bit.ly/3D6ehI1 (accessed November 2, 2023).

difficulties, one might suspect that the organization of *violines* and related music would decline, yet conversations with contacts in Havana suggests that this is not the case.[17] It appears that, despite the ongoing crisis, the religious community continues to grow and musicians report constant demand for their services.

Given that *violines* generate new understandings of the sacred and the secular and make frequent incursions into new repertoires, they are perhaps best understood as a musical crossroads. Crossroads are spaces of encounter in which decisions are made, alternatives are pondered, and new directions are taken. *Violines* demonstrate more crossings than most music, even in a region such as the Caribbean, long recognized as a space of encounter and exchange in contexts of colonial dominance. Cultural crossroads contain both residual and emergent elements; they speak to dangers and opportunities (Lipsitz 1994, 19). *Violines* evoke the spirit of the crossroads and, by extension, of Eleggúa in opening artistic pathways, suggesting new forms of spirituality and leading to a more expansive religious understanding. Angelina Tallaj understands the staged Dominican religious performances she studies in this way, as existing at the intersection of entertainment and devotion, the commercial and the ritualistic, and ultimately as challenging the confines of all such binaries (Tallaj 2018, 102). Much like Eleggúa (and particularly in his incarnation as Esu Odara, messenger *orisha* of transformation), *violines* change the ways that religious music is experienced and understood. Fa'lokun Fatunmbi (1993) reminds us that the spirit of Eleggúa is that of a trickster who confounds or deceives so as to upend limited visions of the world and related perceptions or practices: "When humans become too set in their ways, too rigid in their thinking and too dogmatic in their response to other points of view, it is Esu who stirs up the mix and forces the kind of re-evaluation that can lead to enlightenment" (4). As a transformative practice, *violines* offer new ways of thinking and acting, new forms of worship, and they expand our understanding of the sacred so that it extends further into everyday life.

---

[17] Melena Francis Valdés, personal WhatsApp message, October 24, 2023, in consultation with other performers.

References

BOOKS AND ARTICLES

Aijmer, Göran, ed. 1995. *Syncretism and the Commerce of Symbols*. Göteborg: IASSA.

Altmann, Thomas. 1998. *Cantos Lukumí a los Orishas*. Brooklyn, NY: Descarga.

Amira, John and Steven Cornelius. 1999. *The Music of Santería: Traditional Rhythms of the Batá Drums*. Reno, NV: White Cliffs Media.

Averill, Gage and David Yuen-Ming Yi. 2003. "Militarism in Haitian Music." In Ingrid Monson, ed., *The African Diaspora: A Musical Perspective*. New York: Routledge, 263–89.

Ayoh'Omidire, Félix. 2014. "Petrodollar, Bolivarianism, and the Re-Yorubanization of Santería in Chávez's Socialist Venezuela." In Ingrid Kummels, Claudia Rauhut, Stefanie Rinke, and Birte Timm, eds., *Transatlantic Caribbean: Dialogues of People, Practices, Ideas*. Bielefeld: International Conference Proceedings, 201–24.

Balbuena, Bárbara. 2003. *Las celebraciones rituales festivas en la Regla de Ocha*. Havana: Centro de Investigación y Desarrollo de la Cultura Cubana Juan Marinello.

2005, *El casino y la salsa en Cuba*. Havana: Letras Cubanas.

Barnet, Miguel. 2001 [1995]. *Afro-Cuban Religions*, transl. Christine Renata Ayorinde. Princeton, NJ: Markus Wiener Publishers.

Barnet, Miguel and Esteban Montejo. 1994 [1966]. *Biography of a Runaway Slave*, transl. W. Nick Hill. Willimantic, CT: Curbstone Press.

Barreal Fernández, Isaac. 1966. "Tendencias sincréticas de los cultos populares en Cuba." *Etnología y folklore*, vols. 1–2, 17–24.

Barreal Fernández, Isaac, ed. 1998. *Fiestas populares tradicionales cubanas*. Havana: Editorial de Ciencias Sociales.

Basail Rodríguez, Alain and M. Yoimy Castañeda Seijas. 1999. "Conflictos y cambios de Identidad Religiosa en Cuba." *Convergencia: Revista de Ciencias Sociales* vol. 6 no. 20 (Sept.), 173–94.

Bastide, Roger. 1971. *African Civilizations in the New World*. New York: Harper and Row.
Becker, Judith and Alton Becker. 1981. "A Musical Icon: Power and Meaning in Javanese Gamelan Music." In Wendy Steiner, ed., *The Sign in Literature and Music*. Austin, TX: University of Texas Press, 203–12.
Beliso-De Jesús, Aisha M. 2015. *Electric Santería: Racial and Sexual Assemblages of Transnational Religion*. New York: Columbia University Press.
Benítez-Rojo, Antonio. 1996. *The Repeating Island: The Caribbean and the Postmodern Perspective*. Durham, NC: Duke University Press.
Bermúdez, Armando Andrés. 1967. "Notas para la historia del espiritismo en Cuba." *Etnología y folklore* no. 4 (July–December), 5–22.
Betancourt Estrada, Víctor. 2007. *La santería: Una tradición en decadencia*. Caracas: Graficas Reus, CA.
Bilby, Kenneth. 1985. "The Caribbean as a Musical Region." In Sidney Mintz and Sally Price, eds., *Caribbean Contours*. Washington, DC: Johns Hopkins University Press, 181–218.
Bolívar, Natalia. 1990. *Los orichas en Cuba*. Havana: Ediciones Unión.
Bolívar, Natalia and Carmen González. 2007. *Corrientes espirituales en Cuba*. Havana: Editorial José Martí.
Brandon, George. 1990. "Sacrificial Practices in Santería, an Afro-Cuban Religion in the United States." In Joseph E. Holloway, ed., *Africanisms in American Culture*. Bloomington, IN: Indiana University Press, 119–47.
  1993. *Santería from Africa to the New World: The Dead Sell Memories*. Bloomington, IN: Indiana University Press.
Brennan, Timothy. 2008. *Secular Devotion: Afro-latin Music and Imperial Jazz*. New York: Verso.
Brown, David H. 2019 [2003]. *Santería Enthroned: Art, Ritual, and Innovation in an Afro-Cuban Religion*. New York: Routledge.
Buisseret, David and Steven G. Reinheardt, eds. 2000. *Creolization in the Americas*. College Station, TX: Texas A&M University Press.
Burdick, John. 2013. *The Color of Sound: Race, Religion, and Music in Brazil*. New York: New York University Press.
Cabrera, Lydia. 1970 [1957]. *Anagó: Vocabulario lucumí*. Miami, FL: Ediciones Universal.
  1989 [1954]. *El monte*. Havana: Letras Cubanas.
  1996 [1974]. *Yemayá y Ochún: Kariocha, Iyalorichas y Olorichas*. Miami, FL: Ediciones Universal.
  2001 [1984]. *Vocabulario congo (El bantú que se habla en Cuba)*. Miami, FL: Ediciones Universal.
  2023 [1954]. *El Monte: Notes on the Religions, Magic, Superstitions, and Folklore of the Black and Creole People of Cuba*, trans. David Font-Navarrete. Durham, NC: Duke University Press.
Camal, Jérôme. 2019. *Creolized Aurality: Guadeloupean Gwoka and Postcolonial Politics*. Chicago: University of Chicago Press.
Cano Miranda, Diana. 2016. "Santería cubana en la ciudad de México: Estudio de case en una colonia popular al sur de la Ciudad de México." *Revista Brasileira do Caribe* vol. 17 no. 33 (July/Dec), 161–86.

Carranza Fuentes, Lázara Y. and Fundación Fernando Ortiz. 2011. *Las relaciones raciales en Cuba: Estudios contemporáneos*. Havana: Fundación Fernando Ortiz.
Casanova Oliva, Ana Victoria. 1988. *Las manifestaciones musicales en el municipio 10 de Octubre, de Cuidad de La Habana*. Havana: Centro de Investigación y Desarrollo de la Cultura Cubana Juan Marinello.
Castellanos, Isabel. 1996. "From Ulkumí to Lucumí: A Historical Overview of Religious Acculturation in Cuba." In Arturo Lindsay, ed., *Santería Aesthetics in Contemporary Latin American Art*. Washington, DC: Smithsonian Institution Press, 39–50.
Castellanos, Jorge and Isabel Castellanos. 1992. *Cultura afrocubana: 3: Las religiones y las lenguas*. Miami, FL: Ediciones Universales.
Castro Ramírez, Luis Carlos. 2017. "Cordones espirituales, cordones de identidad: La misa de investigación en el espiritismo cruzao en Cali (Colombia)." *Chungara: Revista de antropología chilena* vol. 49 no. 1, 133–42.
Cavalcante Rosa, Laila Andresa. 2009. "As juremeiras da nação Xambá (Olinda, PE): músicas, performances, representações de feminino e relações de gênero na jurema sagrada." Unpublished doctoral thesis in ethnomusicology, Universidade Federal da Bahia.
Chaudenson, Robert, ed. 2001. *Creolization of Language and Culture*. New York: Routledge.
Coburg, Adrian. 2004. *Toques Especiales: Batá Scores*, 5th ed. Bern: [self-published].
Cortes, Carlos. 2016. "Regla de Osha y su Legado." Facebook post, October 14. www.facebook.com/yemaya0907/posts/1132189936864123/ (accessed July 18, 2019).
Crookes, William. 2012. *Cantos para misas espirituales*. Spain: Iridium Books.
Cuéllar Vizcaino, Manuel. 1950. "Un bembé." *Bohemia*, vol. 42 no. 37, September 10, 55–8, 97.
Cueto, Emilio. 2014. *La Virgen de la Caridad en el alma del pueblo cubano*. Guatemala City: Ediciones Polymita.
De León, Carmela. 1990. *Sindo Garay: Memorias de un trovador*. Havana: Letras Cubanas.
Delgado, Kevin M. 2001. *Iyesá: Afro-Cuban Music and Culture in Contemporary Cuba*. Los Angeles, CA: University of California Press.
    2008. "Iyesá Complexes: Reexamining Perceptions of Tradition in Cuban Iyesá Music." *Black Music Research Journal* vol. 28 no. 2 (Fall), 1–39.
Dodson, Jualynne E. 2008. *Sacred Spaces and Religious Traditions in Oriente Cuba*. Santa Fe, NM: University of New Mexico Press.
Domínguez Encinas, Andrés. 1958. *Villancicos para el niño de Belén*. Salamanca: Imp. Calatrava.
Dos Ventos, Mario. 2008. *Sea el Santísimo: A Manual for Misa Espiritual and Mediumship Development*. Breinigsville, PA: Nzo Quimbanda Exu Ventania Press.
Droogers, André and Sidney M. Greenfield. 2001. "Recovering and Reconstructing Syncretism." In Sidney M. Greenfield and André Droogers,

eds., *Reinventing Religions: Syncretism and Transformation in Africa and the Americas*. Lanham, MD: Rowman and Littlefield, 21–42.

Duany, Jorge. 2017. "Cuban Migration: A Post-Revolution Exodus Ebbs and Flows." *Migration Information Source* (July 6, 2017). Washington, DC: Migration Policy Institute. https://bit.ly/3WvEKoQ (accessed February 22, 2025).

Eli Rodríguez, Victoria, Ana Victoria Casanova Olivia, Jesús Guanche Pérez, et al., eds. 1997. *Instrumentos de la música folklórica-popular de Cuba*, 2 vols. Havana: Editorial de Ciencias Sociales.

Espinosa Mendoza, Norge. 2012. "Escenarios para la Virgencita." *La Gaceta de Cuba* Jan–Feb, 22–3.

Espírito Santo, Diana. 2015. *Developing the Dead: Mediumship and Selfhood in Cuban Espiritismo*. Gainesville, FL: University of Florida Press.

Fa'lokun Fatunmbi, Awo. 1993. *Esu–Elegba: Ifá and the Divine Messenger*. Old Bethpage, NY: Original Publications.

Feld, Steven. 1984. "Communication, Music, and Speech about Music." *Yearbook for Traditional Music* vol. 16 (1984), 1–18.

Fernández Olmos, Margarite and Lizabeth Paravisini-Gebert. 2011. *Creole Religions of the Caribbean*, 2nd ed. New York: New York University Press.

Fernández Robaina, Tomás. 2001. *Hablen paleros y santeros*. Havana: Editorial de Ciencias Sociales.

Feraudy Espino, Heriberto. 1999. *Irna: Un encuentro con la santería, el espiritismo y el palomonte*. Guadalajara: Editorial Conexión Grafico.

Fishbane, Michael. 1998. *The Exegetical Imagination: On Jewish Thought and Theology*. Cambridge, MA: Harvard University Press.

Font-Navarrete, David. 2021. "Writing Orisha Music: Text, Tradition, and Creativity in Afro-Cuban Liturgy." *Religions* 12 (11). https://doi.org/10.3390/rel12110964.

Fonseca, Brian, John Polga-Hecimovich, and Richard E. Feinberg. 2020. "Venezuela and Cuba: The Ties that Bind." Washington, DC: Wilson Center Latin America Program. www.wilsoncenter.org/publication/venezuela-and-cuba-ties-bind (accessed February 22, 2025).

Font-Navarrete, David and Akinsola Akiwowo. 2015. "Awo Ayan: Metaphysical Dimensions of the Yoruba Divinity of Drumming." In *The Yorùbá God of Drumming: Transatlantic Perspectives on the Wood That Talks*, edited by Amanda Villepastour. Jackson, MS: University Press of Mississippi, 35–50.

Frías, Johnny. 2015. "A Violín for Ochún," *Cuba Counterpoints* https://cubacounterpoints.com/archives/4265.html.

Garcés Marrero, Roberto. 2020. "La Santa Muerte en la música mexicana." *Mitológicas*, vol. XXXV, 133–54.

García Canclini, Néstor. 1995. *Hybrid Cultures: Strategies for Entering and Leaving Modernity*, transl. Christopher L. Chiappari and Silvia L. López. Minneapolis, MN: University of Minnesota Press.

García Lacerra, Miraima. 2015. "Para dar un violín. Estudio de caso. La Habana 2012–2014." Unpublished thesis, Instituto Superior de Arte, Havana.

García Pérez, Tahtiali M. 2012. "Migración cubana en México." Repositorio Leopoldo Zea: Migración Cubana. https://rilzea.cialc.unam.mx/jspui/handle/CIALC-UNAM/CL437 (accessed February 22, 2025).
Geertz, Clifford. 1973. *The Interpretation of Culture*. New York: Basic Books.
Gidal, Marc. 2016. *Spirit Song: Afro-Brazilian Religious Music and Boundaries*. New York: Oxford University Press.
Gilroy, Paul. 1993. *The Black Atlantic: Modernity and Double Consciousness*. Harvard, MA: Harvard University Press.
Giro, Radamés, ed. 2002. *Diccionario enciclopédico de la música cubana*, 4 vols. Havana: Editorial Letras Cubanas.
    2007. *Diccionario enciolopédico de la música en Cuba*, 4 vols. Havana: Letras Cubanas.
González Bello, Neris and Liliana Casanella. 2002. "La timba cubana: Un intergénero contemporáneo." *Clave* 4 no. 1, 2–9.
González-Wippler, Migene. 1995. "Santería: Its Dynamics and Multiple Roots." In *Enigmatic Powers: Syncretism with African and Indigenous Peoples' Religions Among Latinos*, ed. Anthony M. Stevens-Arroyo and Andres I. Pérez y Mena. New York: Bildner Center series on religion; v. 3.; PARAL studies series ; v. 3, 99–111.
Guanche, Jesús. 1983. *Procesos etnoculturales de Cuba*. Havana: Editorial Letras Cubanas.
Guerra, Ramiro. 1989. *Teatralización del folklore y otros ensayos*. Havana: Editorial Letras Cubanas.
Guevara, Florencio. 2014. *Mesa Blanca: White Altar*. Bloomington, IN: Author House LLC.
Hagedorn, Katherine. 2001. *Divine Utterances: The Performance of Afro-Cuban Santería*. Washington, DC: Smithsonian Institution Press.
    2002. "Long Day's Journey to Rincón: From Suffering to Resistance in the Procession of San Lázaro/Babalú Ayé." *British Journal of Ethnomusicology* vol. 11 no. 1, 43–69.
    2014. "Resorting to Spiritual Tourism: Sacred Spectacle in Afro-Cuban Regla de Ocha." In Timothy Rommen and Daniel T. Neely, eds., *Sun, Sea, and Sound: Music and Tourism in the Circum-Caribbean*. New York: Oxford University Press, 289–305.
Hall, Stuart. 1993. "What Is This 'Black' in Black Popular Culture? *Social Justice* vol. 20 no. 1/2 (51–2), Rethinking Race edition (Spring–Summer 1993), 104–14.
Hernández Reguant, Ariana. 2009. *Cuba in the Special Period: Culture and Ideology in the 1990s*. New York: Palgrave Macmillan.
Hesse, Axel. 1971. "Das Transmissionen-Singen im kubasnischen Spiritismus. Musikethnologische und sosiologischen Untersuchungen zur Transkulturationes-Problematik im stüdtich-halbproletarischen Kontakbersich der afroiden und europäiden Gruppenkulturen Kubas." Unpublished PhD dissertation, University of East Berlin.
    1975. "La genesis de las transmisiones espiritistas cubanas y la dialéctica transculturativa en el semiproletariado poliétnico urbano." *Revista venezolana de folklore* no. 6 (Oct 1975)), 67–91.

Iglesias Utset, Marial. 2011. *A Cultural History of Cuba During the US Occupation, 1898–1902*, transl. Russ Davidson. Chapel Hill, NC: University of North Carolina Press.
Iyanga, Michael. 2015. "Why Saints Love Samba: A Historical Perspective on Black Agency and the Rearticulation of Catholicism in Bahia, Brazil." *Black Music Research Journal* vol. 35, no. 1 (Spring 2015), 119–47.
  2023. *Alegria é Devoçã: Santos, sambas e novenas numa tradição afro-diaspórica da Bahía*. Campinas, São Paulo: Editora da Unicamp.
Johnson, Paul Christopher, (ed.), 2014. *Spirited Things: The Work of "Possession" in Afro-Atlantic Religions*. Chicago: The University of Chicago Press.
Johnson, Paul Christopher and Stephan Palmié. 2018. "Afro-Latin American Religions." In Alejandro de la Fuente and George Reid Andrews, eds., *Afro-Latin American Studies. An Introduction*. New York: Cambridge University Press, 438–85.
Juárez Huet, Nahayeilli B. 2013. "Los procesos de la relocalización en México: Algunos ejemplos etnográficos." *Debates du Ner* (Porto Alegre, ano 14 no. 23, Jan/June 2013), 167–99.
Koprivica, Ana. 2002. "La pratique du *toque de violin*, un exemple de syncrétisme musico-religieux." Unpublished Master's thesis in musicology. Paris, France: Université Paris IV (Paris-Sorbonne).
  2010. "The *Toque de Violín*: An Emerging Tradition in Cuba." *International Journal of Cuban Studies* vol. 2 no. 3–4 (Autumn/Winter 2010), 276–85.
Kubik, Gerhard. 1994. "Ethnicity, Cultural Identity, and the Psychology of Culture Contact." In Gerard Béhague, ed., *Music and Black Ethnicity: The Caribbean and South America*. New Brunswick, NJ: Transactions Publishers and the North South Center, University of Miami, 17–46.
Lachatañeré, Rómulo. 1992. *El sistema religioso de los afrocubanos*. Havana: Editorial de Ciencias Sociales.
LaFevers, Cory. 2019. "Jurema in the Folk Fiddle Music of Maciel Salú." Unpublished conference paper presented at the annual Society for Ethnomusicology meeting in Bloomington, IN.
Larduet Luaces, Abelardo. 2016. "Las transmisiones en el espiritsmo de altar o de mesa." *Del Caribe* no. 65 (2016), *Espiritsmos en Cuba*. Santiago de Cuba), 78–87.
Leé Llossas, Marta. 2005. *Sincretismo y religisiosidad popular: Influencias en la sociedad cubana*. Havana: CENDA.
León, Argeliers. 1984. *Del canto y el tiempo*. Havana: Editorial Letras Cubanas.
Lionnet, Françoise and Shu-mei Shih, eds. 2011. *The Creolization of Theory*. Durham, NC: Duke University Press.
Lipsitz, George. 1994. *Dangerous Crossroads: Popular Music, Postmodernism, and the Poetics of Place*. New York: Verso.
Livari, Ville. 2023. "Violin Improvisation in Afro-Cuban Religious Ceremonies." Doctoral dissertation, University of Turku. www.utupub.fi/handle/10024/1 75198 (accessed February 22, 2025).

López Martínez, Manuel. n.d. "De canto religioso al exilio popular: Tras los derroteros del *Sun-Sun Babaé*," www.academia.edu/10772165/Articulo_sobre_el_Sun (accessed February 22, 2025).
Lowenthal, Ira. 1978. "Ritual Performance and Religious Experience: A Service for the Gods in Southern Haiti." *Journal of Anthropological Research* vol. 34 no. 3 (Autumn 1978), 392–414.
Madrid, Alejandro and Robin Moore. 2013. *Danzón: Circum Caribbean Dialogues in Music and Dance*. New York: Oxford University Press.
Martiatu, Inés María. 2008. *Over the Waves and Other Stories*, transl. Emmanuel, Harris II. Chicago: Swan Ile Press.
Mason, John. 1992. *Orin Orisa: Songs for Selected Heads*. Brooklyn, NY: Yoruba Theological Ministry.
Matera, Mónica. 2013. "El violín para Oshún." Alafia con Iré blog, http://alafiaconire.blogspot.com/2013/12/el-violin-para-oshun.html (accessed July 18, 2019).
Matory, J. Lorand. 2005. *The Black Atlantic Region: Tradition, Transnationalism, and Matriarchy in the Afro-Brazilian Candomblé*. Princeton, NJ: Princeton University Press.
  2018. *The Fetish Revisited: Marx, Freud, and the Gods Black People Make*. Durham, NC: Duke University Press.
Martiatu, Inés María. "Costumbres y tradiciones: un violín para Ochún?" *Cuba Internacional*, no. 312 (May–June 1998), 44.
Matibag, Eugenio. 1996. *Afro-Cuban Religious Experience: Cultural Reflections in Narrative*. Gainseville, FL: University of Florida Press.
Meadows, Ruthie. 2023. *Efficacy of Sound: Power, Potency, and Promise in the Translocal Ritual Music of Cuban Ifá-Orisà*. Chicago: University of Chicago Press.
Meintjes, Louise. 1990. "Paul Simon's Graceland, South Africa, and the Mediation of Musical Meaning." *Ethnomusicology* vol. 34, no. 1 (Winter, 1990), 37–73.
Menéndez Vásquez, Lázara. 2005a. "Cake para Obatalá?" *Temas* no. 4 (Oct–Dec 1995), 38-51.
  2005b. "Para amanecer mañana hay que dormir esta noche." In Joseph S. Tulchin, ed., *Cambios en la sociedad cubana desde los noventa*. Washington, DC: Woodrow Wilson International Center for Scholars, 335–57.
  2012. "Por más que el tronco permanezca en el río, el agua no lo convierte en cocodrilo." *La Gaceta de Cuba*, Jan–Feb 2012, 9–12.
Mikelsons, Nancy B. 2005. "Homage to Eva Fernandez Bravo, Espiritista Cruzado." In *Fragments of Bone: Neo-African Religions in a New World*, ed. Patrick Bellegard-Smith. Urbana, IL: University of Illinois Press, 224–49.
Miller, Ivor. 2009. *Voice of the Leopard: African Secret Societies and Cuba*. Jackson, MI: University of Mississippi Press.
Millet, José. 1993. *Del mundo terrenal a las fuerzas ocultas (hablan los espíritus cubanos)*. Mex. D. F. Editorial Travesía.
  1996. *El espiritismo: Variantes cubanas*. Santiago de Cuba: Editorial Oriente.

Mintz, Sidney W. and Richard Price. 1992 [1976]. *The Birth of African-American Culture: An Anthropological Perspective*. Boston, MA: Beacon Press.
Moore, Robin. 1997. *Nationalizing Blackness: Afrocubanismo and Artistic Revolution in Havana, 1920–40*. Pittsburgh, PA: University of Pittsburgh Press.
  2006. *Music and Revolution: Cultural Change in Socialist Cuba*. Berkeley, CA: University of California Press.
  2010. *Music in the Hispanic Caribbean*. New York: Oxford.
  2018a. "A Century and a Half of Scholarship on Afro-Latin American Music." In George Reid Andrews and Alejandro de la Fuente, eds., *Afro-Latin American Studies: An Introduction*. New York: Cambridge University Press, 406–37.
  2018b. "Introduction. Fernando Ortiz: Ideology and Praxis of the Founder of Afro-Cuban Studies." In R. Moore, ed., *Fernando Ortiz on Music: Selected Writings on Afro-Cuban Culture*. Philadelphia, PA: Temple University Press, 1–41.
Moore, Robin and Elizabeth Sayre. 2006. "An Afro-Cuban Batá Piece for Obatalá, King of the White Cloth." In *Analytical Studies in World Music*, ed. Michael Tenzer. New York: Oxford University Press, 120–60.
Morán Soto, Edixsandro de Jesús. 2015. "La santería cubana en Venezuela, nuevo campo de acción para la pastoral." *RAM* 6.1 (2015), 199–218.
Moten, Fred. 2018. *Stolen Life*. Durham, NC: Duke University Press.
Murphy, Joseph M. 1994. *Working the Spirit: Ceremonies of the African Diaspora*. Boston, MA: Beacon Press.
Nederveen, Pieterse, Jan. 2001. "Hybridity, So What? The Anti-Hybridity Backlash and the Riddles of Recognition." *Theory, Culture & Society* 18, 2–3: 219–45.
Ochoa, Todd Ramón. 2010. *Society of the Dead: Quita Manaquita and Palo Praise in Cuba*. Berkeley, CA: University of California Press.
  2020. *A Party for Lazarus: Six Generations of Ancestral Devotion in a Cuban Town*. Berkeley, CA: University of California Press.
Ochoa Gautier, Ana María. 2014. *Aurality: Listening and Knowledge in Nineteenth-Century Colombia*. Durham, NC: Duke University Press.
Ortiz, Fernando. 1955. *Los instrumentos de la música afrocubana*, 5 vols. Havana: Ministerio de Educación.
  1965 [1950]. *Africanía de la música folklórica de Cuba*. Havana: Universidad Central de Las Villas.
  1973 [1906]. *Los negros brujos*. Miami, FL: Ediciones Universal.
  1981 [1951]. *Los bailes y el teatro de los negros en el folklore de Cuba*. Havana: Letras Cubanas.
  1991. "El golpe de la Sunsundamba." In *Estudios Etnosociológicos*, ed. Isaac Barreal Fernández. Havana: Editorial Ciencias Sociales, 114–22.
  2012. *La Virgen de la Caridad del Cobre: Historia y etnografía*. Compilación, prólogo y notas por José A. Matos Arévalos. Havana: Fundación Fernando Ortiz.
Orozco, Danilo. 2001. *Nexos globales desde la música cubana con rejuegos de son y no son*. Havana: Ediciones Ojalá.

Otero, Solimar. 2020. *Archives of Conjure: Stories of the Dead in Afrolatinx Cultures*. New York: Columbia University Press.
Palmié, Stephan. 1986. "Afro-Cuban Religion in Exile." *Journal of Caribbean Studies* vol. 5 no. 3 (1986), 171–9.
  2002. *Wizards and Scientists: Explorations in Afro-Cuban Modernity*. Durham, NC: Duke University Press.
  2013. *The Cooking of History: How Not to Study Afro-Cuban Religion*. Chicago: University of Chicago Press.
Paquette, Robert. L. 1988. *Sugar Is Made With Blood: The Conspiracy of La Escalera and the Conflict Between Empires over Slavery in Cuba*. Middleton, CT: Wesleyan University Press.
Pavez Ojeda, Jorge. 2016. "Músicos y tambores en la etnomusicología de la transculturación: Fernando Ortiz, los tamboreros de Regla y la etnografía afrocubana." *Latin American Music Review*, vol. 37 no. 2 (Fall/Winter), 208–38.
Pedroso, Lázaro. 2013. *Edigbe*. English translation by Christiane Hayashi. Self-published.
Peñate, Cary. 2021. "Rum, Tobacco, Dance, and Music: The Cuban *Mulata* as Signifier in Twentieth-Century Cinema of the Americas." Unpublished PhD dissertation, University of Texas at Austin.
Perera, Ana Cecilia and Ofelia Pérez Cruz. "Crisis social y reavivamiento religioso. Una mirada desde lo sociocultural." *Cuicuilco* no. 46 (May–Aug 2009), 135–57.
Pérez, Elizabeth. 2013. "Nobody's Mammy: Yemayá as Fierce Foremother in Afro-Cuban Religions." In Solimar Otero and Toyin Falola, eds. *Yemoja*. Albany, NY: State University of New York Press, 9–41.
Pérez Fernández, Rolando. 1986. *La binarización de los ritmos ternarios africanos en América Latina*. Havana: Casa de las Américas.
Perna, Vincenzo. 2005. *Timba: The Sound of Cuban Crisis*. London: Ashgate.
Quintero Rivera, Ángel "Chuco." 1998. *Salsa, sabor y control: Sociología de la música tropical*. San Juan: Siglo Veintiuno Editores.
Quiñones, Tato. 2014. *Asere núncue itiá ecobio enyene abacuá*. Havana: Editorial José Martí.
Ramírez Calzadilla, Jorge. 1995. "Religión, cultura, y sociedad en Cuba." *Papers* 52 (1997), 139–53.
Reyes Fortún, José "Pepe." 2006 [1998]. "Violín a Oshún." Liner notes to the recording *Violín a Ochún* (BIS Music 1998), re-released in the collection *Estudios musicológicos*, ed. Olavo Alén. Havana: Letras Cubanas, 89–94.
Rommen, Timothy. 2007. *"Mek Some Noise": Gospel Music and the Ethics of Style in Trinidad*. Berkeley, CA: University of California Press.
  2016. "Sounds Transcendant. Gospel Music and the Negotiation of Proximity in Trinidad." In *Resounding Transcendence. Transitions in Music, Religion, and Ritual*. New York: Oxford University Press, 97–110.
Rosaldo, Renato. 1995. *"Forward"* to Néstor Canclini's *Hybrid Cultures*, transl. Christopher L. Chiappari and Silvia L. López. Minneapolis, MN: University of Minnesota Press, xix–xviii.

Rossbach de Olmos, Lioba. 2007. "De Cuba al Caribe y al mundo: La santería afrocubana como religión entre patrimonio nacional(ista) y transnacionalización." *Memorias: Revista digital de historia y arqueología desde el Caribe*, año 4 no. 7 (May 2007), 129–60.
  2014. "Cruces y entrecruzamientos en los caminos de los orichas: Tradiciones en conflicto." *Indiana* vol. 31 (2014), 9–107.
Sanchez, Sara M. 2000. "Afro-Cuban Diasporan Religions: A Comparative Analysis of the Literature and Selected Annotated Bibliography." Miami, FL: Institute for Cuban and Cuban-American Studies, Occasional Paper Series.
Sánchez-Boudy, José. 1999. *Diccionario mayor de cubanismos*. Miami, FL: Ediciones Universal.
Sarria, Leonardo. 2012 "El país de amarillo." *La Gaceta de Cuba* Jan–Feb 2012, 64.
Schulman, George. 2021. "Fred Moten's Refusals and Consents: The Politics of Fugitivity." *Political Theory* vol. 49 no. 2, 272–313. https://journals.sagepub.com/doi/10.1177/0090591720937375
Seeman, Sonia. 2019. *Sounding Roman. Representation and Performing Identity in Western Turkey*. New York: Oxford University Press.
Shiloah, Amnon. 1992. *Jewish Musical Traditions*. Detroit, MI: Wayne State University Press.
Sotto, Arturo. 2012. "El misterio de las aguas." *La Gaceta de Cuba* no. 1 (Jan–Feb 2012), 13-17.
Stewart, Charles, ed. 2007. *Creolization: History, Ethnography, Theory*. Walnut Creek, CA: Left Coast Press.
  2009. "El sincretismo y sus sinónimos: Reflexiones sobre la mezcla cultural." *Criterios* no. 36 (2009), 196–203.
Stewart, Charles and Rosalind Shaw, eds. 1994. *Syncretism/Anti-syncretism: The Politics of Religious Synthesis*. London: Routledge.
Stokes, Martin. 2004. "Music and the Global Order." *Annual Review of Anthropology* 33, 47–72.
Tallaj, Angelina. 2018. "Religion on the Dance Floor: Afro-Dominican Music and Ritual from Altars to Clubs." *Civilisations* vol. 67, 95–109.
Toledo, Armando, ed. 1981. *Presencia y vigencia de Brindis de Salas*. Havana: Letras Cubanas.
Turino, Thomas. 1999. "Signs of Imagination, Identity, and Experience: A Peircian Semiotic Theory for Music." *Ethnomusicology* vol. 43, no. 2 (Spring–Summer, 1999), 221–55.
Valdés Garriz, Yrmino. 1991. *Ceremonias fúnebres de la santería afrocubana: Ituto y honras de egun*. San Juan: Sociedad de Autores Libres.
Vaughan, Umi and Carlos Aldama. 2012. *Carlos Aldama's Life in Batá: Cuba, Diaspora, and the Drum*. Bloomington, IN: Indiana University Press.
Vélez, María Teresa. 2000. *Drumming for the Gods: The Life and Times of Felipe García Villamil, Santero, Palero and Abakuá*. Philadelphia, PA: Temple University Press.
Vidal, Pavel and Luis R. Luis. 2024. "Cuba's Monetary Reform and Triple-Digit Inflation." *Latin American Research Review* (2024), 59, 274–91. https://doi.org/10.1017/lar.2023.59.

Wallace, David. 2018. "Fred Moten's Radical Critique of the Present." *The New Yorker* vol. 94 no. 11 (30 April 2018). www.newyorker.com/culture/persons-of-interest/fred-motens-radical-critique-of-the-present (accessed February 22, 2025).

Warden, Nolan. 2006. "Cajón pa' los muertos: Transculturation and Emergent Tradition in Afro-Cuban Ritual Drumming and Song." Unpublished Master's thesis, Tufts University.

Watson, Carolyn. 2009. "Citizenship, Religion and Revolution in Cuba." Unpublished Master's dissertation, University of New Mexico. http://digitalrepository.unm.edu/cgi/viewcontent.cgi?article=1080&context=hist_etds (accessed February 22, 2025).

Williams, Raymond. 1977. *Marxism and Literature.* New York: Oxford University Press.

Wirtz, Kristina. 2014. *Performing Afro-Cuba: Image, Voice, Spectacle in the Making of Race and History.* Chicago: University of Chicago Press.

Yi, David Yuen-Ming. 1995. "Music and Dance of Haitian Vodoun: Diversity and Unity in Regional Repertoires." Unpublished PhD dissertation, Wesleyan University. Middleton, CT: University Microfilms International.

AUDIOVISUAL MATERIAL

Álvarez, Lázaro, dir. 1997. *Los Nani: Espiritistas ¡a cantar!* Uniko Records CD UNK-80765. Canada.

Brandoli, Luca and Grupo Barracón. 2011. *Cajón pa el muerto.* www.youtube.com/watch?v=uTR8ZMabRMc (accessed February 22, 2025).

Font-Navarrete, David and Kenneth Schweitzer, directors. 2015. *Lucumí Music: Singing, Dancing, and Drumming Black Divinity* [video]. Durham, NC: Center for African and African-American Research at Duke University.

Ortega, Manuel, dir. 2008. *Estampas de fe.* Havana: Instituto Superior de Arte, 5 PA Films. www.YouTube.com/watch?v=M9AgLFNBofo (accessed July 23, 2022).

Oviedo, Ernesto and Tony Pinelli, prods. 2011 [1998]. *Orquesta Estrellas Cubanas: Violín a Ochún.* Havana: BIS Music CD 137.

Sotto, Arturo, dir. 2009. *El misterio de las aguas.* Havana: Seseo Films, in collaboration with the Consejería de Cultura de la Junta de Andalucía.

INTERVIEWS CONDUCTED BY THE AUTHOR

Juan Mesa, anthropologist, June 13, 2018
María Teresa Gómez Noguera, violinist and band director, June 23, 2018
Luis Peña, *batalero*, and Miguel Amín, violinist, May 30, 2022
Octavio Rodríguez, *santero* and percussionist, June 14, 2018
Lázaro Dagoberto González Siones, violinist, May 25, 2018
Lisbet Soto, violinist, August 9, 2023
Yunior Terry, violinist, February 23, 2022 and October 5, 2023
Roy Vázquez, musician, July 31, 2018
Roberto Zurbano, scholar and activist, June 11, 2018

References

INTERVIEW CONDUCTED BY JOHNNY FRÍAS

Abraham Rivero, violinist, October 23, 2023

INTERVIEWS CONDUCTED BY MELENA FRANCIS VALDÉS IN HAVANA CUBA, 2020–24

Yenny Bahi, "Oshun Guere," *santera*, April 24, 2022
Abilio Betancourt Bejerano, violinist and musical director of the Orquesta Sublime, 12, 15, May 2021, April 1, 8 2024, and personal communication, WhatsApp, April 24, May 7, 13, and June 2 2024
Eduar Marzán Betancourt, *santero* and violinist, April 26, 2022
Rafael Espinosa Casanova, percussionist, *santero*, and *babalawo*, March 7, 2022
Marcel Fernández Díaz, *akpwón*/lead *cajón* singer, Tata Nkisi, January 21, 2021
Danai Pérez Domínguez, "Ibú Añá," *santera*, January 14, 2021 and personal communication, WhatsApp, 7 May 2024
José del Pilar Suárez Entenza, musician and *omo Añá*, November 17, 2020, December 26, 2020, and January 12, 2021
Carmen Julia Canto Herrera, Spiritist and *santera*. December 12, 2023 and
    February 18, 2024.
Santa Villas Junco, *santera*, March 4, 2021
Luis Manuel Leyro, Spiritist, Tata Nkisi and Obá Oriate, April 24, 2022
Ileana Hodge Limonta, February 4 and March 19, 2021
Joaquín Fernández Miranda, spiritual advisor, March 17, 2021
Emilio Gordillo Miraval, *santero*, January 27, and March 8, 2021
Jorge Alberto Duquesne Mora, *santero*, Spiritist, Tata Nkisi, and musician, April 14, 2022, and personal communication, WhatsApp, April 5, 2023 and March 11, 2024.
Nicolás Martínez Palacios, "Adde Añá," *babalawo* and *omo Añá*, January 30, 2021, and personal communication, WhatsApp, May 19 and 21, 2024
Santiago "Chaguito" Garzón Rill, musician, February 4, 2021 and personal
    communication, WhatsApp, April 26, 2024
Tomás Fernández Robaina, historian, April 26, 2022
Gladys Sivico Sulueta "Omi Elekun," *santera*, January 14, 2021
Emir Molina del Valle, Spiritist, Tata Nkisi, *santero* and composer, April 14, 2022

ANONYMOUS CONTRIBUTORS

A few of the individuals interviewed asked that their names not be included in the
    book. Information taken from them appears accompanied by the phrase
    "anonymous interview."

Index

Afrocubanismo, 7, 47, 117
Altars
   in *violines espirituales*, 86, 187, Figure 3.1. See also *bóveda*
   in *violines de santo*, 107, 108, 110, 126, 130, 140, 198, Figure 4.1
Amín Miguel. See Peña, Luis and Miguel Amín
"A remar," 75, 152, 179, Figure 5.12
"Ave María" by Schubert and Bach-Gounoud, 84, 87, 95, 110, 114, 128, 135, 137, 140, 169, 173, 191, 192. See also "O María"
"Awoyó aé," 125, 152, Figure 4.12. See also Yemayá, songs to

Babalú Ayé, songs to, 68, 73, 88, 92, 114, 115–16. See also San Lázaro
"Babalú Ayé" chorus, 116, Figure 4.4
Bastide, Roger, 38, 195
Beliso-De Jesús, Aixa, 13
"Beroní abebe Ochún," 126, 127, Figure 4.13, 4.14. See also Ochún, songs to
Betancourt Estrada, Víctor, 198, 199, 205
Borotitilawa rhythm, 176, 192, Figure 6.5. See also *violines*, *batá* drums in
Bóveda, 57, 60, 61, 62, 63, 99, 107, 130, 131
Brindis to Ochún. See also Ochún, songs to
Brindis de Salas, Claudio, 32, 33
Burdick, John, 201

Cajón de muerto, 41–7, 205, 206, 208, Figure 2.6
"Canción a San Lázaro," 91, Figure 3.7, 3.17
"Canto al indio," 78, Figure 3.11
Caridad del Cobre, 111–13
   Divergent representations of, 103, 104
   Relation to Ochún, 105
Chachalokafun, 43, 177
Changó, songs to, 73, 114, 120, 121, 122, 130, 143, 158
"Cheke cheke," 174, Figure 6.8. See also Ochún, songs to
"Como soy tan chiquitico." 111 See also Elegguá, songs to
"Congo de Guinea soy," 81, 82, 156, Figure 3.13
"Corre el agua," 58, 75, 123, 175, Figure 3.9
Creolization, 16, 17, 30
Crespo, Aurelia, 34, 35, 109
Cuadro espiritual, 58, 59, 60, 61, 62, 68, 76, 95, 107, 157

Domain collapsing, 200
Dones de gracia, 6, 28, 29, 85

"Elegguá, Elegguá, asokere," 140, 143, 182, Figure 6.7. See also Elegguá, songs to
Elegguá, songs to, 111–13, 140
"El hombre de la guayabera," 122, Figure 4.9. See also Changó, songs to

222

Index

Espiritismo cruzado, 4, 10, 12, 44, 54, 57, 58. *See also* Spiritism
Espiritismo de cordón, 57, 67
Espiritismo de mesa, 57
"Estaba la langosta" chorus, 159, Figure 5.15

Fantasía Yoruba ensemble, 189, 192, 194, Figure 6.10. *See also* Peña, Luis and Miguel Amín
"Francisca," 94, Figure 3.20
Fugitivity, 131, *See also* Moten, Fred

"Gitana de mis amores, bendíceme," 92, Figure 3.19
Gómez Noguera, María Teresa, 1, 136, Figure 2.5
Gypsy spirits, 10, 58, 59, 76, 77, 88

Hybridity, 15, 16

Indian spirits, 10, 34, 58, 59, 61, 73, 76, 78, 88
Iyanga, Michael, 201, 202
Iyesá music and culture, 43, 45, 106, 128, 129, 141, 144, 175, 176

Kardec, Alain, 34, 56, 57, 60, 61, 70
"Ko ko ko iroko omo iyesá," 176, Figure 6.4. *See also* Ochún, songs to
Kongo religions, 5, 29, 34, 43, 44, 58, 59, 73, 76, 79, 82, 88, *See violines*, Palo influences in
Kongo spirits, 5
Kunduru, 188, 189

"La gitana,", 77, Figure 3.10
"La luz redentora," 62, 87, 208, Figure 3.3
Liminality, 199
Los Nani, 41, 43, 77
"Lumbe lumbe," 83, 95, Figure 3.14

"Mamá Francisca," 81, 174, Figure 3.12
Mariachi repertoire in *violines*, 109, 170, 184, 190
"Marinero, marinero," 44, 74, 75, Figure 3.8
Migration, Cuban
　Historical, 166
　To Mexico, 167
　To Venezuela, 166

Misas espirituales, 13, 19, 53, 55, 58, 59, 79, 84, 97, 98, 99, 100, 106
　Music of, 62–84
Moten, Fred, 6. *See also* fugitivity

Nigerian influence on Cuban religion, 38, 40, 54, 115, 176, 198
Ñongo, 118, 145, 163

Obatalá, songs to, 5, 63, 116, 117, 118, 180, 184, 192
"Obatalá kunawa," 117, 118, Figure 4.6, 4.7
"Ochimini," 111, Figure 4.2 *See also* Elegguá, songs to
Ochún, songs to, 2, 5, 34, 35, 36, 41, 44, 46, 114, 126, 127, 128, 129, 137, 138, 157, 169, 170, 173, 174, 176, 178, 193
Ogbe-She, Wilson, 207, 208
"Ole con ole gitana," 93, Figure 3.18
"O María,", 67, 69, Figure 3.5, 3.16. *See also* "Ave María"
"Onileo vamp," Figure 4.10. *See also* Changó, songs to
Orama, Yilian, 178, 180, 181, Figure 6.6
Orquesta Estrellas Cubanas, 25, 27, 36, 89, 90, 92, 120, 125, 168
Ortiz, Fernando, 42, 102, 146, 197
"O venid protectores," 43, 62, 64, 65, 110, Figure 3.4
Oyá, songs to, 119, 120
"Oyansa ma terema," 120, Figure 4.8. *See also* Oyá, songs to

"Padrenuestro," 60, 86, 87, 96, 110, 135, 140, 169, Figure 3.15
Palo influences in *violines*. *See violines*, Palo influences in
Peña, Luis and Miguel Amín, 180, 189, 190, 191, 192, 193
"Plegaria a Obatalá," 117 Figure 4.5. *See also* Obatalá, songs to
"Plegaria a Yemayá," 125 Figure 4.11. *See also* Yemayá, songs to
"Porque soy tan chiquitico," 112, 140 Figure 4.3. *See also* Elegguá, songs to

Regla de Ocha, music of. *See* Santería, music of
Religious persecution in Cuba, 37, 194, 195, 196

Religious revival of 1990s Cuba, 38, 39, 40
Religious tolerance in Cuba, 38
Religiosidad popular, 12
Rivero, Abraham and Tania, 171, 173, 174, 175, 176, Figure 6.2
Rommen, Timothy, 200
Rumba para Ochún, 46

San Lázaro/St. Lazarus, 3, 55, 58, 73, 74, 115, 116, 138, 149
San Miguel/St. Michael, 3, 70, 71, 72, 90, 92, 145, 156, 203
"San Miguel bendito,", 71, Figure 3.6
Santería, musical formats of, 106
"Sea el Santísimo," 62, 63, 69, 90, 169, 187, Figure 3.2
Servicio al muerto, 100, 101, 106
"Siento una voz," 82
Soto, Lisbet, 169, 184, 185, 186, 187, Figure 6.9
Spiritism, 4, 52, 53, 55, 56, 57, 58, 188, 196. See also *espiritismo cruzado*, *misas espirituales*
    Influence on Santería, 99, 100, 101
Syncretism, 14, 15

Tallaj, Angelina, 203, 204, 209
Terry, Yunior, 37, 167, 186, Figure 6.1
Transculturation, 16

Vázquez, Roy, 35, 87, 123, Figure 2.5
Violines
    And class or taste, 47, 48, 49
    Batá drums in, 41, 173, 176, 180, 189, 190, 191, 192
    Cost of, 27, 28
    Definition of, 22
    de santo, 98, 106–32
    Divergent attitudes toward, 129, 130
    Divination leading to, 24
    Developing out of religious persecution, 37
    Espirituales, 5, 28, 52, 84–97, 114, 145
    History of, 21
    Improvised choruses in, 145, 148, 149
    Influence of dance music on, 4, 6, 36, 91, 92, 148, 200, 201, 207
    In Canada, 170
    In Mexico City, 188–9
    In Miami, 170–81
    In New York, 167–9
    In Venezuela, 181–7
    Instrumentation of, 26
    Loss of ritual knowledge in, 205–7
    Oblique lyrics in, 82, 163
    Origins in Spiritist rites, 33
    Palo influences in, 58, 66, 68, 82, 83, 85, 94, 110, 114, 130, 145, 175
    Percussion-only sections in, 94, 95, 98, 114, 115, 122, 128, 142, 144, 145, 148, 155, 157, 163
    Performers of, 25, 27
    Possession in, 29, 30, 34
    Reasons for offering, 22
    Repertoire in, 1, 2, 3, 24, 36
    Rhythmic shifts in, 146–8, Figure 5.8, 5.9
    Spanish and Lucumí lyrical shifts in, 143, 149
    Structure of performances, 5
    Transitions between ritual and non-ritual music in, 143
Virgin of Regla, 23, 48, 58, 68, 88, 107, 123, 125, 189
"Vuela la paloma" chorus, 157, Figure 5.14

White, José, 21, 32, 33, 137

"Y qué tú quieres que te den?", 180, 181
Yemayá, songs to, 74, 75, 126, 155
Yoruba Cultural Association, 40

For EU product safety concerns, contact us at Calle de José Abascal, 56–1°, 28003 Madrid, Spain or eugpsr@cambridge.org.

 www.ingramcontent.com/pod-product-compliance
Ingram Content Group UK Ltd.
Pitfield, Milton Keynes, MK11 3LW, UK
UKHW012113041225
465605UK00002B/169